CLUES

E169.12.I37
IMAGES AND IDEAS IN AMER   CC CS

W9-CAE-823

I CUM 00 0078058 O

81-693

E
169.12
I37   Images and ideas in
          American culture

JUL   2000

DATE   JUN   2004

JUN 0 9

JUL X X 2015

WITHDRAWN

© THE BAKER & TAYLOR CO.

Images and Ideas in
American Culture:
The Functions of Criticism

Images and Ideas in American Culture

The Functions of Criticism

Essays in Memory of Philip Rahv

Arthur Edelstein, editor

Cumberland County College
Library
P.O. Box 517
Vineland, NJ 08360

Published by Brandeis University Press
Distributed by the University Press of New England
Hanover, New Hampshire 1979

E
169.12
I36

81-693

Copyright © 1979 by Trustees of Brandeis University
All rights reserved
Library of Congress Catalog Card Number 78-63584
International Standard Book Number 0-87451-164-X
Printed in the United States of America.

Library of Congress Cataloging in Publication data
will be found on the last printed page of this book.

Preface

This book is dedicated to the late Philip Rahv, literary and cultural critic, polemical editor, and influential teacher—one of the significant intellectuals of our time. His achievements as a critic, as co-founder and co-editor of *Partisan Review* (with William Phillips), and as founder and editor of the periodical *Modern Occasions* are well known. What is not well known is his influence as a teacher; so, a few words on that. From 1957 until his death on December 22, 1973, he was a professor in the Department of English and American Literature at Brandeis University. Solemn and thick-mannered, often intolerant of disagreement, always intellectually rigorous, he was not the sort of teacher who becomes a legend for generations of students. He was decidedly a man of opinions, and since he had not reached these casually, he was not dainty about asserting them. In short, his air was dogmatic. He was not, consequently, a good teacher for those who sought quick approval, nor for the tender and hesitant who wished merely to dip their toes; but for anyone willing to swim in deep waters, he was a powerful and invigorating example.

Among his students in a course on modern literature one summer was Anne Sexton, who later credited Rahv's powerful lectures and personality with her decision to begin writing poetry in earnest. And he encouraged a number of other young writers and intellectuals, among them the novelist Alan Lelchuk, who was not formally his student but a colleague on the Brandeis faculty. His teaching, that is, was not confined to the classroom. It could occur anywhere, everywhere, and it may well be that his colleagues were the prime beneficiaries of his wisdom, though his influence was always strong among the brightest of his students. It was in fact several of these—Nancy Wiener, Daniel Krakower, and Joan Forman—who came up with the idea of a memorial volume for Rahv and who helped significantly thereafter with the project. Their initial suggestion was that the brief talks given by Rahv's friends at the memorial services after his death be brought between covers as a tribute. That idea evolved until it became the present volume, not a chorus of eulogies for the dead but a series of critical essays on what had long been the live substance of Rahv's own reflections: literature and politics in American culture.

The essays were prepared especially for this collection by writers who knew and respected Rahv (respected him even when they disagreed with him). It would have been particularly gratifying if more people from the *Partisan Review* group had been able to contribute. The collection, however, does constitute a solid sampling of Rahv's colleagues. First thanks must go to them for having given so generously of their time and talent in writing these essays. But thanks must go as well to a great many others who made this volume possible—to John Hazel Smith, Chairman of the Department of English and American Literature at Brandeis, for his voluntary and long-term services in surmounting the inevitable difficulties that attend upon a project of this kind; to Andrew Dvosin, now completing a book-length study of Rahv's life and work; Arabel Porter, Rahv's editor at Houghton Mifflin; and Irving Karg, his literary executor—all for their valuable advice; to Abram Sachar, Chancellor of Brandeis University, for providing early encouragement and helping to arrange financial support; to Mrs. Nathan S. Goldstein for generously supplying the seed money; to David Steinberg, Vice-President at Brandeis, and Jack Goldstein, Dean of Faculty, for offering helpful suggestions and for solving the difficult problem of printing costs in a time of severe academic austerity; to

David Horne, Director of the University Press of New England, for his expert unraveling of the knotty editorial and production problems; and to Aiko Adachi and Arlene Durkin for their skillful secretarial aid.

Wellesley, Massachusetts   A.E.
October 1978

Contents

Prologue

To begin: some postulates. Since literature is apprehended differently in different times, one of the responsibilities of the literary critic—even if he is concerned with works of the past—is to assess the assumptions of his own time. To do so, he must be alert to the immediate world in which he lives, as well as to the worlds in which he reads. That world will embrace varying and often contradictory assumptions. Consequently, he will have to repudiate some of these. He will be, then, a critic not only of literature but of his society, his culture, his time.

That was emphatically the case for Philip Rahv, as we can see, for instance, from his work with *Partisan Review*, a periodical that emerged from political circumstances. His own view on the matter is indicated in a brief passage quoted in Milton Hindus' essay on Rahv's work: "The true function of criticism is now frequently to resist the *Zeitgeist* rather than acquiesce in its more rampant aberrations." To resist the *Zeitgeist*—that expresses Rahv's sense of mission as a critic and also something of the capacity for morose contentiousness in his personality. Though his combativeness sometimes got the better of him and caused him to make war even on his allies, his judgment was usually exquisite, and the totality of his work will surely stand up under the scrutiny of the future. And of the past as well, for his conception of the critical role fits the thrust of American criticism since its true beginnings in the early nineteenth century.

Though it would seem axiomatic that literary criticism cannot be born until there is a mature body of literature to nourish it, criticism in America came alive prematurely but fervently and set about the labor of invoking its own parentage. Before the great literary genesis of the 1850's, the decade that F. O. Matthiessen would honor a century later as an "American Renaissance," a native criticism had swelled into voice. It had two voices really, and they would sound themselves across much of the century. One was a tone of lamentation that mourned the presumed absence of imaginative resources in the American experience. In 1828 Cooper articulated an early version of the theme:

[An] obstacle against which American literature has to contend is in the poverty of materials. There is scarcely an ore which contributes to the wealth of the author that is found here in veins as rich as in Europe. There are no annals for the historian; no follies (beyond the most vulgar and commonplace) for the satirist; no manners for the dramatist; no obscure fictions for the writer of romance; no gross and hardy offences against decorum for the moralist; nor any of the rich artificial auxiliaries of poetry. The weakest hand can extract a spark from the flint, but it would baffle the strength of a giant to attempt kindling a flame with a pudding-stone . . . . There is no costume for the peasant (there is scarcely a peasant at all), no wig for the judge, no baton for the general, no diadem for the chief magistrate.

Along with the later versions produced by Hawthorne and James, this catalogue of negatives has perhaps become so familiar as to appear merely quaint. And since these lamentations assumed an energy crisis that did not exist, assumed that only the fuels derived from Europeanate social strata could fire a literature, they can seem essentially futile, a cultural nervousness. Yet they constituted a seminal anxiety. For a nation that was as yet without a resonant literature of its own, they raised a fundamental issue: the relation of literature to the broad actualities of society. And in so doing they helped to strike into being the other voice of our early nineteenth-century criticism, a voice prophetic and generative.

"Our age is retrospective." In opening the first of his major essays, "Nature," with that admonitory charge, and in calling upon America to discover "an original relation to the universe," Emerson was by no means limiting himself to a concern for literature. But his exhortations could well have served as a response to Cooper. "Why should we not have a poetry and philosophy of insight and not of tradition . . . ?" And when Emerson turned his vision directly upon the issue of literature, in a later essay, he looked back far beyond the analogy with recent European writing to observe that the materials of American life were at bottom the same materials from which all of Western literature had sprung. The connection was root and branch. In "The Poet" he invoked an American genius

with tyrannous eye, which knew the value of our incomparable materials, and saw, in the barbarism and materialism of the times, another carnival of the same gods whose picture he so much admires in Homer; then in the Middle Age; then in Calvinism. Banks and tariffs, the newspaper and caucus, Methodism and Unitarianism, are flat and dull to dull people, but rest on the same foundations of wonder as the town of Troy and the temple of Delphi, and are as swiftly passing away.

Though Emerson's invocation rang the most powerfully and has become part of the very literature he called for, his was not at all a solitary voice but only the deepest in a chorus that filled the journals and lecture halls of the time with promptings toward original relation, a chorus that struck the first rhythms and themes of the literature to come.

The force of this projective criticism derived from the fact that it was not simply belletristic. Though Emerson, and his neighbor and disciple Thoreau, were given to empyrean flights of mood, to mounting arias on the cosmic magnitude of the isolated self, both intimated the vital connection between literary imagination and social fact. Despite the inconsistencies of Emerson on this matter—and it was he, of course, who first attempted to raise inconsistency to a philosophic principle—he asserted this connection with sufficient power to provoke into being the social catalogues of Whitman. Having delivered the birth slap, he was dismayed at this particular result. But even Whitman's extended naming of parts, a telling of American places and types, was an element in that genesis of the imagination, a setting of the scene for American literary effort.

From the embarkation point of Emerson's essays, through the Howellsian call for realism, to the vehement cultural admonitions of Van Wyck Brooks, and on into the politically oriented critiques of the 1930's—from which Rahv emerged as one of the enduring instances—the prime impulse of American criticism was social, its practitioners resisting the *Zeitgeist*, steering a course past the shallows of genteel fashion that threatened to leave our literature high and dry, poised loftily and vainly above the full flow of American experience. Ultimately, under the pressure of enormous changes in American life, the direction set by that long critical discourse was taken into depths even its originators could not have foreseen. Though Emerson and Thoreau had anchored their social sensibilities within the world of nature, it was the literary determinists of the end of the century who produced the true nature literature of the world's most profoundly industrial society by charting the barbarism and materialism of the times all the way to their primal sources. The nurturing elements of the mid-century writers—Thoreau's symbol-stocked pond and the blithe air of Emerson's woods—were replaced by the streets and factories and clamor of an industrial edifice, all of these apprehended as the unalterable ingredients of existence, the essential facts: nature. Whereas this "realism on all fours," as it has been called, established an iron connection between man and nature, that connection was by no means the shining link sought by Emerson but a chain that fastened humanity to the same principles of force that governed the predatory animals and the nucleus of the atom. Nevertheless this unromantic literature solved the romantic dilemma; it broke the polarity of nature and society that had persisted in the writings of the transcendentals despite all their assaults against it. In its own grim way, literary naturalism fused the two, perceiving the natural as the nucleus of the social, presenting the social as a manifestation of the natural.

It was only after our novelists had entered firmly into the wilderness of the cities, to record the struggles for survival among the new industrial primates, that our criticism—as though it had in some uncomfortable way fulfilled its first mission—backed almost entirely out of those streets, away from the hard social facts, to enter the textual intricacies of literature itself. Though the New Criticism emerged during the desperate social upheavals of the Great Depression and the Second World War, it sidestepped the novelistic literature that had become the major mode of literary address to such circumstances and gave itself to the tighter forms of poetry, forms that were more amenable to close analysis. But the brilliance of this developing body of theory helped to thrust criticism of the novel in a formal direction too, encouraging into fuller being a counterpart criticism that had its basis in the prefaces of Henry James, its first synthesis in the work of Percy Lubbock and some of its methods from the poetic criticism itself. The new methods were so strikingly effective that they became virtually irresistible, and to this day they govern in the teaching of literature and in the practical criticism that is published. But like other technologies, they have turned out to be a blight as well as a blessing. That there has been tireless mass production of tiresome textual analyses is by now an old story. It needs no explication here. And critical overproduction is only a storage problem anyway, for no one need feel obliged to read those endless disputations on Prufrock's tie pin or Quentin Compson's watch. The real problem lies deeper: there is evidence—to be touched upon later—that the long affair with New Critical methods has weakened our relation to literature while strengthening our grip upon it, softened our sense that its visions matter while enhancing our capacity to take command of them. Among graduate students of literature, who wrote New Critical essays throughout high school and college without even knowing they did so, there has lately been a growing impatience with those methods and a high receptivity to the striking positions of the most recent critical theories: the encodements and intertextualities of the structuralists, and the daemonizations and poetic misreadings of the Yale critics. No doubt this receptivity is due in part to the appeal of novelty; but very likely it has more substantial causes in the sensed debility of the old critical rituals. Whatever the reasons for this hospitality, the new arrivals are unsettling the critical situation, and another battle of the books has already begun. It is likely to intensify as those who are now in the graduate schools become teaching and publishing professionals—those, among them, that is, who can manage to do so despite the employment crisis that has fallen upon the academy.

There is plenty to be disturbed about also in the recent critical modes. Structuralism, which derives much of its procedure and terminology from anthropology and linguistics, has already achieved a vastly more formidable array of measuring and weighing and codifying instruments than any critical technique that preceded it. To its practitioners, all that shining and intricate machinery is often so alluring in itself that they wind up running it solely for its exquisite complexity of motion. As for the Yale school of critics, there is a rather ponderous air of self-display about much of their work, a willingness to use literature as a kind of subway platform for a sensational (it must be hoped) baring of the critic's private emotional parts. There has been a Panglossian zeal about some of the recent theorizings, an implication that to discover a new way of looking at things is to foreclose all other ways. Since our bread is after all only a collection of atoms, we must no longer butter it.

Nevertheless, there is great value in recent critical orientations, not only in what they offer by way of insight but in the very fact of their existence as a challenge to the assumptions we have settled so comfortably into. We have been so accustomed, for instance, to assuming the primacy of literature as a form of discourse that we automatically regard any exploration of that assumption as aberrant, even shocking. Yet a thing that is venerated automatically (by custom, as it were) is a thing that is being sentimentalized—and thereby trivialized. To see this sentimentalizing habit in its clearest form, we need only look at our undergraduates, who catch the habit from their educators but manifest it with less subtlety and therefore with higher visibility. What teacher of English has not read countless papers expressing admiration for a work of literature in a way that indicates sheer rituality of response? One can be sure that the writers of those papers will never again take the revered first book of *The Faerie Queene* down from the shelf. Yet those students are not necessarily falsifying. They often mean what they say, though they only mean it when there is occasion to say so. It is the occasion they respond to, not the work.

Though we professors are vastly more skillful at rationalizing our reflexes of response, we are subject to similar contradictions about what we believe. It has become all too apparent of late that our behavior can be deeply inconsistent with what we profess. The study of humane letters, we urge, is different from the study of, say, the natural sciences; it is value oriented. That is one of our major arguments whenever we have to justify the allocation of scarce funds to our impractical disciplines. We are big on values. But for some time now we have gone on professing humane values while paying almost no meaningful attention to the crisis that has descended upon our graduate students, the young who wish to join us in the professing of literature but will be lucky indeed if they can find a place even remotely connected to that enterprise. The evidence for a disastrous decline in opportunities for those aspiring to teach in the humanities has been before us for a decade now. And what has been our response? Consider a statistic or two from a 1976 report of the Higher Education Research Institute: whereas first-time graduate enrollments in physics were reduced by 37 percent between 1965 and 1975, first-time enrollments in humanities rose throughout that period; and among graduate programs in English reporting their first-time enrollments for 1975-76, in that year alone the figure was up 6.5 percent over the previous year. Dorothy Harrison (a contributor to the HERI study), after reporting similarly disturbing figures, notes that "thus far the contraction in the academic job market has not affected degree production in the humanities; it appears it has been one important factor influencing production in the physical sciences."

Professors of literature cannot be expected to solve the employment problems of American society. We would not know how to in any case (any more than do those who are entrusted with such matters). But we can and should be expected to address seriously, however arduous that may be, the terrible human problem among those who consider us their mentors. Instead, either through innocence or indifference, we have blindly helped to deepen it. This suggests that despite all the sophisticated signs to the contrary, our regard for what we profess is sentimental, simply automatic, and that the celebrated crisis of the humanities is not only something that afflicts us from without, not only a matter of money shortages and public indifference, but also a sickness within. And it is likely that the way in which we have addressed ourselves to literature over the past several decades has something to do with the matter. The extraordinary sophistication of our criticism—New and new—is all to the good. But what has faded dangerously in the spectrum of critical orientations is the powerful sense of actuality, the large concern for contemporary experience that was for so long the foundation of literary life in America.

That is what the *Partisan Review* of Philip Rahv and William Phillips promoted in its attention to the imaginative and circumstantial aspects of American culture, both literature and politics—terms that could well have been the title for this collection of new essays, which makes its dedication to Rahv by addressing the continuum of cultural circumstances, of modern occasions as he called them, that are embraced by those terms. And it is fitting that in honor of so serious a critic of politics and literature these essays give their attention in the main to modes and instances of criticism—again political and literary.

From quite differing positions, Noam Chomsky and Stephen Whitfield examine the polity and its critics. Like many of our novelists in the twentieth century, from Fitzgerald to Ellison, they probe the beliefs to which Americans so readily give themselves. Chomsky argues against the assumption that American intellectuals since Vietnam have opposed the abuses of state power. Instead, he urges, they have been eager to join the apologists who have emerged here as in every society, "a caste of propagandists who labor to disguise the obvious, to conceal the actual workings of power, and to spin a web of mythical goals and purposes, utterly benign, that allegedly guide national policy." Whitfield, while ranging critically across American cultural phenomena from politics to poetry, and across the political spectrum from right to left, levels his case mainly against the critics of American policy. They have often, he says, overstated their positions irresponsibly by drawing analogies to the Holocaust that have blurred significant moral and historical distinctions.

With varying emphases, the essays of Robert Alter, Richard Poirier, Milton Hindus, and Robert Brustein involve themselves with literature and the criticism of literature within social, political, and philosophical contexts. Alter speculates on the social-political factors behind the recent upsurge of structuralist criticism in the United States and mounts an argument against the critical view that literary texts cannot refer us to nontextual circumstances. While he allows that recent theory has shown us how tenuous the relation is between "*verba* and *res*, book and world," we seem, he says, "to run some danger of being directed by the theoreticians to read in a way that real readers, on land or sea, have never read."

Striking at a different angle, Poirier too raises the issue of how a literary text has its "meaning." His focus is on the works of literary modernism, which, he urges, achieve their relation with us in a quite different way from most of the texts of the past, a way that has been misconceived by mainstream criticism. Though he is uneasy also with the "ahistoricism" of the newest critical theories and rejects "the fashion that proposes an infinite variety of possible readings," he lauds the efforts of recent criticism "to break down the coherencies that have passed for literary history and to invalidate the principles on which that coherency has traditionally depended." What Poirier offers is a new way of examining and determining the history of literature, especially in its modernist phase.

The historical sense also figures importantly in Hindus' examination of the critical works of Rahv, whose "massive, sturdy common sense"—a perfect phrase for Rahv's quality as a critic—had its source, Hindus suggests, in "a powerful awareness of the historical dimension of reality." This awareness, "which may have been awakened initially in him by Marxism, survived when the special theory which had given rise to it lost its hold upon his mind." And one might add that Rahv's immersion in the historical dimension included a powerful moral concern with the immediate political history of his time. This is evident even in the brief passage from Rahv that Chomsky uses as his epigraph, a passage expressing revulsion from recent American behavior in Latin America and Asia.

.Robert Brustein, in his exploration of contemporary American drama, carries the discourse into another historical dimension, by apprehending in plays the history of ideas. Though Ibsen's *The Master Builder*, he argues, broke with the assumptions of realist drama, American playwrights have been long in departing from the sequential patterns of cause and effect, of sin, guilt, and expiation: "even now, toward the end of the 1970's, our most highly acclaimed playwrights are still shaping their works to sequential diagrams." But recent dramatists like Sam Shepard and (especially) Robert Wilson, he indicates, have started to move beyond the Newtonian universe into the world envisioned by modern scientific philosophy. In so doing, they are carrying our theater past the modes of assumption that formerly dominated our sense of reality: "Just as the dominant strain of our religious life has been a form of Judaeo-Christian Puritanism, and the dominant strain of our politics a form of liberal reform democracy, so the dominant strain of our stage has been social, domestic, psychological, and realistic—which is to say, *causal*—and its dominant theme, the excavation, exposure, and expiation of guilt."

Even when it is perceived at its most mysterious, there is—by the report of these critics, from Chomsky to Brustein—a world of extratextuality, a world where things are more and less than semiotic, where things matter in themselves, where they may simultaneously signify and simply be. Howard Nemerov's meditative essay on poetry and childhood explores the sense of being that precedes all signification. Though it is not specifically about literature or criticism or that broad range of human affairs we call politics, it draws near to the place where all of these have their source. The sense of being it gravitates toward is antecedent to literature and criticism and politics because it is antecedent to the categories of language itself. It is an Ur-sense—and seems strange indeed when it expresses itself, through the perceptions of the child, in the alien formulations of language, for those slide into striking patterns that affect us simultaneously as disoriented and somehow significant. In its resonant idiosyncracy, that expression approaches the literary. While literature cannot exist without access to the social—that maze of relations and perceptions and formulations from which it draws and into which it speaks—neither can it exist without a tie to the sheer sense of being. In literature, that is the ultimate validation. Nemerov's swift essay, then, has its affinity with the other side of Emerson's social exhortations, with the Emerson of the "transparent eyeball," the Emerson who celebrated the self as the sensorium of utter existence. It is fitting that this anchor should have been provided for the collection by an important contemporary poet, a man given to sounding the intricate simplicities of language and experience.

It is fitting, too, that we should be introduced to the motive for this whole collection, to Philip Rahv the man, by Alan Lelchuk, a novelist whose works have dealt so audaciously with the life of the intellect, desublimating the hidden promptings, the stirrings and primalities that are, finally, the yeasts and cultures of mentality. Though Philip Rahv was a man of the mind, committed to a struggle with all that he felt to be false to the intellect in his time, we can see from Lelchuk's account of the last years of his complicated and difficult friend that Rahv was resisting not the *Zeitgeist* alone. Like all of us, he had spirits and times of his own to contend with. And like all of us, he sometimes failed in this struggle, occasionally even carrying personal resentments into the tone of his essays on contemporaries. Unlike most of us, however, he left his mark upon his time, for he had those rarest and most fundamental of all critical capacities: sheer clarity of perception, and a moral commitment to human events both literary and literal. To that the body of his work will attest. And to that and to him we dedicate these essays.

Part I

The Literature and

Language of Politics

Chapter 1

Foreign Policy and the Intelligentsia

Noam Chomsky

So it would seem that our repeated interventions, covert and overt, in Latin America and elsewhere, our brutal assault on the Vietnamese people, not to mention our benign inattentiveness to the abolition of democracy in Greece by a few crummy colonels wholly dependent on American arms and loans, are all mere accidents or mistakes perhaps.
—Rahv, *New York Review of Books,* October 12, 1967

If we hope to understand anything about the foreign policy of any state, it is a good idea to begin by investigating the domestic social structure: Who sets foreign policy? What interests do these people represent? What is the domestic source of their power? It is a reasonable surmise that the policy that evolves will reflect the special interests of those who design it. An honest study of history will reveal that this natural expectation is quite generally fulfilled. The evidence is overwhelming, in my opinion, that the United States is no exception to the general rule—a thesis that is often characterized as a "radical critique," in a curious intellectual move to which I will return.

Some attention to the historical record, as well as common sense, leads to a second reasonable expectation: in every society there will emerge a caste of propagandists who labor to disguise the obvious, to conceal the actual workings of power, and to spin a web of mythical goals and purposes, utterly benign, that allegedly guide national policy. A typical thesis of the propaganda system is that *the nation* is an agent in international affairs, not special groups within it, and that *the nation* is guided by certain ideals and principles, all of them noble. Sometimes the ideals miscarry, because of error or bad leadership or the complexities and ironies of history. But any horror, any atrocity will be explained away as an unfortunate—or sometimes tragic—deviation from the national purpose. A subsidiary thesis is that the nation is not an active agent, but rather responds to threats posed to its security, or to order and stability, by awesome and evil outside forces.

Again, the United States is no exception to the general rule. If it is exceptional at all, its uniqueness lies in the fact that intellectuals tend to be so eager to promulgate the state religion and to explain away whatever happens as "tragic error" or inexplicable deviation from our deepest ideals. In this respect the United States is perhaps unusual, at least among the industrial democracies. In the midst of the worst horrors of the American war in Vietnam, there was always a Sidney Hook to dismiss "the unfortunate accidental loss of life" or the "unintended consequences of military action"[1] as B–52s carried out systematic carpet bombing in the densely populated Mekong Delta in South Vietnam, or other similar exercises of what Arthur Schlesinger once described as "our general program of international good will" (referring to United States Vietnam policy in 1954).[2] There are many similar examples.

Here is one case, not untypical. William V. Shannon, liberal commentator for the *New York Times*, explains how "In trying to do good, we have been living beyond our moral resources and have fallen into hypocrisy and self-righteousness."[3] A few passages convey the flavor:

For a quarter century, the United States has been trying to do good, encourage political liberty, and promote social justice in the Third World. But in Latin America where we have traditionally been a friend and protector and in Asia where we have made the most painful sacrifices of our young men and our wealth, our relationships have mostly proved to be a recurring source of sorrow, waste and tragedy . . . Thus through economic assistance and the training of anti-guerrilla army teams we have been intervening with the best of motives [in Latin America]. But benevolence, intelligence and hard work have proved not to be enough. Chile demonstrates the problem [where with the best of motives] by intervening in this complicated situation, the C.I.A. implicated the United States in the unexpected sequel of a grim military dictatorship that employs torture and has destroyed the very freedom and liberal institutions we were trying to protect.

And so on. He concludes that we must observe Reinhold Niebuhr's warning that "No nation or individual, even the most righteous, is good enough to fulfill God's purposes in history." Not even the United States, that paragon of righteousness and selfless benevolence, which has been a friend and protector for so long in Nicaragua and Guatemala and has made such painful sacrifices for the peasants of Indochina in the past 25 years. We must therefore be more constrained in our efforts to "advance our moral ideals," or we will be trapped in "ironic paradoxes" as our efforts to fulfill God's purposes lead to unexpected sequels.

Had these words been written twenty years earlier, they would have been disgraceful enough. That they should appear in September 1974 surpasses belief, or would do so were it not that such depraved submissiveness to the state propaganda system is so typical of substantial segments of the liberal intelligentsia as virtually to go unnoticed.

It is commonly believed that an adversary relationship developed between the government and the intelligentsia during the Vietnam war. We read, for example, that "Most American intellectuals have since Vietnam come to believe that the exercise of American power is immoral" and that a new "convergence is emerging now around [a new] objective: the dismantling of American power throughout the world."[4] This is largely myth, akin to the belief that the media have become a "notable new source of national power," opposed to the state.[5] In fact, through the war and since, the national media remained properly subservient to the basic principles of the state propaganda system, with a few exceptions,[6] as one would expect from major corporations. They raised a critical voice when rational imperialists determined that the Vietnam enterprise should be limited or liquidated, or when powerful interests were threatened, as in the Watergate episode.[7]

As for the intellectuals, while it is true that an articulate and principled opposition to the war developed, primarily among students, it never passed quite limited bounds. Illusions to the contrary are common, and are fostered often by those who are so frightened by any sign of weakening of ideological controls that they respond with hysteria and vast exaggeration. Critics of new initiatives in strategic weapons development are commonly denounced for their "call for unilateral disarmament." Correspondingly, a "pragmatic" retreat from the exuberant interventionism of earlier years is transmuted into a demand for "the dismantling of American power throughout the world."

The remarkable submissiveness of the intelligentsia to the state ideological system through the Vietnam period is graphically indicated in a study of "the American intellectual elite" carried out at the height of opposition to the war in 1970.[8] This detailed investigation revealed that the "elite" opposed the war "mainly on pragmatic grounds—the war did not work—rather than on ideological or even moral grounds" (opposition in principle to aggression is here stigmatized as "ideological," a revealing choice of terms: would we describe someone who protested the Russian invasion of Czechoslovakia—which did work—as an "ideological" opponent of the aggression?). In contrast, substantial segments of the unwashed masses were opposed to aggression and massacre for reasons of principle and acted accordingly, much to the horror of more delicate souls who now explain that their sense of irony and the complexities of history prevented them from participating in popular actions (however non-violent) against the war.[9]

A typical version of the dominant "pragmatic" position is presented by columnist Joseph Kraft, commenting on Kissinger's diplomacy and the reaction to it:

The balance-of-power approach was acceptable as long as it worked. More specifically, while the Vietnam war lasted, particularly while chances of an indecisive or happy end seemed open, the Kissinger diplomacy commanded general approval. But the debacle in Vietnam showed that the United States has broken with its traditional policy of selflessly supporting the good guys. It demonstrated that American policymakers had used all the dirty tricks in the game on behalf of the baddies.[10]

Note the curious reasoning: our clients become "baddies" when they lose, and our tricks become "dirty" when they fail. Kraft's comment is characteristic in its reference to our alleged "traditional policy" and is accurate in noting that Kissinger's attempt to maintain an American client regime in South Vietnam in explicit violation of the 1973 Paris Agreements did command substantial support until events revealed that it could not succeed.

In a revealing study of public attitudes toward the Vietnam war, Bruce Andrews discusses the well documented fact that "lower-status groups" tended to be less willing than others to support government policy.[11] One reason, he suggests, is that "with less formal education, political attentiveness, and media involvement, they were saved from the full brunt of Cold War appeals during the 1950s and were, as a result, inadequately socialized into the anticommunist world view." His observation is apt. There are only two avenues of escape from the awesome American propaganda machine. One way is to escape "formal education" and "media involvement," with their commitment to the state propaganda system. The second is to struggle with near fanatical resolve to extract the facts that are scattered in the flood of propaganda, while searching for "exotic" sources not considered fit for the general public—needless to say, a method available to very few.

In discussing the intellectuals, we may invoke a distinction sometimes drawn between the "technocratic and policy-oriented intellectuals" and the "value-oriented intellectuals," in the terminology of the study of the Trilateral Commission cited above.[12] With reference to our enemies, we dismiss the technocratic and policy-oriented intellectuals as *commissars* or *apparatchiks*, and we honor the value-oriented intellectuals as democratic dissidents. But at home the values are reversed (the two major world propaganda systems are alike in this respect, and the observation generalizes to the minor systems as well). The technocratic and policy-oriented intellectuals at home are the good guys, who make the system work and raise no annoying questions. If they oppose government policy, they do so on "pragmatic" grounds, like the bulk of the "American intellectual elite." Their occasional technical objections are "hard political analysis" in contrast to the "moralism" or "dreamy utopianism" of people who raise objections of principle to the course of policy.[13] As for the value-oriented intellectuals, who "devote themselves to the derogation of leadership, the challenging of authority, and the unmasking and delegitimation of established institutions," they constitute "a challenge to democratic government which is, potentially at least, as serious as those posed in the past by the aristocratic cliques, fascist movements, and communist parties," in the judgment of the Trilateral scholars. Much of the current writing on "the time of troubles" in the 1960's is a variation on the same theme, and a fantastic "history" of the period is in the process of creation, to be exposed, perhaps, by the "revisionist historians" of a future generation.

A variant of the Trilateral argument, not uncommon, is that the "American commitment to democracy is being undermined by analyses—generally from the liberal and left part of the political spectrum—which assert that concern for democracy has played no role in American foreign policy."[14] In fact, a strong case can be made—and often is made, by no means from the left—that "it is only when her own concept of democracy, closely identified with private, capitalistic enterprise, is threatened by communism [or, we may add, by mild reform, as in Guatemala, for example] that [the United States] has felt impelled to demand collective action to defend it," or to intervene outright: "There has been no serious question of her intervening in the case of the many right-wing coups, from which, of course, this [anticommunist] policy generally has benefited."[15] Is it such analyses, or the facts which they accurately describe, that "undermine the American commitment to democracy," or, better, reveal how shallow is the commitment? For the statist intelligentsia, it does not matter that such analyses may be correct; they are dangerous, because they "challenge the existing structures of authority" and the effectiveness of "those institutions which have played the major role in the indoctrination of the young," in the terminology of the Trilateral theorists, for whom such categories as "truth" and "honesty" are simply beside the point.[16]

We can distinguish two categories among the "secular priesthood"[17] who serve the state. There are, in the first place, the outright propagandists; and alongside them are the technocratic and policy-oriented intellectuals who simply dismiss any question of ends and interests served by policy and do the work laid out for them, priding themselves on their "pragmatism" and freedom from contamination by "ideology," a term generally reserved for deviation from state doctrine. Of the two categories, the latter are probably far more effective in imposing attitudes of obedience and in "socializing" the public.

Perhaps I may interpolate two personal remarks, to illustrate the effectiveness of the cult of the technocratic and policy-oriented intellectuals in the United States. As it happens, my own work over the years has often ranged rather far from what is supposed to be my professional discipline. For example, I have done some work in mathematics and some in political analysis and social commentary, two fields in which I have no professional training whatsoever. In the course of these efforts, I have noticed a rather striking fact. When I deliver a lecture to a mathematics colloquium at a major university here or abroad, no one ever asks me what my professional credentials are (that they are slight is surely obvious to the participants). Rather, quite different questions are raised: are the ideas and results of any interest, can they be improved, etc.? In sharp contrast, in discussing social and political issues in the United States I am repeatedly challenged by professionals on grounds that I lack the credentials to speak about these matters, and interest in content or implications is rare. It is a fair generalization, I believe, that the greater the intellectual content of a discipline and the higher its intellectual standards, the less concern there is for professional credentials. To a certain extent, the latter concern serves to insulate the ideological disciplines from criticism from without; "professional standards" generally suffice rather well to insulate them from criticism from within.

A second and related personal experience is this. Like many others who have been involved in writing and actions opposed to state policy, I am frequently asked for comments on current affairs or social and political issues by press, radio, and television in Canada, Western Europe, Japan, Latin America, and Australia—but almost never in the United States. Here, commentary is reserved for professional experts, who rarely depart from a rather narrow ideological range; as Henry Kissinger has accurately commented, in our "age of the expert" the "expert has his constituency—those who have a vested interest in commonly held opinions; elaborating and defining its consensus at a high level has, after all, made him an expert."[18] The academic profession has numerous devices to ensure that professional expertise remains "responsible," though it is true that this sytem of control was partially threatened in the 1960's. Since the media, in part perhaps from naiveté, conform virtually without question to the cult of expertise in the United States, there is little danger that dissident analyses will be voiced, and if they are, they are clearly labeled "dissident opinion" rather than dispassionate, hard, political analysis. This is another example of "American exceptionalism" within the world of industrial democracies.

To return to the main theme: the United States, in fact, is no more engaged in programs of international good will than any other state has been. Furthermore, it is just mystification to speak of the nation, with its national purpose, as an agent in world affairs. In the United States, as elsewhere, foreign policy is designed and implemented by narrow groups who derive their power from domestic sources—in our form of state capitalism, from their control over the domestic economy, including the militarized state sector. Study after study reveals the obvious: top advisory and decision-making positions relating to international affairs are heavily concentrated in the hands of representatives of major corporations, banks, investment firms, the few law firms that cater to corporate interests,[19] and the technocratic and policy-oriented intellectuals who do the bidding of those who own and manage the basic institutions of the domestic society, the private empires that govern most aspects of our lives with little pretense of public accountability and not even a gesture to democratic control.

Within the nation-state, the effective "national purpose" will be articulated, by and large, by those who control the central economic institutions, while the rhetoric to disguise it is the province of the intelligentsia. An Arthur Schlesinger can write, presumably without irony, that under the Carter Administration, "human rights is replacing self-determination as the guiding value in American foreign policy" (*Boston Globe*, March 13, 1977). In the era of Vietnam and Chile, Guatemala and the Dominican Republic, "self-determination" was our "guiding value"—and to the same extent, no doubt, "human rights" will be our guiding value tomorrow. In such pronouncements we see very clearly the contribution of the technocratic and policy-oriented intellectual to what we properly call "thought control" in the totalitarian states, where obedience is secured by force rather than by density of impact. Ours is surely a more effective system, one that would be used by dictators if they were smarter. It combines highly effective indoctrination with the impression that the society really is "open," so that pronouncements conforming to the state religion are not to be dismissed out of hand as propaganda.

Much of the writing on the "national interest" serves to obscure the basic social facts. Consider, for example, the work of Hans Morgenthau, who has written extensively and often perceptively on this topic. In a recent presentation of his views, he states that the national interest underlying a rational foreign policy "is not defined by the whim of a man or the partisanship of party but imposes itself as an objective datum upon all men applying their rational faculties to the conduct of foreign policy." He then cites in illustration such commitments as support for South Korea, containment of China, and upholding of the Monroe Doctrine. He further observes that "the concentrations of private power which have actually governed America since the Civil War have withstood all attempts to control, let alone dissolve them [and] have preserved their hold upon the levers of political decision."[20] True, no doubt. Under such cirumstances, do we expect the "national interest" as actually articulated and pursued to be simply the outcome of the application of rational faculties to objective data, or to be an expression of specific class interests? Obviously the latter, and a serious investigation of the cases Morgenthau cites will demonstrate, again, that the expectation is amply fulfilled. The real interests of Americans were in no way advanced by "containing China" (where was it expanding?) or crushing the popular forces in South Korea in the late 1940's and imposing a series of dictatorial regimes since, or ensuring that Latin America remains subordinated to the needs of United States-based international corporations—the real meaning of our upholding of the Monroe Doctrine in the modern period. But it can be argued that the interests of the "concentrations of private power" in the United States that dominate the world capitalist system have been advanced by this pursuit of the "national interest." The same holds generally. The idea that foreign policy is derived in the manner of physics, as an objective datum immune to class interest, is hardly credible.

Or, consider a recent analysis by Walter Dean Burnham in the journal of the Trilateral Commission.[21] He notes that the "basic functions" of the state are "the promotion externally and internally of the basic interests of the dominant mode of production and the need to maintain social harmony." The formulation is misleading. These basic functions are not a matter of metaphysical necessity but arise from specific social causes. Furthermore, the "dominant mode of production" does not have interests; rather, individuals or groups who participate in it have interests, often conflicting ones, a distinction that is no mere quibble. And since those who manage this system are also in effective control of the state apparatus—a fact that should be sufficiently obvious to those familiar with the Trilateral Commission, which dominates the Carter Administration in a rather surprising way—the "basic interests" pursued will tend to be theirs. There are no grounds in history or logic to suppose that these interests will coincide to any significant extent with interests of those who participate in the dominant mode of production by renting themselves to its owners and managers.

A standard and effective device for obscuring social reality is the argument that the facts are more complex than as represented in the "simplistic theories" of the "value-oriented" critics. Note first that the charge is of course correct: the facts are always more complex than any description we may give. Faced with this contingency of empirical inquiry, we may adopt several courses: (1) we may abandon the effort; (2) we may try to record the facts in enormous detail, a course that reduces in effect to the first, for all the understanding it provides; (3) we may proceed in the manner of rational inquiry in the sciences and elsewhere to try to extract some principles that have explanatory force over a fair range, thus hoping to account for at least the major effects. Pursuing the third—i.e., the rational—approach, we will always be subject to the criticism that the facts are more complex, and if rational, we dismiss the charge as correct but irrelevant.

Attempting to pursue a rational course, let us consider American foreign policy since World War II. We are faced at once with some striking features of the world that emerged from the wreckage of the war. Primary among them is the enormous preponderance of American power with respect to the other industrial societies, and *a fortiori*, the rest of the world. During the war, most of the industrial world was destroyed or severely damaged, while industrial production rose dramatically in the United States. Furthermore, long before, the United States had become the leading industrial society, with unparalleled internal resources, natural advantages, scale, and social cohesion. It was natural to expect, under these circumstances, that the United States would use its enormous power in an effort to organize a global system, and it is uncontroversial that this is exactly what happened, though the question, what were the guiding principles, is indeed controversial. Let us consider these principles.

Where should we look to discover some formulation of them? In a totalitarian society this would pose problems, but the United States really is open in this respect, and there is considerable documentary evidence concerning the vision of the postwar world developed by the very people who were to play the major part in constructing it.

One obvious documentary source is the series of memoranda of the War and Peace Studies Project of the Council on Foreign Relations (CFR) during the war. Participants included a fair sample of the "foreign policy elite," with close links to government, major corporations, and private foundations.[22] These memoranda deal with the "requirement[s] of the United States in a world in which it proposes to hold unquestioned power," foremost among them being "the rapid fulfillment of a program of complete re-armament" (1940). In the early years of the war it was assumed that part of the world would be controlled by Germany. Therefore, the major task was to develop "an integrated policy to achieve military and economic supremacy for the United States within the non-German world," including plans "to secure the limitation of any exercise of sovereignty by foreign nations that constitutes a threat to the world area essential for the security and economic prosperity of the United States and the Western Hemisphere." (The concern for the "prosperity of the Western Hemisphere" is adequately revealed by United States policies, say, in Central America and the Caribbean, before and since). These areas, which are to serve United States prosperity, include the Western Hemisphere, the British Empire, and the Far East, described as a natural integrated economic unity.

The major threat to United States hegemony in the non-German world was posed by the aspirations of Britain. The contingencies of the war served to restrict these, and the American government consciously exploited Britain's travail, to help the process along. Lend-lease aid was kept within strict bounds: enough to keep Britain in the war but not enough to permit it to maintain its privileged imperial position.[23] There was a mini-war between the United States and Great Britain within the context of the common struggle against Germany, where, of course, Britain was on the front line—more accurately, the overwhelming burden of fighting Nazi Germany fell to the Russians,[24] but let us keep now to the Anglo-American alliance. In this conflict within the alliance, American interests succeeded in taking over traditional British markets in Latin America and in partially displacing Britain in the Middle East, particularly in Saudi Arabia, which was understood to be "a stupendous source of strategic power, and one of the greatest material prizes in world history," in the words of the State Department. I will return to this matter, but let us continue to explore the CFR planning documents.

The United States-led non-German bloc was entitled the "Grand Area" in the CFR discussions. Actually, a United States-dominated Grand Area was only a second-best alternative. It is explained in June 1941 that "The Grand Area is not regarded by the Group as more desirable than a world economy, nor as an entirely satisfactory substitute." The Grand Area was seen as a nucleus or model that could be extended, optimally, to a global economy. It was soon recognized that at least Western Europe could be integrated into the Grand Area. Participants in the CFR discussions recognized that "the British Empire as it existed in the past will never reappear and . . . the United States may have to take its place." One stated frankly that the United States "must cultivate a mental view toward world settlement after this war which will enable us to impose our own terms, amounting perhaps to a pax-Americana." Another argued that the concept of United States security interests must be enlarged to incorporate areas "strategically necessary for world control." It is a pervasive theme that international trade and investment are closely related to the economic health of the United States, as is access to the resources of the Grand Area, which must be so organized as to guarantee the health and structure of the American economy.

The notion of "access to resources" is marvellously expressed in a State Department memorandum of April 1944 called "Petroleum Policy of the United States," dealing with the primary resource.[25] There must be equal access for American companies everywhere, but no equal access for others, the document explained. The United States dominated Western Hemisphere production[26] and this position must be maintained while United States holdings are diversified elsewhere. The policy "would involve the preservation of the absolute position presently obtaining, and therefore vigilant protection of existing concessions in United States hands coupled with insistence upon the Open Door principle of equal opportunity for United States companies in new areas." That is a fair characterization of the principle of the "Open Door."[27]

All of this is in accord with the concepts of Grand Area planning, and it also corresponded to the evolving historical process. The United States retained its dominance of Western Hemisphere petroleum resources while the American share of Middle East oil rapidly increased.[28] The British maintained their control of Iranian oil until 1954, when the United States government imposed an international consortium after the CIA-backed coup that restored the Shah, with American companies granted a 40 percent share.[29] Similarly, in the Far East "occupied Japan was not permitted to reconstruct the oil-refining facilities that had been destroyed by Allied bombings, a policy widely attributed in the oil industry of Japan to the fact that the oil bureau of General MacArthur's headquarters was heavily staffed with American personnel on temporary leave from Jersey Standard and Mobil." Later,

American-based companies were able to take over a dominant position in controlling Japan's energy resources. "Under the Allied occupation the Japanese government was powerless to block such business links."[30]

Much the same was true elsewhere. For example, the United States succeeded in expelling French interests from Saudi Arabia in 1947 by some legal legerdemain, alleging that French companies were "enemies" as a result of Hitler's occupation of France, so that the 1928 Red Line agreement on sharing oil in the former Ottoman Empire was abrogated (MNOC, pp. 50f.). British interests in Saudi Arabia were excluded by a different device—namely, when American companies expressed their fear that "the British may be able to lead either Ibn Saud or his successors to diddle them out of the concession and the British into it" (Navy Under Secretary William Bullitt), and "told the Roosevelt Administration that direct U.S. Lend Lease assistance for King Saud was the only way to keep their Arabian concession from falling into British hands," the President obligingly issued the following directive to the Lend Lease Administrator: "in order to enable you to arrange Lend Lease aid to the Government of Saudi Arabia, I hereby find that the defense of Saudi Arabia is vital to the defense of the United States"—its defense from whom, he did not stipulate, though a cynic might remark that the tacit identification of the United States with the Aramco concession is consistent with the actual usage of the phrase "national interest." Lend Lease had been authorized by Congress for "democratic allies." In other ways as well the Roosevelt Administration acted to support the American companies against their British rivals, through aid (Saudi Arabia received almost $100 million under Lend Lease, including scarce construction materials) or direct government intervention.[31]

As an aside, recall what happened when Iranians experimented with the curious idea of taking control of their own oil in the early 1950's. After an oil company boycott, a successful CIA-backed coup put an end to that, installing the regime of the Shah which remains, today, a powerful United

States client state purchasing vast quantities of American arms, conducting counterinsurgency in the Arabian peninsula, and, of course, subjecting the Iranian people to the Shah's pleasant whims.

We should bear in mind that the CIA-backed coup that ended the experiment in Iranian democracy and led to a further displacement of British power was welcomed as a great triumph here. When the agreement was signed between Iran and the new oil consortium organized by the United States government, the *New York Times* commented editorially (Aug. 6, 1954) that this was "good news indeed"; "Costly as the dispute over Iranian oil has been to all concerned, the affair may yet be proved worth-while if lessons are learned from it." The crucial lessons are then spelled out as follows:

Underdeveloped countries with rich resources now have an object lesson in the heavy cost that must be paid by one of their number which goes berserk with fanatical nationalism. It is perhaps too much to hope that Iran's experience will prevent the rise of Mossadeghs in other countries, but that experience may at least strengthen the hands of more reasonable and more far-seeing leaders.

Like the Shah. With typical ruling-class cynicism, the *Times* then goes on to say that "The West, too, must study the lessons of Iran" and must draw the conclusion that "partnership, even more in the future than the past, must be the relationship between the industrialized Western nations and some other countries, less industrialized, but rich in raw materials, outside Europe and North America," a statement that must have been most inspiring for the underdeveloped countries that had enjoyed the great privilege of partnership with the West in the past.

The "costs" incurred in this affair, according to the *Times*, do not include the suffering of the people of Iran but rather the propaganda opportunities offered to the Communists, who will denounce the whole affair in their wicked fashion, and the fact that "In some circles in Great Britain the charge will be pushed that American 'imperialism'—in the shape of the American oil firms in the consortium—has once again elbowed Britain from a historic stronghold." The implication is that this charge, or even the concept of American "imperialism," is too obviously absurd to deserve comment, a conclusion based as always on the doctrines of the state religion rather than an analysis of the facts. The exuberance over the "demonstration effect" of the CIA achievement is also typical, though the vulgarity of the *Times* account perhaps goes beyond the ordinary. The theme became familiar with reference to Vietnam in subsequent years. One might add that the delight in the American success in destroying Iranian democracy persists to the present, though the rhetoric is now somewhat more modulated, and propagandists are unlikely to speak of countries as "going berserk with fanatical nationalism" when they try to take control of their own natural resources.

But let us return to the CFR global planning, which laid out a program for organizing the Grand Area, or if possible, the world, as an integrated economic system that would offer the American economy "the 'elbow room' . . . needed in order to survive without major readjustments"—that is, without any change in the distribution of power, wealth, ownership, and control.

The memoranda, which are explicit enough about Grand Area planning, are careful to distinguish between principle and propaganda. They observe in mid-1941 that "formulation of a statement of war aims for propaganda purposes is very different from formulation of one defining the true national interest." Here is a further recommendation:

If war aims are stated, which seem to be concerned solely with Anglo-American imperialism, they will offer little to people in the rest of the world, and will be vulnerable to Nazi counter-promises. Such aims would also strengthen the most reactionary elements in the United States and the British Empire. The interests of other peoples should be stressed, not only those of Europe, but also of Asia, Africa and Latin America. This would have a better propaganda effect.

The participants must have been relieved when the Atlantic Charter, suitably vague and idealistic in tone, was announced a few months later. The CFR studies were extended in subsequent years to include analyses of prospects and plans for most parts of the world. The sections on Southeast Asia are interesting in the light of developments there. The analyses that issued from CFR study groups closely resemble the National Security Council memoranda and other material now available in the Pentagon Papers, a remarkable documentary record of the design and execution of imperial planning.[32] The similarity is hardly accidental. The same interests and often the same people are involved. The basic theme is that Southeast Asia must be integrated within the United States-dominated global system to ensure that the needs of the American economy are satisfied, and also the specific needs of Japan, which might be tempted again to set its independent course or to flood Western markets unless granted access to Southeast Asian markets and resources, within the overarching framework of the Pax Americana—the Grand Area. These principles were firmly set by the 1950's and guided the course of the American intervention, then outright aggression, when the Vietnamese, like the Iranians, went "berserk with fanatical nationalism," failing to comprehend the sophisticated Grand Area concepts and the benefits of "partnership" with the industrialized West.

The material that I have been reviewing constitutes a primary documentary source for the study of formation of American foreign policy, compiled by those who carried out this policy. We might ask how this material is dealt with in academic scholarship. The answer is simple: it is ignored. The book by Shoup and Minter (see note 22) seems to be the first to examine these records. American scholars justly complain that the Russians refuse to release documentary materials, thus raising all sorts of barriers to the understanding of the evolution of their policies. Another just complaint is that American scholars avoid documentary materials that might yield much insight into the formation of American policy, a fact easily explained in this instance, I believe: the documentary record is no more consistent with the doctrines of the state religion, in this case, than is the historical record itself.

Parenthetically, it might be noted that the Pentagon Papers, which provide a record of high-level policy planning that is incomparable in its richness, have suffered the same fate. This record too is ignored—indeed, often misrepresented. There is a spate of scholarly work on United States Vietnam policy, some of which makes extensive use of material in the Pentagon Papers. Typically, attention is focused on the 1960's. Then we have a detailed microanalysis of bureaucratic infighting, political pressures, and the like, completely disregarding the general framework, set long before and never challenged by those who were simply applying imperial doctrine as carefully elaborated ten to twenty years earlier. This is a marvellous device for obscuring the social reality by diverting attention from the documentary record concerning the guiding principles of state policy, as clearly revealed in the basic documentation that is characteristically ignored.

Space prevents a detailed review here, but one example may suffice to illustrate. Consider a review of several recent books on Vietnam by William S. Turley, one of the more critical and independent American academic scholars with a professional involvement in Indochina.[33] He discusses two "prevailing images of American policy-making on Vietnam": the "quagmire hypothesis," which "held that involvement was the result of incremental decisions made without adequate understanding of probable consequences," and "the interpretation that American policy was stalemated by the need of successive administrations, for domestic political reasons, to do what was minimally necessary to avoid losing a war." The book he reviews, by Robert Galluci,[34] finds both of these images too simple and seeks a more complex interpretation through application of a bureaucratic process model. Turley points out that the Pentagon Papers provide important evidence bearing on the questions.

In fact, the Pentagon Papers provide extensive evidence for a different hypothesis that goes unmentioned, as it is passed over in silence in the scholarly literature—namely, the hypothesis that American policy in Vietnam was a conscious application of principles of imperial planning that formed part of a consensus established long before the specific period, the 1960's, to which attention is generally restricted. This hypothesis is massively documented in the Pentagon Papers and elsewhere, but the documentary record is never so much as mentioned in the book under review, the review itself, or academic scholarship generally. The hypothesis in question is simply not fit for discussion in polite company, no matter what the documentation may be. It is not even a competitor, to be rejected.[35]

I do not suggest that, in refusing to consider the hypothesis in question or the substantial documentation supporting it, scholars are being dishonest. It is simply that nothing in their training or in the literature generally available to them makes this hypothesis comprehensible. It is a reflection of the success of the educational system in "socialization," the success of what the Trilateral authors call the "institutions which have played the major role in the indoctrination of the young," that certain ideas, however natural and well-supported, do not even come to mind or, if noticed, can be dismissed with derision. People who break away from the consensus have little future in the media or the academy, in general. The resulting subversion of scholarship is systematic, not individual. Similar phenomena are familiar from the history of organized religion. Anyone who has spent some time in a university knows how it is done. Some young scholars are "hard to get along with" or are "too strident" or "show poor taste in their choice of topics" or "don't use the proper methodology," or in other ways do not meet the professional standards that not infrequently serve to insulate scholarship from uncomfortable challenge.

The ideological disciplines are particularly subject to these tendencies.

Primary documentary sources like the CFR studies and the Pentagon Papers must be investigated with a critical eye and supplemented by much additional evidence if one wants to reach any serious understanding of the evolution of American policy. It might turn out to be the case that the analyses cited above, which are among the few even to concern themselves with the basic documentary record, are inadequate or even seriously in error in the interpretations they provide. What is remarkable and noteworthy, however, is how consistently American scholarship takes a different tack, simply ignoring the documentary record that does not accord with received opinion.

Consider one final example of how the central questions are evaded in academic scholarship. Let us return again to our hypothetical rational observer attempting to discern some of the major factors in foreign-policy formation and consider some further facts that should immediately strike him as significant.

Since World War II there has been a continuing process of centralization of decision-making in the state executive, certainly with regard to foreign policy. Secondly, there has been a tendency through much of this period toward domestic economic concentration. Furthermore, these two processes are closely related, because of the enormous corporate influence over the state executive. And finally, there has been a vast increase in overseas investment, marketing, and resource extraction in the postwar period, greatly increasing the stake of the masters of the corporate economy in foreign affairs. To cite one indication, "It has been estimated that earnings from these foreign operations by 1970 contributed between 20 and 25 percent of total U.S. corporate profits after taxes, a very considerable magnitude indeed."[36] The basic facts are uncontroversial. They suggest, perhaps, a certain hypothesis for investigation: corporations have some influence, perhaps considerable influence, in setting foreign

policy. How does academic scholarship deal with this issue?
There is a (rare) discussion of the question by political
scientist Dennis M. Ray in the volume on the multinational
corporation just cited.[37] He observes that "we know virtually
nothing about the role of corporations in American foreign
relations." Scholarship has "clarified the influence of Congress, the press, scientists, and non-profit organizations,
such as RAND, on the foreign policy process. The influence
of corporations on the foreign policy process, however, remains clouded in mystery."

Is this "mystery" somehow inherent in the difficulty of
discerning the corporate role, as distinct from the massive
impact of scientists and the press on foreign policy? Not at
all. As Ray points out, the issue remains clouded in mystery
because it is systematically evaded:

*My search through the respectable literature on international
relations and U.S. foreign policy shows that less than 5 percent of some two hundred books granted even passing attention to the role of corporations in American foreign relations. From this literature, one might gather that American
foreign policy is formulated in a social vacuum, where national interests are protected from external threats by the
elaborate machinery of governmental policymaking.* There
is virtually no acknowledgement in standard works within
the field of international relations and foreign policy of the
existence and influence of corporations. *[My emphasis]*

Note that Ray limits himself to the "respectable literature." He excludes what he calls the literature of "advocacy,"
which includes two streams: statements by corporate execu-
tives and business school professors, and "radical and often
neo-Marxist analyses." In this literature, particularly the
latter category, there is much discussion of the role of corporations in foreign policy formation. Furthermore, as Ray
turns to the topic itself, he discovers that the conclusions
reached seem to be correct. "Few if any interest groups,
outside of business, have generalized influence on the broad

range of foreign policy," he observes, citing one of the few works in the "respectable literature" that raises the question. Ray believes that scholars will discover these facts if they "begin to examine the question."

In short, if scholars begin to study the question, they will discover the truth of truisms that have been discussed and documented for years outside of the "respectable literature," exactly as one would expect in the light of such basic and fundamental facts about American society as those noted earlier.

It is interesting that Ray never inquires into the causes of this strange lapse in "respectable" scholarship. In fact, the answer does not seem obscure. If we are interested in careful investigation of the inner workings of the Politburo, we do not turn to studies produced at Moscow and Leningrad Universities, and we know exactly why. There is no reason not to apply the same standards of rationality when we find something similar in the United States, though undoubtedly here the mechanisms are different: willing subversion of scholarship rather than obedience to external force.

Moreover, consider Ray's attitude toward those who do study the major and dominant themes, providing the obvious answers that he himself repeats. They are not respectable scholars, in his view, but are engaged in "advocacy"—while the scholarly mainstream, which carefully skirts the major formative influence on foreign policy, does not lose its "respectability" for this curious oversight, and does not seem to him to be engaged in "advocacy."

If an anthropologist were to observe the phenomenon I have been discussing, he would have no hesitation in concluding that we are dealing here with a form of taboo, a deep-seated superstitious avoidance of some terrifying question: in this case, the question of how economic power functions in American society. Among the secular priesthood of academic scholars, the issue can be mentioned only, if at all, in hushed tones. Those who do raise the question seriously are no longer "respectable." As diplomatic historian Gaddis Smith asserts in a review of recent work by

William Appleman Williams and Gabriel Kolko, they are
"essentially pamphleteers" rather than authentic historians.[38]

In a free society we do not imprison those who violate
profound cultural taboos or burn them at the stake. But
they must be identified as dangerous radicals, not fit to be
counted among the priesthood. The reaction is appropriate.
To raise the dread question is to open the possibility that
the institutions responsible "for the indoctrination of the
young" and the other propaganda institutions may be in-
fected by the most dangerous of plagues: insight and understanding. Awareness of the facts might threaten the social
order, protected by a carefully spun web of pluralist mys-
ticism, faith in the benevolence of our pure-hearted leadership, and general superstitious belief.

It is to be expected, of course, that in any society the prevailing ideology will be designed to protect privilege, while
the experts in legitimation construct a mask for privilege.
As Marx expressed it, intellectuals are "the thinkers of the
[ruling] class (its active, conceptive ideologists, who make
the perfecting of the illusion of the class about itself their
chief source of livelihood)," giving its ideas "the form of
universality, and represent[ing] them as the only rational,
universally valid ones."[39]

An ideological structure, to be useful for some ruling
class, must conceal the exercise of power by this class either
by denying the facts or more simply ignoring them—or by
representing the special interests of this class as universal
interests, so that it is seen as only natural that representatives of this class should determine social policy, in the
general interest. As Ray notes, it is not unexpected that
foreign policy decision-makers should perceive the world
from the same perspective as businessmen: "In this context,
we are not dealing simply with phenomena of influence, for
national goals may in fact be synonymous with business
goals." Extricating the expression "national goals" from its
typical mystical usage, the remark approaches tautology.

Outside the ranks of the priesthood the facts are clearly
presented in the socially marginal literature of "advocacy"

by "pamphleteers" who make extensive and often very insightful use of the relevant documentary sources. Here, it is recognized that the notion of "national goals" is merely a device of mystification, and that the often conflicting goals of various social groups can be conceived in terms other than those set by the masters of the private economy. But the universities, the scholarly professions, the mass media, and society at large are carefully insulated from these dangerous heresies in a highly indoctrinated society, which is commonly described—the ultimate irony—as "pragmatic" and "nonideological." All of this is the more interesting when we realize that the society really is free from ugly forms of totalitarian control and coercion that are prevalent elsewhere.

Carl Landauer, who participated in the short-lived revolutionary government in Bavaria after World War I, remarked that the censorship of the bourgeois press by the revolutionary government marked the "beginning of freedom of public opinion."[40] His point was that the organs of propaganda and opinion, firmly in the hands of ruling groups, destroyed freedom of opinion by their dominance of the means of expression.[41] Clearly one cannot accept the view that state censorship is the answer to the distortion and deceit of intellectual servants of ruling groups. Just as surely, we cannot pretend that there is freedom of opinion in any serious sense when social and cultural taboos shield the formation of policy from public awareness and scrutiny.

It is, in fact, quite true that the business press sometimes tends to be more honest about social reality than academic scholarship. Consider, for example, this reaction to the American failure in Vietnam (and elsewhere) in *Business Week* (April 7, 1975). The editors fear that "the international economic structure, under which U.S. companies have flourished since the end of World War II, is in jeopardy." They go on to explain how

Fueled initially by the dollars of the Marshall Plan, American business prospered and expanded on overseas orders

despite the cold war, the end of colonialism, and the crea-
tion of militant and often anti-capitalistic new countries.
No matter how negative a development, there was always
the umbrella of American power to contain it. . . . The rise
of the multinational corporation was the economic expres-
sion of this political framework.

But "this stable world order for business operations is falling
apart" with the defeat of American power in Indochina.
Nothing here about our unremitting campaign "to do good"
and "advance our moral ideals." They explain further how
Congressional obstinacy is undermining our efforts to persuade our European allies to support our concept of "a
floor price on oil," and the "debilitating impact on international economics" with "the collapse of U.S. foreign
policy around the globe," particularly, "If Japan cannot
continue to export a third of its products to Southeast
Asia." Unless a new "bipartisan foreign policy" (i.e., one-
party state) is reestablished, it may be "impossible to maintain a successful international economic framework."

A year later, however, things were looking up, and "it
appears that the future of the West again lies in the hands
of the U.S. and, to a lesser extent, West Germany," American oil policies being one reason, as a matter of fact.[42] As
the editors note, "trends now at work in the world have
greatly strengthened the competitive position of the U.S.
economy" with the result that "Washington will have more
freedom to maneuver in formulating foreign economic policies than it has had since the early 1960s."[43] In short, the
Grand Area is being successfully reconstituted.

Occasionally, the light breaks through in statements of
public officials as well. Consider for example a Statement
by Frank M. Coffin, Deputy Administrator, Agency for
International Development (AID), outlining "Objectives
of the AID Program":

Our basic, broadest goal is a long-range political one. It is
not development for the sake of sheer development . . . An

*important objective is to open up the maximum opportunity
for domestic private initiative and enterprise and to insure
that foreign private investment, particularly from the United
States, is welcomed and well treated . . . The fostering of a
vigorous and expanding private sector in the less developed
countries is one of our most important responsibilities. Both
domestic private initiative and management and outside
investment are important . . . Politically, a strong and progressive private business community provides a powerful
force for stable, responsible Government and a built-in
check against Communist dogma.*[44]

Another "built-in check" is counterinsurgency, as Mr. Coffin
goes on to explain, "and we in AID of course have a public
safety program which, perhaps to oversimplify, seeks to
equip countries to utilize the civilian police in preventive
action so that they do not have to place excessive reliance
on the military." Many thousands of people in Latin America
and Asia have benefited from this particular element in their
"partnership with the West" over the years.[45] Needless to
say, all of this is spiced with rhetoric on how our aid program
seeks "partnership" in contrast to that of the Russians and
the Chinese which seeks "domination," and so on. Spec-
tacularly lacking is a comparative analysis of the aid programs
to support this claim.

While noting occasional flashes of honesty in the business
press, I would not want to imply that businessmen are free
from the cant of much academic scholarship. Here is a single
example, which could easily be duplicated in years before
and since, to the present:

*You will point an accusing finger and you will hurl the chal-
lenging question: "What about Hayti [sic] and San Domingo,
what about Nicaragua, Honduras, and so forth?" It is true
we did send military forces to these countries. There did,
most regrettably, occur some bloodshed. In the execution of
our program we did commit some errors in judgment and in
manners. We did, in certain measures, proceed bunglingly*

*and clumsily, as Governments and their agents not infre-
quently do, especially when, as in the cases under discussion,
the task to be undertaken is an unusual and unexpected one,
and there are neither traditions which afford guidance nor a
trained personnel to attend to the execution. (Incidentally,
the very absence of such personnel tends to prove how little
the thoughts of our Government and people were on Imperialism.)*

*But the test is in the answer to the question which in my
turn I ask of you: "What was our purpose? Did we go to
oppress and exploit, did we go to add these territories to our
domain? Or did we go to end an inveterate rule of tyranny,
malefactions and turmoil, to set up decent and orderly
government and the rule of law, to foster progress, to establish stable conditions and with them the basis for prosperity
to the population concerned?"*

*I think there can be no doubt that it was these latter things
we aimed to attain. And having measurably accomplished the
task, we did withdraw, or shall withdraw. We left behind, or
shall leave behind, a few persons charged with the collection
and proper administration of certain revenues, but such
arrangements . . . are no more in the nature of exploitation
or oppression than the appointment of a person under deed
of trust is in the nature of exploitation and oppression.*[46]

It would be superfluous to discuss how the United States
proceeded to foster progress, prosperity and an end to
tyranny and malefactions in Haiti, San Domingo, Nicaragua
(see note 45), Honduras, and the other parts of Latin America
"where we have traditionally been a friend and protector"
(see p. 16). The immunity of doctrine to mere fact, in such
cases, easily compares with the so-called "communist"
countries. Such pronouncements closely resemble the blather
produced by pundits of the press as the Vietnam war came to
an end: The United States involvement was "honorable"
though "fraught with mistakes and misjudgments"; "good
impulses came to be transmuted into bad policy"; it would
be unfair to leave "the impression somehow the United

States was responsible for the carnage in Southeast Asia"; our "blundering efforts to do good" turned into a "disastrous mistake"; and so on.[47] Again, it is remarkable how impervious the state religion is to mere factual evidence, extended now over 80 years of imperial aggression, following upon the bloody conquest of the national territory.

I have been discussing one major persistent theme of United States foreign policy, and not a very surprising one — namely, the attempt to create a Grand Area, a global economy, adapted to the needs of those who design United States government policy and the corporate interests that they largely represent. One concomitant of this dominant commitment is the repeated reliance on military force. This is, of course, only the most visible and dramatic device — United States policy toward Chile under Allende or Brazil since the early 1960's illustrates more typical and preferred procedures. But military force is the ultimate weapon to preserve a Grand Area. It is not exactly something new in American history.

James Chace, editor of *Foreign Affairs*, comments on this matter in a recent article. He counts up 159 instances of United States armed intervention abroad prior to 1945. Since World War II, he adds, "we have used military forces in Korea, Indochina, Lebanon, the Dominican Republic and the Congo." He then cites various reasons why we should expect all of this to continue: fears of resource scarcity, concern for the United States sphere of influence in the Caribbean and "regional balances of power" elsewhere, and, finally, the American "concern for human rights and the espousal of liberal, pluralistic democracies."[48]

Recall the cases cited, or other examples of intervention not cited: Iran, Cuba, Guatemala, Chile. In which of these cases was American intervention motivated by concern for human rights and espousal of liberal, pluralistic democracies? It remains a matter of great interest and importance that such utter nonsense can be produced with a straight face and be taken seriously in journalism, academic scholarship, and other propaganda institutions.

Chace points out correctly that the American people continue to support an activist, interventionist foreign policy. One of the contributing factors is the ideology of American benevolence and international good will, as illustrated in his own remarks. I have cited a number of examples to show how this doctrinal framework governs scholarship, as well as the mass media, journals of current affairs, and the like. Most of these examples illustrate how the facts are simply ignored in the interests of doctrinal purity. But it is interesting to see that even direct and overt self-contradiction poses no particular problem for the secular priesthood, which rarely achieves the sophistication of its theological counterparts. As an illustration, consider another article in which Chace returns to the same themes.[49] Here he discusses the "ironies and ambiguities" of "the American experience," referring to the "moral concern" that is "a typical expression of the American spirit" though "We have found that the pursuit of justice sometimes leads to consequences contrary to those we had intended [and] that, at times, our proclaimed ideals serve to hide—from ourselves even more than from others—motivations of a darker and more complex character." "Experience should have taught us," he concludes, "that we do not always completely understand our own motivations," though he does not discuss the elaborate system of deceit that has been constructed to prevent such understanding. What is remarkable, however, is his discussion of particular cases, for example the *Realpolitik* of the Nixon-Kissinger period. "We were determined to seek stability," Chace asserts, and as an illustration—literally—he offers "Our efforts to destabilize a freely elected Marxist government in Chile." Even a direct self-contradiction in successive sentences[50] does not suffice to raise a question about "our own motivations." Rather, the example falls under the category of "irony."

This category serves in the most astonishing ways to disguise reality in the ideological disciplines. Here is a final example, particularly revealing, I think, because of the source. Norman Graebner is an outstanding historian, a critic of cold war idiocies, a "realist" of more or less the variety of George Kennan, to whom the study from which I will now quote is dedicated.[51] Graebner accepts the conventional belief that American foreign policy has been guided by the "Wilsonian principles of peace and self-determination." The United States is not "an aggressive, imperialist country" in the twentieth century, as we can see from the many "references to principle" in "its diplomatic language." The "traditional American dilemma" lies in the delusion that, given "the energy or determination of its antagonists," nevertheless "the nation was always assured that it could anticipate the eventual collapse of its enemies and the creation of the illusive world of justice and freedom." He asserts without qualification that "Certainly all fundamental American relations with the U.S.S.R. and mainland China after 1950 were anchored to that assumption." It is this "American idealism" that caused so many problems in the postwar period.

Having laid down these basic principles, Graebner proceeds to investigate some particular examples of foreign policy in action. He then makes the following observation: "It was ironic that this nation generally ignored the principles of self-determination in Asia and Africa where it had some chance of success and promoted it behind the Iron and Bamboo curtains where it had no chance of success at all."

Consider the logic. A general principle is proposed: The United States follows the Wilsonian principle of self-determination. Then specific examples are surveyed. We discover that where the principles could be applied, they were not applied; where they could not be applied, they were advocated (and their advocacy demonstrates that we are not aggressive and imperialistic). Conclusion: it is ironic that the general thesis fails when tested. But the general principle remains in force. In fact, Graebner goes on to lament that "This nation's selfless search for order in world affairs could not sustain the gratitude of a troubled world."

By similar logic a physicist might formulate a general hypothesis, put it to the test, discover that it is refuted in each specific instance, and conclude that it is ironic that the facts are the opposite of what the principle predicts—but the principle nevertheless stands. The example illustrates the difference between ideological disciplines such as academic history and political science, on the one hand, and subjects that are expected to meet rational intellectual standards, on the other.

This example is interesting precisely because the historian in question was an early critic of cold war doctrine. He argues, on Kennanesque lines, that United States policy was in error. "Error," however, is a socially neutral category. To invoke it is to remain safely within the bounds of the primary dogma: that the United States simply responds to external challenges, and that its policy reflects no special material interests of dominant social groups.

This discussion has so far been fairly abstract. I have not tried to deal with the human consequences of the policy of military intervention against those too weak to strike back, or other measures undertaken to ensure the stability of the Grand Area—policies that it is only reasonable to assume will continue in the future, since there have been no significant institutional changes, and even the critique that developed in some circles during the Indochina war has been fairly well deflected and contained. We may recall how all of this looks from the wrong end of the guns. Seventy-five years ago a Filipino nationalist wrote that the Filipinos "have already accepted the arbitrament of war, and war is the worst condition conceivable, especially when waged by an Anglo-Saxon race which despises its opponent as an alien or inferior people. Yet the Filipinos accepted it with a full knowledge of its horror and of the sacrifices in life and property which they knew they would be called upon to make."[52] It will be recalled that on that occasion too, our selfless leadership was merely attempting "to fulfill God's purposes in history." Even James Chace concedes that in this case, though there were "moral purposes" alongside of self-interest, "we were hard put to find a moral defense for our behavior. The atrocities committed by American troops there were horrifying, as they resorted to a no-quarter war, taking no prisoners, burning villages and often shooting innocent men, women and children."[53]

One might think that after Vietnam it would be superfluous to go into this matter. Unfortunately, that supposition would be false. When President Carter, in the midst of one of his sermons on human rights, explains that we owe no debt and have no responsibility to Vietnam because "the destruction was mutual,"[54] there is not a comment nor a whisper of protest in the American press. And the history of that "tragic error" is now being rewritten to make the people of Indochina the villain of the piece. And when Ford and Kissinger sent their bombers over Cambodia in one final act of violence and murder in that land ravaged by American terror at the time of the Mayaguëz incident in May 1975, even Senator Kennedy, one of the very few Senators to have shown genuine concern over the human consequences of the American war, saw fit to state that "the President's firm and successful action gave an undeniable and needed lift to the nation's spirit, and he deserves our genuine support."[55] The world was put on notice—as if notice were needed—that the world's most violent power had not renounced its commitment to the use of force as a consequence of its defeat in Indochina, at least when the victims are defenseless.

The pattern has continued since. Consider what happened in the demilitarized zone between North and South Korea in August 1976, when two American soldiers were killed by North Korean troops as they attempted to trim a tree under circumstances that remain disputed. For the sake of discussion, let us assume the American account to be entirely accurate: the North Koreans simply murdered them in cold blood. The United States army then cut down the tree, with a considerable show of force, including a flight of B-52s. An important account of this incident was given by William Beecher, former Deputy Assistant Secretary of Defense for Public Affairs, now a diplomatic correspondent. He writes that the original plan was to have the B-52s drop "about 70,000 tons of bombs on a South Korean bombing range only about 10 miles from Panmunjom . . . But well-placed sources say that at the eleventh hour it was decided that to drop the bombs would be too provocative and might trigger a military response from the truculent North Koreans."[56]

Let us assume that the figure of 70,000 tons—more than three Hiroshima equivalents—is mistaken. But why should heavy bombing a few miles from Panmunjom appear "provocative" to the "truculent North Koreans"? Perhaps because they retain some memories of things that happened a quarter-century ago when the United States air force so thoroughly devastated their land that there were simply no remaining targets. In keeping with the principle of believing only the American side of the story, let us recall how these events were officially perceived in an Air Force Study of "an object lesson in air power to all the Communist world and especially to the Communists in North Korea," a "lesson" delivered a month before the armistice:

On 13 May 1953 twenty USAF F-84 fighter-bombers swooped down in three successive waves over Toksan irrigation dam in North Korea. From an altitude of 300 feet they skip-bombed their loads of high explosives into the hard-packed earthen walls of the dam. The subsequent flash flood scooped clean 27 miles of valley below, and the plunging flood waters wiped out large segments of a main north-south communication and supply route to the front lines. The Toksan strike and similar attacks on the Chasan, Kuwonga, Kusong, and Toksang dams accounted for five of the more than twenty irrigation dams targeted for possible attack—dams up-stream from all the important enemy supply routes and furnishing 75 percent of the controlled water supply for North Korea's rice production. These strikes, largely passed over by the press, the military observers, and news commentators in favor of attention-arresting but less meaningful operations events, constituted one of the most significant air operations of the Korean war. They sent the Communist military leaders and political commissars scurrying to their press and radio centers to blare to the world the most severe, hate-filled harangues to come from the Communist propaganda mill in the three years of warfare.

In striking one target system, the USAF had hit hard at two sensitive links in the enemy's armor—his capability to supply his front-line troops and his capability to produce food for his armies. To the U.N. Command the breaking of the irrigation dams meant disruption of the enemy's lines of communication and supply. But to the Communists the smashing of the dams meant primarily the destruction of their chief sustenance—rice. The Westerner can little conceive the awesome meaning which the loss of this staple food commodity has for the Asian—starvation and slow death. "Rice famine," for centuries the chronic scourge of the Orient, is more feared than the deadliest plague. Hence the show of rage, the flare of violent tempers, and the avowed threats of reprisals when bombs fell on five irrigation dams. [57]

Recall that this is not quoted from Communist propaganda or from Nazi archives but from an official United States Air Force study.

The North Koreans, truculent as ever, could not see the beauty of this magnificent air operation, and might find heavy bombing "provocative" today as well, so the original plan was called off.

Only a few years after the USAF succeeded in bringing starvation and slow death to the Asian in Northeast Asia, they were at it again in Southeast Asia. As that war ended, after vast destruction and massacre, the United States insisted on a show of force against defenseless Cambodia during the Mayagüez incident. Sihanoukville was bombed, but a planned B–52 attack was called off—wisely, the *New Republic* commented, because of "predictable domestic and world reaction" and possible adverse effects on the Mayagüez crewmen—not because it would have constituted another major massacre of Cambodians. [58] A year later United States planes almost carried out heavy bombing in Korea to impress the truculent North Koreans. The American people continue to support an activist foreign policy, so the polls indicate, and the articulate intelligentsia are as usual urging us to forget the "errors" and "miscalculations" of the past and to set forth again on our campaign to instill our moral ideals in an evil and ungrateful world. The institutional structures that lie behind the military episodes and other interventions of the postwar years, the ideological framework of Grand Area planning—all remain intact, subjected to little public challenge, effectively removed from popular scrutiny or, in part, even scholarly analysis. It is only reasonable to conclude that the editor of *Foreign Affairs* is quite right when he predicts that military intervention will continue, as will other attempts to enforce "stability" through "destabilization" and to contain and destroy movements that threaten the Grand Area.

A high-level study group of the foreign policy elite once accurately described the primary threat of Communism as the economic transformation of the Communist powers "in ways which reduce their willingness and ability to complement the industrial economies of the West"[59]—that is, in ways that draw them out of the Grand Area, where the United States, as Kissinger has explained, is concerned "with the over-all framework of order" while lesser powers take over "the management of . . . regional enterprise[s]."[60] It is this threat, whether called "Communist" or something else, that the United States government will bend every effort to contain and destroy, by force if need be, by more delicate means if they suffice, while the intelligentsia divert us with tales about our selfless devotion to principle and moral idealism.

Notes

1. For references and further comment, see my *For Reasons of State* (New York, Pantheon, 1973).
2. *New York Times*, February 6, 1966.
3. Ibid., September 28, 1974.

4. Peter L. Berger, "When Two Elites Meet," *Washington Post*, April 18, 1976, reprinted from *Commentary* (March 1976).

5. Samuel P. Huntington, in M. J. Crozier, S. P. Huntington, and Joji Watanuki, *The Crisis of Democracy: Report on the Governability of Democracies to the Trilateral Commission* (New York, New York University Press, 1975).

6. For some discussion of recent examples, see my "Reporting Indochina: the News Media and the Legitimation of Lies," *Social Policy* (September/October 1973), dealing with press distortion of events surrounding the Vietnam peace negotiations and the explicit American government commitment to violate every significant commitment in them, as it proceeded to do; cf. Gareth Porter, *A Peace Denied* (Bloomington, Indiana, 1975); "The Remaking of History," *Ramparts* (August–September 1975), dealing with interpretations of the war in the liberal press; "Distortions at Fourth Hand" (with E. S. Herman), *Nation* (June 25, 1977), dealing with the press version of events in Indochina since the war's end.

7. See my articles "Watergate: A Skeptical View," *New York Review* (September 20, 1973); editorial, *More* (December 1975); and the introduction to N. Blackstock, ed., *COINTELPRO* (New York, Vintage Books, 1976).

8. Charles Kadushin, *The American Intellectual Elite* (Boston, Little Brown, 1974).

9. For some acute commentary, see Julius Jacobson, "In Defense of the Young," *New Politics* (June 1970).

10. *Boston Globe*, October 18, 1976. Variants of this argument are common. Consider Martin Peretz, editor of the *New Republic*: "the American collapse [in Indochina] will read in history as among the ugliest of national crimes" (June 11, 1977). It is not what the United States did in Indochina, but rather its failure to continue, that was criminal. Peretz makes an interesting contribution to the new version of history now being created. He states that the book he is reviewing "stakes out significant independent ground—implicitly against the peace movement" by arguing "that a political settlement was possible," thus implying that "the peace movement" was against a political settlement. Of course, everyone on every side was in favor of a political settlement, but they differed on the terms: crucially, should the National Liberation Front, which the United States government always knew to be the only mass-based political force in South Vietnam, be permitted to share in (hence presumably to dominate) the governance

of the South? The "peace movement," to the extent that such an entity can be identified, argued for a political settlement on these terms, which the United States government rejected on the grounds that if the group it supported were to enter a coalition with the NLF, "the whale would swallow the minnow," in the picturesque phrase of the government expert Douglas Pike. Until it committed the ugly crime of failing, the United States government was committed to blocking any such political settlement; cf. references of notes 1 and 6 for background, particularly Porter. Placed against the background of the actual history, which he knows well enough, Peretz's argument that it was criminal for the United States to desist can be understood in its full significance.

11. Bruce Andrews, *Public Constraint and American Policy in Vietnam*, SAGE Publications, International Studies Series, Vol. 4, 1976. Note that the facts are somewhat ambiguous, as Andrews explains, in that much of this opposition was of the "win or get out" variety.

12. *Crisis of Democracy* (above, note 5).

13. For an inane analysis along these lines, see Sandy Vogelsang, *The Long Dark Night of the Soul* (New York, Harper and Row, 1974).

14. Nathan Glazer, "American Jews and Israel: The Last Support," *Interchange* (November 1976).

15. Gordon Connell-Smith, *The Inter-American System* (Oxford, Royal Institute of International Affairs, 1966), p. 343.

16. Consider Henry Kissinger's characterization of the "statesman": "he judges ideas on their utility and not on their 'truth'." The word "truth" is placed in quotes, reflecting the contempt that Kissinger has always felt for this concept. In the same essay he complains of the difficulty of dealing with the "ideological leadership" of the Communist states: "The essence of Marxism-Leninism . . . is the view that 'objective' factors such as the social structure, the economic process, and, above all, the class struggle are more important than the personal convictions of statesmen . . . Nothing in the personal experience of Soviet leaders would lead them to accept protestations of good will at face value," as we do all the time.

A few pages later Kissinger identifies "the deepest problem of the contemporary international order": it is nothing like starvation, war, oppression, or other trivia that occupy superficial minds, but rather a "difference of philosophical perspective" that separates the West, which "is deeply committed to the notion that the real world is external to the observer," from "cultures which escaped the early impact of Newtonian thinking," and still believe "that the real world is almost completely *internal* to the observer." The French Enlightenment (which revered Newton), Lenin, Mao, and others failed to cross this philosophical barrier (though Russia, he concedes, has partly come to recognize that there is a real world outside of our heads). Just how this squares with the idea that the Communists are difficult because of their absurd concern for objective reality is not easy to determine, but perhaps this all-too-typical nonsense should simply be dismissed as a parody of the academic intellectual, which was in fact quite effective with the media, and remarkably, with the academic world as well.

17. The term is used by Isaiah Berlin, "The Bent Twig," *Foreign Affairs* (October 1972). The context suggests that he has in mind primarily the subservient intelligentsia of the state socialist societies, an apt usage.

18. Above, note 16. It is worth noting Kissinger's uncritical acceptance of the legitimacy of this concept of "the expert."

19. In the article cited in note 16, Kissinger observes that "law and business . . . furnish the core of the leadership groups in America." So far, he is correct. But which lawyers? Those who defend civil rights of Blacks? Obviously not. Rather, overwhelmingly, those linked to corporate power. And which businessmen? The corner grocer? Evidently it is the "business élite," whose special talent, Kissinger adds, is their "ability to manipulate the known"—an ability that they share with carpenters and the peasants who have yet to learn about the existence of the external world. Putting aside the typical obfuscation, the fact that Kissinger carefully skirts is that foreign policy is largely in the hands of those with private power. Some ideologists are more straightforward, e.g., Huntington, who writes (in *The Crisis of Democracy*) that "Truman had been able to govern the country with the cooperation of a relatively small number of Wall Street lawyers and bankers," though he fears that these happy days are gone, since other groups have been "mobilized and organized" to protect their interests, leading to a "crisis of democracy."

20. *New Republic* (January 22, 1977).

21. *Trialogue* (Fall 1976).

22. The following remarks on the War-Peace Studies Project relies on Laurence H. Shoup, "Shaping the Postwar World," *Insurgent Sociologist*, 5, no. 3 (Spring 1975), where there are explicit references for the quotes that appear below. See now also the

important study by L. Shoup and W. Minter, *Imperial Brain Trust* (Monthly Review Press), to my knowledge the first serious study of the CFR, issued in early 1977 to a resounding silence.

23. Cf. Gabriel Kolko, *The Politics of War* (New York, Random House, 1968), and David P. Calleo and Benjamin M. Rowland, *America and the World Political Economy* (Bloomington, Indiana, 1973). Kolko is, to my knowledge, the first historian to have seriously investigated this question. Calleo and Rowland conclude that "the war had exhausted British economic power. To a considerable extent, the United States was responsible. Throughout the War, Hull, determined to break up the British bloc, had used the leverage of Lend-Lease skillfully and systematically to reduce Britain to a financial satellite." The British, of course, were aware of what was going on; Calleo and Rowland quote an "outraged" communication from Churchill to Roosevelt on the subject.

24. There has been much debate over the question of how or whether Western policy deliberately contributed to this outcome. Albert Speer recalls "one single case" of direct cooperation between Hitler and the West—namely, an arrangement for the transfer of German troops cut off by the British fleet on a Greek island to the Russian front, to allow the British, rather than the Russians, to take Salonika. Albert Speer, *Inside the Third Reich* (New York, Macmillan, 1970; Avon books, 1971), p. 509.

25. Cf. Kolko, pp. 302f.

26. The Western Hemisphere was then and for many years after the major producing area. Until 1968 North America surpassed the Middle East in oil production. Cf. John Blair, *The Control of Oil* (New York, Pantheon, 1976).

27. For discussion of how this principle was applied to extend the power of the American oil companies, see *Multinational Oil Corporations and U.S. Foreign Policy* (henceforth, MNOC), Report to the Committee on Foreign Relations, U.S. Senate, January 2, 1975 (Washington, D.C., Government Printing Office, 1975).

28. Cf. Michael Tanzer, *The Energy Crisis* (Monthly Review Press, 1974).

29. This plan was actually imposed on the oil companies by the government, naturally over the strong objections of the British. This is one of several instances that reveal how the government may disregard the parochial short-term interests of even major segments of the corporate system in order to safeguard the more general interests of American capitalism. For discussion, see my

"Stratégie pétrolière ou politique de paix?", *Le Monde diplomatique* (April 1977). The 40 percent American share was distributed among the five major American companies, who were persuaded to relinquish one percent each to American independent companies for "window dressing," according to the Middle East coordinator for Exxon (MNOC, p. 71). It should be remembered that this was shortly after President Truman had killed a grand jury investigation of the oil cartel on grounds of "national security," on recommendation of the Departments of State, Defense, and Interior, who advised that the "American oil operations are, for all practical purposes, instruments of our foreign policy"–and who might have added, reciprocally, that our foreign policy is to a significant extent guided by long-term oil company interests.

30. Yoshio Tsurumi, "Japan," in "The Oil Crisis: In Perspective," *Daedalus* (Fall 1975). Discussing the prewar period, the same author has commented on "the American myth that the government and business circles of the United States operate at arms-length, if not in outright adversary relationships"–Reviews, *Journal of International Affairs* (Spring/Summer 1976). It should be noted that under the conditions cited in the preceding note, local conflict may occasionally arise, since as a generalized agency of American capitalism the government may have concerns different from those of some particular segment.

31. MNOC, pp. 36f.

32. For a review of the contents of these memoranda, see Richard B. Du Boff, "Business Ideology and Foreign Policy," in N. Chomsky and H. Zinn, eds., *Critical Essays*, published as Volume 5 of the Gravel edition of the Pentagon Papers (Boston, Beacon Press, 1972). For further analysis of the contribution of the Pentagon Papers to the understanding of United States imperial planning, see my *For Reasons of State*, particularly pp. 31-66.

33. Reviews in *Annals* of the American Academy of Political and Social Science (March 1976).

34. Robert L. Gallucci, *Neither Peace nor Honor: the Politics of American Military Policy in Vietnam* (Baltimore, The Johns Hopkins University Press, 1975). The limitation to "military policy" is crucial; basic decision-making with regard to the American involvement in Vietnam is nowhere discussed.

35. Largely as a result of the impact of the student movement, it became difficult to ignore completely the so-called "radical critique"–though, as noted, it is not obvious why the assumption

56 *The Literature and Language of Politics*

that the United States behaves much as all other great powers do should be considered particularly "radical." There are, in fact, several publications attempting to deal with it. The most serious, to my knowledge, is Robert W. Tucker, *The Radical Left and American Foreign Policy* (Baltimore, The Johns Hopkins University Press, 1971). For a discussion of gross errors of fact and logic that entirely undermine his analysis (and others), see my *For Reasons of State*. For a very penetrating discussion of critical literature on the "radical critique," see Stephen Shalom, "Economic Interests and United States Foreign Policy," unpublished, adapted from the author's Boston University Ph.D. dissertation: "US–Philippine Relations: A Study of Neo-Colonialism," 1976.

36. Laurence B. Krause, "The International Economic System and the Multinational Corporation," in *The Multinational Corporation*, Annals of the American Academy of Political and Social Science (September 1972).
37. Ray, "Corporations and American Foreign Relations."
38. Gaddis Smith, "The United States as Villain," *New York Times Book Review*, October 10, 1976.
39. Cited by Ralph Miliband, *The State and Capitalist Society* (London, Weidenfeld and Nicolson, 1969), in an excellent discussion of this whole matter.
40. Cited in Charles B. Maurer, *Call to Revolution* (Detroit, Wayne State University Press, 1971), p. 174.
41. A fact of which the business press is not unaware, though businessmen constantly whine of their difficulties in reaching public opinion with their "message." Cf. "Business Is Still in Trouble," editorial, *Fortune*, 39, no. 5 (1949): "The daily tonnage output of propaganda and publicity . . . has become an important force in American life. Nearly half of the contents of the best newspapers is derived from publicity releases; nearly all the contents of the lesser papers . . . are directly or indirectly the work of PR departments." The further conclusion that "it is as impossible to imagine a genuine democracy without the science of persuasion as it is to think of a totalitarian state without coercion" is consistent with the doctrine that propaganda is essential in a democracy because "men are often poor judges of their own interests" and must therefore be controlled by propaganda (Harold Lasswell); "The engineering of consent is the very essence of the democratic process, the freedom to persuade and suggest" (Edward Bernays). Cited in an important article by Alex Carey, "Reshaping the

Truth: Pragmatists and Propagandists in America," *Meanjin Quarterly* (Australia) Vol. 35, no. 4.

42. See my "Stratégie pétrolière," above, note 29.

43. "International Economics," *Business Week* (March 29, 1976).

44. *Winning the Cold War: The U.S. Ideological Offensive*, Hearings before the Subcommittee on International Organizations and Movements of the Committee on Foreign Affairs, House of Representatives, 88th Congress, second session, Part VIII, U.S. Government Agencies and Programs, January 15 and 16, 1964 (Washington, D.C., U.S. Government Printing Office), pp. 953f.

45. Consider, e.g., Nicaragua, where a recent National Guard offensive resulted "in thousands of deaths in the countryside, where whole villages suspected of harboring guerillas were destroyed," and villagers describe "aerial bombings, summary executions and gruesome tortures . . . it is also believed by many that an ongoing American-backed 'peasant welfare' program [heavily financed by AID] is actually a cover for anti-guerilla activities" in the north, where these military exercises are being conducted. Furthermore, "about 85 percent of the National Guard leadership is directly trained in anti-guerilla warfare by the United States" in Nicaragua, which is "the only country which sends the entire annual graduating class of its military academy for a full year of training" at the United States Army school in the Panama Canal Zone. Stephen Kinzer, "Nicaragua, a Wholly Owned Subsidiary," *New Republic* (April 9, 1977). In a pastoral letter the seven principal Catholic prelates of Nicaragua have denounced the "atrocious climate of terror" that reigns in the country. Jean-Claude Buhrer, "Les Droits de l'homme en Amérique centrale," *Le Monde diplomatique* (May 1977). Even the generally ludicrous State Department *Human Rights Reports* concede that there may be a few problems in Nicaragua (primarily, as a result of Cuban-supported guerilla activities), while naturally ignoring entirely the United States role. Cf. *Human Rights Reports,* submitted to the Subcommittee on Foreign Assistance of the Committee on Foreign Relations of the U.S. Senate, March 1977 (Washington,) D.C., Government Printing Office, 1977).

46. Otto H. Kahn, *The Myth of American Imperialism*, publication of the Committee of American Business Men, an address given December 30, 1924, at a meeting on the subject of American imperialism organized by the League for Industrial Democracy, p. 4, section entitled "The Allegation of Political or Military Imperialism."

47. For references, see above, note 6, "The Remaking of History."
48. James Chace, "American Intervention," *New York Times*, September 13, 1976.
49. Chace, "How 'Moral' Can We Get?" *New York Times Magazine*, May 22, 1977.
50. To be sure, the contradiction can easily be resolved. We can take these statements as an indication of what is really meant by the term "stability" in the rhetoric of American political analysis.
51. Norman A. Graebner, *Cold War Diplomacy: 1945-60* (New York, D. Van Nostrand, 1962).
52. Sixto Lopez, "The Philippine Problem: A Proposition for a Solution," *The Outlook* (April 13, 1901).
53. "How 'Moral' Can We Get?"
54. News conference, March 24, 1977; reprinted in the *New York Times*, March 25.
55. Commencement address at Bentley College. *Boston Globe*, May 18, 1975. See below, note 58.
56. William Beecher, "US show of force impressed N. Korea," *Boston Globe*, September 3, 1976.
57. Quarterly Review Staff Study, "The Attack on the Irrigation Dams in North Korea," *Air Universities Quarterly Review*, 6, no. 4 (Winter 1953-54). Cf. Robert Frank Futrell, *The United States Air Force in Korea, 1950-1953* (New York, Duell, Sloan and Pearce, 1961), pp. 623f.
58. John Osborne, *New Republic* (June 7, 1975). Osborne goes on to denounce those "journalistic thumb-suckers" who raised questions about this glorious incident in the wrong "manner and tone" in "a disgrace to journalism." Top Administration officials informed the press that it was Henry Kissinger who advocated the B-52 bombing of Cambodia, but he was overruled by others who felt that carrier-based bombers would be punishment enough. James McCartney, *Boston Globe*, May 29, 1975. The first bombing took place almost four hours after the Cambodian radio announced that the ship, which they claimed had been intercepted within three miles of a Cambodian island, would be released; the second strike against civilian targets took place 43 minutes after the captain of the U.S. destroyer *Wilson* reported to the White House that the crew was safe. Though B-52s were ruled out, The Pentagon announced that it had used its largest bomb, 15,000 pounds. For further discussion, see my article,

"U.S. Involvement in Vietnam," *Bridge*, 4, no. 1 (November) 1975).

59. William Y. Elliott, ed., *The Political Economy of American Foreign Policy* (New York, Holt, 1955), p. 42.

60. Henry Kissinger, "Central Issues of American Foreign Policy," reprinted in *American Foreign Policy*, p. 97.

Chapter 2

"Totalitarianism" in Eclipse:

The Recent Fate of an Idea

Stephen J. Whitfield

For many intellectuals the mid-1930's was the fault line of the landscape of modern history. The hope that revolution could be both decent and successful was dashed, the tremors of an imminent barbarism were experienced, the belief that reason could be injected into history was shaken. Indeed, "history stopped in 1936," George Orwell once told Arthur Koestler, who quickly understood and agreed, for both were thinking especially about the Spanish Civil War and about the general phenomenon of totalitarianism. "The end of a historical period and the horror of the one to come were announced in the simultaneity of the civil war in Spain and the trials in Moscow," Herbert Marcuse recalled, adding that the horror that had culminated in Auschwitz had made his own earliest essays "perhaps not false, but a thing of the past."[1] Even in the haven of America, the editors of *Partisan Review* were irrevocably affected; and in propelling themselves out of the orbit of Communist sponsorship in 1936–37, Philip Rahv and his associates neither ceased their opposition to capitalist economics nor stifled their repugnance toward bourgeois philistinism. Rather they asserted, in the name of democracy, the primacy of the struggle against totalitarianism.

That term was born in the Italian language in 1925, three years after the Fascist seizure of power, when Mussolini boasted of "la nostra feroce volontà totalitaria" (our fierce totalitarian will). He considered the term an apt description of the Italian political system ("lo stato totalitario") and, along with the philosopher Giovanni Gentile, made the word part of official expositions of Fascist doctrine. Gentile, for example, introduced it to Americans in an article in *Foreign Affairs* in 1928.

Hitler himself rarely used the term, but the German counterpart of Gentile, the political philosopher Carl Schmitt, attempted to formulate a Nazi version of *lo stato totalitario* that proved incompatible with the supremacy of race over state in the ideology of the Third Reich. In the Russian language, from the Thirties until the present, the label "totalitarian" has been pejorative, applied by official spokesmen only to Fascist states and never to the Soviet regime or to the ruling Communist party. It is noteworthy that in his most systematic attack on Stalinism, in 1937, Trotsky referred to the "present totalitarian regime" as a bureaucratic betrayal of the October Revolution.[2]

The ascription of the term to Stalinist Russia, Nazi Germany and often to Fascist Italy was common to American political discourse from the mid-Thirties until the Sixties. Then, however, a transmutation occurred; what once had a certain categorical precision became diffuse, ambiguous in its historical relationship to European tyranny, and disturbingly accessible as an instrument of invective and demagogy. The waning of the Cold War and the persistent fear of nuclear war weakened earlier hostility to Stalinism, and in both scholarly and polemical literature the distinction between democracy and totalitarianism became blurred. Americans in recent years have exploited the portentous memories of Nazism in particular to engage in radical excoriation of national conduct and to justify military intervention in Vietnam, but the inferences drawn from the history of foreign totalitarianism were erroneous. Three of the consequences are that the language, which intellectuals are supposed to safeguard, was corrupted; understanding of the past, which is the best antidote to both innocence and despair, was obscured; and the martyrdom of those who were subjected to Nazi and Soviet brutality was demeaned and insulted. Such, at any rate, is the argument of this essay.

The intellectuals most responsible for the abuse of the idea were on the left, and they are therefore frequently placed between the cross-hairs of critical scrutiny. But this essay is not intended to offer a general assessment of the radicalism of the Sixties; I am not concerned with the justice of a cause but with the intellectual quality of its expression. The thinkers who are discussed are necessarily treated briefly, without direct consideration of their overall contributions to scholarship or of the value of their other criticisms of American life. For many of them the issue of totalitarianism was undoubtedly peripheral to their concerns and not central to their own contexts, but I hope that requiring them to sit briefly for portraits here will not result in disfigurement. Totalitarianism has commonly been the purview of students of comparative politics; here it is regarded as part of the history of ideas and is traced among writers who have disagreed about its meaning, its application, its implications, and its importance. But my own conviction should at least be noted that only Germany under Hitler and Russia under Stalin can properly be called totalitarian, and that the recent imprecision and inflation of the term constitutes not only a semantic but a cultural problem which this essay attempts to identify.

Any sketch of the historical background of this development must mention the influential odyssey of Philip Rahv, in whom the recognition of the specter of totalitarianism coincided with the waning of radical estrangement. For with the realization that capitalism was less dangerous than unprecedented tyranny came the dissipation of the energies of revolt. Under the spell of the Trotskyist critique, Rahv explained in 1938 that *Partisan Review* was "revolutionary" but "independent" in its opposition to the Soviet Union, where, "for the first time in history, the individual has been deprived of every conceivable means of resistance. Authority is monolithic: Property and politics are one."[3] Such thorough control was even more awesome than in Nazi Germany, where the institution of private property had not been abolished. The historical impetus toward collectivism might not offer hope of liberation but might lead instead only to a more efficient form of domination. After Pearl Harbor *Partisan Review* supported the military resistance of Western capitalist democracies allied with the Soviet Union against the aggressive and peculiarly barbaric totalitarianism of Germany.

The Allied victory did not eradicate the memories of the Thirties or impugn the lessons of that decade, however, and *Partisan Review* remained haunted by the Stalinist destruction of the humane spirit that had animated classical socialism. Rahv dismissed Bolshevism as "an alibi for mass-murder" while still adhering, more out of its moral appeal than any sense of its political imminence, to socialism as "the only possible perspective, despite its present vulnerability in a world dominated by Soviet totalitarianism on the one hand and American capitalism on the other." In the postwar period, resistance to the aggrandizement of the Soviet Union clearly took precedence over the Marxist injunction to accelerate the collapse of capitalism. In 1948 the editors of *Partisan Review* announced their willingness to "support, if necessary, any force opposed not only to Stalinism, but to all forms of totalitarianism."[4] The editors' appreciation for the relative safety and openness of one party to the Cold War was enhanced, as the difference between intimidation and accommodation, between authoritarian control and democratic consensus sharpened. This sense could be expressed in the contrast between a Lenin who took responsibility for the red terror of the secret police by remarking, "We are all Chekists," and a Jefferson who tolerated conflict with an idealistic Inaugural assurance that "we are all republicans—we are all federalists."

So fully had the dread of totalitarianism pervaded American life after the war that, as George Kennan complained in his memoirs, by 1950 it was "hard to get the Pentagon to desist from seeing in Stalin another Hitler." The generals "viewed the Soviet leaders as absorbed with the pursuit of something called a 'grand design' for world conquest." In that period Kennan himself had observed that totalitarianism "has overshadowed every other source of human woe in our times; for it has demeaned humanity in its own sight, attacked man's confidence in himself, made him realize that he can be his own most terrible and dangerous enemy. . . . To many of our countrymen it has come to appear as the greatest of all our American problems."[5] Evidence for such concern ranged across the political spectrum—from Clinton Rossiter's sympathetic view of *Conservatism in America* (1955), which contrasted constitutional democracy with "totalitarian radicalism," to Arthur Schlesinger, Jr.'s *The Vital Center* (1949), which limned the parallel Nazi and Communist solution to the fear of that freedom essential to the faith of the chastened liberal. The spectrum included the beleaguered socialism of Norman Thomas, forced to deny that he shared the same moral universe as Communists, to the quondam tutor of Senator McCarthy, Father Edmund Walsh, whose *Total Power* (1948) not only emphasized the menace of Stalinism but also showed its similarities with Nazism.

Daniel Boorstin struck a characteristic Fifties note in identifying "the genius of American politics" as antimetaphysical, devoid of the European susceptibility to the "philosophies" of Nazism, Fascism, and Communism. American politicians were supposed to make deals, not ideals; European leaders were not born in log cabins but were "garret-spawned" agitators like Hitler, Mussolini, and Lenin. It was therefore possible to exaggerate the danger of McCarthy, Will Herberg argued, because "the totalitarian demagogue operates with something positive, with some idea or cause, which he himself believes in"—whereas the junior Senator from Wisconsin was simply a wrecker without a crew, a bully without an ideology.[6] The political discourse of the period therefore typically acknowledged, often with complacency and rigidity, the immunity of the American system to the totalitarian bacillus.

This then was roughly the consensus that had emerged in the mid-Thirties and which endured largely intact till the end of the Fifties. Its most brilliantly compelling expression was undoubtedly Hannah Arendt's *The Origins of Totalitarianism* (1951), which identified ideology and terror as the characteristics which made the phenomenon a novel and horrifying form of tyranny. The term was therefore applicable only to Nazi Germany and to Stalinist Russia, not to the country where the word originated; and the struggle against its influence transcended in political and moral urgency the conventional conflicts of left and right. Arendt's work was authoritative in its assessment of the gruesome peculiarities of totalitarianism, uncompromising in the bleakness of its interpretive scheme, courageous in the willingness of its author to stare into the abyss. "Her thinking," Alfred Kazin concluded, "has a moral grandeur suitable to the terror of her subject."[7]

Other retrospective judgments were less generous and accused her of exaggerating evil, and can be taken as symptomatic of a common failure of those reared in liberal democracies to comprehend what is, after all, incomprehensible. "It is my duty to describe something beyond the imagination of mankind," began the dispatch of the London *Times* correspondent who witnessed the liberation of Belsen; and evil for its own sake has continued to elude understanding. Arendt's conception of totalitarianism as a crime against common sense was so baffling that even the hard-boiled British Sovietologist Robert Conquest once asked Tibor Szamuely about the rationale of the military purges of the Thirties. Conquest could grasp why Stalin had killed Marshal Tukhachevsky, but why shoot Marshal Yegorov? Szamuely, himself a survivor of the Gulag Archipelago, replied: "Why not?" It is therefore unsurprising that a very sensible historian like H. Stuart Hughes should find Arendt's book "overwrought, highly colored, and constantly projecting interpretations too bold for the data to bear." Hughes was unsettled by the extreme pitch of "ethical revulsion" that she brought to her subject, by the "historical amateurishness" and "striving for shock effect" displayed in *The Origins of Totalitarianism*. Calling Arendt's parallels between Nazi Germany and Stalinist Russia grossly overdrawn and quickly "dated," Hughes dismissed her book as an icicle of the Cold War.[8]

As her title indicated, Arendt had produced essentially a

work of history. Hughes seemed to blame her because the world itself changed rather than holding her responsible for her views of the world as of 1951, when purge trials were sweeping Eastern Europe and a pogrom against Soviet Jewry may have been in the planning stage. The word "totalitarian," Hughes noted, "began to dissolve as the 1950's came to a close in an ideological situation whose complexities defied any simple scheme of classification. The notion of a bipolar world lapsed; so too did the clear contrast between freedom and totalitarianism." Hughes was indisputably right about the thaw since the death of Stalin, which is why Arendt herself, in the preface to the 1966 edition, did not classify post-Stalinist Russia as totalitarian. But surely that does not alter the earlier distinction between freedom and totalitarianism, for which considerable historical evidence could be marshalled. Nor incidentally was Arendt especially enamored of the Western democracies, which she considered typical of mass society—the matrix of totalitarianism itself. Her theory was therefore suitable as a weapon in the Cold War only in the sense that Koestler had justified the military struggle against Nazism: "We are fighting against a total lie in the name of a half-truth."[9]

Hughes' historical criticism was of a piece with his politics, which in the Sixties was to make him an emblematic intellectual. As an independent candidate for the U.S. Senate from Massachusetts in 1962, he conducted the first of the "new politics" campaigns; and in serving thereafter as national chairman of SANE, he articulated the belief that the threat of atomic catastrophe transcended the political differences between Russia and the West. The legitimate fear of such an unparalleled disaster drove Hughes and others strongly influenced by pacifism to advocate a foreign policy approaching neutralism and isolationism. Never, by his own admission, "a strenuous anti-Communist," even during the moral nadir of Stalinism, Hughes proposed unilateral disarmament as "a dramatic gesture of conciliation" toward our Soviet adversary, believing that the Russian leadership had emerged more fully from its totalitarian past than other analysts could discern.

Not the dread of an American nuclear retaliation kept the Red Army out of France or West Germany, Hughes argued, but "the conviction that they would find themselves most unwelcome there."[10] (As though hospitality accounted for the Russian military presence in Poland and East Germany.) A political stance which began with the justifiable horror of nuclear war resulted in a certain evasion of the challenge of modern tyranny.

Revulsion against war also animated the more influential writing of C. Wright Mills, whose political maturity coincided with the birth of the military-industrial complex in the Second World War. From the publication of *The Power Elite* in 1956 until his death eight years later, Mills's sociology went beyond Marxism, focusing less on the means of production than on the means of destruction. Although he almost never used the word "totalitarian" (once, in *The Power Elite*, it appears in a footnote describing the American corporation), he was, in fact, bewitched by the idea of it and saw militarism as central to the totalitarian impulse. Here he noticed little difference between the Soviet Union and the United States. Nor was either society democratic or open to public participation in questions of life and death; both systems were politically constricted and technologically overdeveloped. The Second World War and the Korean War had erected "the principle of obliteration [which] had become totally acceptable as part of the moral universe of the mass society"; and by the Fifties, the "bureaucratic and lethal machines" of both the Soviet Union and the United States endangered human survival. He was appalled by the "lack of indignation when confronted with moral horror."[11]

Mills conveyed the peculiar dread of total war in the nuclear age, but his solution was appeasement—the unreciprocated dismantling of the American and Western European defense establishment. The United States was supposed to abandon all military bases outside its own borders, and Mills told the Western Europeans that "the only sensible defense today is a citizens' army of riflemen."[12] Such advice might have charmed strict constructionists of the Second Amendment like the

National Rifle Association but probably caused few sleepless nights for strategists from the armies of the Warsaw Pact. Mills speculated that the structures of the two superpowers were converging anyway, and he urged American intellectuals to hasten the end of the Cold War by initiating dialogue with their Eastern European counterparts—even though the ones who had not been murdered or jailed were hardly able to talk freely. (*The Power Elite*, which confines its lacerating social criticism to the United States, was translated into Russian within three years of its American publication. *The Causes of World War III*, a pamphlet whose lopsided prescriptions do not smother its attack on both parties to the Cold War, was untranslated. So much for dialogue.)

Mills had no appreciation for the "realist" argument that the peace might be kept by a willingness to fight. His writings stimulated the conviction that peace was worth almost any price, including the price of ignoring the ancient wisdom that it is risky to be a sheep in a world of wolves, that the renunciation of force may only strengthen the rapacious. Harsher on the society he knew best, Mills minimized the legacy of totalitarianism in Soviet society and did not face the consequences of possible Russian rebuffs to the dream of conciliation. Among the young radicals who so admired him, he encouraged an unreflective belief that an often stupid and pernicious anti-Communism was worse than Communism itself.

The notion of totalitarianism as the primary threat to democratic values faded in the Sixties. This decline can be traced in the work of historians, with those on the left especially prone to discredit the political bipolarity that emerged after the Second World War. Perhaps the first salvo was fired in the last chapter of *The New Radicalism in America*, in which Christopher Lasch criticized representative intellectuals of the postwar era for having betrayed the responsibility of opposition and alienation. Lasch blamed this "anti-intellectualism of the intellectuals" upon their assumption that "Soviet totalitarianism was a greater menace than American capitalism." For example, Dwight Macdonald, whose magazine *Politics* had expressed an anarchist animus against Soviet as well as Nazi totalitarianism in the Forties, was scored for announcing in 1952 a preference for the West, making a "choice as if it were a matter of ultimate allegiance." In the battle against totalitarianism, Lasch complained, Arthur Schlesinger, Jr., "tended to raise political issues to the level of philosophical issues." In a similar vein was Lasch's criticism of Reinhold Niebuhr: "The effect of defining a choice as a choice between rival systems was to blind him to the possibility that systems as such were neither moral nor immoral and that the choices confronting the American intellectual in the late Forties were not questions of ultimate allegiance, not questions of allegiance at all, but questions of tactics and strategy."[13]

Dismissing the intellectual defense of an open society as mere "cant," Lasch proved to be a rather inattentive reader of the thinkers he criticized. To depict Macdonald as anything other than a nattering nabob of negativism shows little insight into a journalist whose specialty was skepticism. Macdonald's most consequential essay, "Our Invisible Poor" (1963), based on the socialist critiques of Michael Harrington and Gabriel Kolko, became the *casus belli* of a war on poverty; and even an article from his earlier "apolitical" phase like "America! America!" (1958) had been rejected by *Encounter* for its discomfiting acerbity. Lasch faults Schlesinger for doing what intellectuals, according to the introductory chapter of *The New Radicalism*, are supposed to do, which is to engage in speculation, to articulate meaning on the plane of philosophical issues. Nor did Niebuhr owe Western civilization "ultimate allegiance." *That* he offered to a God whose judgment of humanity—East and West—Niebuhr made no secret of suspecting would be severe. The theologian's ultimate allegiance was not worldly at all, though he tried to infuse politics with the insights of a faith that was prophetic rather than complacent.

Preference for the West was admittedly value-laden, and none of the thinkers Lasch condemned was bereft of principles or reasons for hating Nazism and Stalinism. They were convinced that some systems were indeed "immoral" and could not have agreed with Molotov's *bon mot*, after signing the Nazi-Soviet pact, that Fascism was "a matter of taste." Moreover the assertion that the issues of the Cold War should have been reduced to "questions of tactics and strategy" is, to say the least, odd for a chapter entitled "The Anti-Intellectualism of the Intellectuals." Such questions have normally been left to politicians. *The New Radicalism in America* showed further confusion of purpose and perspective in that its author's objection to an "ultimate allegiance" to the West did not mean that he had found some set of standards outside the boundaries of its civilization. Unlike Sartre, who endorsed Frantz Fanon's apocalyptic appeal for a "new man," Lasch showed no interest in repudiating Western norms of reason and justice or in encouraging the quest for substitute creeds. The imperfect but nevertheless effective containment of the Communist threat to European democracy enabled the beneficiaries of intellectual freedom to be a little frivolous, to disregard the distinctions that postwar authors articulated between a fairly open society and its foes. The high stature of Lasch's book in the historiography of twentieth century America is therefore symptomatic of an altered attitude toward what Arendt called "radical evil."

The earlier view of totalitarianism further disintegrated in the writings of historians further to the left. Howard Zinn's survey of *Postwar America*, for example, presents the aftermath of the Second World War as follows: "The war not only left intact the existing systems, not only concentrated world power even more tightly than before, but . . . perpetuated the identical values the victors claimed to be fighting against. The stockpiling of weapons continued; so, too, did the system of military alliances." Zinn added that "indiscriminate war on civilian populations as an instrument of international politics did not cease, nor did governmental control of information, the political use of racial hatred, the monopolization of wealth by a few, and the destruction of civil liberties—facts as true of the 'totalitarian' Soviet Union as of the 'democratic' United States." Zinn argued that "the term 'totalitarian' to cover both Nazis and Communists" was too facile in not allowing for "important distinctions," but his caveat was not matched by his own effort to weigh the various counts in an indictment so harsh that the destruction of the Third Reich seemed a tangential achievement.[14]

Zinn's facts are all true; but an historian without a sense of proportion may, as Macaulay warned, "by showing nothing but the truth, produce all the effect of the grossest falsehood." Russia and America may have perpetuated some identical values; but the worst example of wartime bigotry and oppression, the disgraceful incarceration of Japanese Americans, compares favorably to the wartime fate of nationalities like the Crimean Tatars, Kalmyks, and Volga Germans, whom the Soviet regime deported with the loss of about half a million lives and whose languages were also prohibited from being taught or printed. Gross and galling disparities of income in the United States can be determined because, in controlling such information, the government makes it available. In the Soviet Union the "monopolization of wealth by a few" is far more difficult to gauge, although it can be assumed, as Trotsky pointed out in his attack on bureaucratization, that "nobody who has wealth to distribute ever omits himself."[15]

The hostility of other historians to American anti-Communism has also meant the loss of nuance. Richard Barnet compared the postwar attitude toward Russian Communism to "the picture Hitler drew for the German people of the six million Jews of Europe." (There were nine million Jews prior to the Final Solution, and during its execution their fate was an official secret.) For many citizens, "abstractions" like "the Soviet Union, Stalin, and communism" served as "convenient explanations of deep feelings of social and psychological distress." Despite a reference to Walter Lippmann's theory of stereotypes, Barnet seems not to have grasped the point in *Public Opinion* (1922) that human beings cannot think *without* stereotypes. Otherwise we would be incorrigibly innocent, swept along by the flow of unpredictable experience—though stereotypes necessarily limit and distort that experience. The analogy with Nazi racism is unpersuasive, for Barnet himself fails to explain why the Americans' "deep feelings of social and psychological distress" did not trigger aggressive war against the Soviet Union. Nor were American Communists hurled into concentration camps, although in 1965 ex-President Eisenhower told Chief Justice Warren what should have been done to Party members: "I would kill the S.O.B.'s."[16] The judiciary did not follow such advice and, compared to its callous irresponsibility in the Red Scare after World War I, sent only twenty-nine Communist leaders to prison, plus Junius Scales, the only person imprisoned for the crime of Party membership. All thirty jailings were unnecessary and unfortunate—but hardly suggestive of the deep distress that in Europe led to the monstrous crime of genocide.

An even more farfetched parallel with Nazism surfaced in the wake of the Cuban missile crisis in *Studies on the Left*. An associate of that journal, Warren Susman, called the United States "clearly and simply a dictatorship" in which, in moments of crisis, "no checks are at all possible. This is as complete a dictatorship as ever existed in history"—a subject Susman has been teaching at Rutgers. He argued that "Hitler had no more power than John F. Kennedy—in fact, he had less. So John F. Kennedy takes the Sudetenland (Cuba)—what will he want next? Who is to stop him or them or whatever power is in the United States?"[17] The sheer audacity of these assertions almost intimidates any effort to refute this bizarre assessment of Kennedy, whom liberals were then blaming for his chronic failure to get Congress to pass legislation he favored. It may be equally tiresome to note that Hitler was willing to light the fuse of war because he wanted to incorporate part of Czechoslovakia into Greater Germany. Kennedy, whose sponsorship of the 1400-man invasion of the Bay of Pigs had failed the year before (some dictatorship), sought not territory but the removal of about fifty-four nuclear missiles which at one stroke would have nearly doubled the Russian capacity to hit American targets. Quite apart from the unsettling ease with which Kennedy is compared to Hitler, the comparison might have been improved had the Sudetenland been suddenly and surreptitiously occupied in 1938 by an army allied with the Czechs, which might have threatened Germany itself.

The facility with which analogies were drawn between American policies and Nazi totalitarianism coincided with the tendency of other scholars to minimize the horror of Soviet totalitarianism. For instance, a brief resurrection of Stalin's reputation took place in a 1968 letter that Eugene D. Genovese wrote to the editor of the *American Historical Review*: "In irreconcilable confrontations, as Comrade Stalin, who remains dear to some of us for the genuine accomplishments that accompanied his crimes, clearly understood, it is precisely the most admirable, manly, principled, and, by their own lights, moral opponents who have to be killed; the others can be frightened or bought."[18] In reading Genovese, one sometimes has, as Guy Davenport said about reading Goethe, "the paralyzing suspicion he is trying to be funny." There could be no doubt, however, about the seriousness of H. Bruce Franklin, the Sixties academician *in extremis*—an authority on Melville and a member of Venceremos. Franklin's praise of Stalin was fulsome (not only in the misused sense of "abundant" but in the precise sense of "excessively offensive") in the introductory essay to a 1973 Anchor paperback entitled *The Essential Stalin*, which fueled speculation whether publication of *The Vintage Attila the Hun* could be far behind.

A more restrained and sophisticated rehabilitation of Stalinism—under the genteel rubric of "authoritarian socialism"—informs Peter Clecak's study of Mills, Marcuse, Paul Baran, and Paul Sweezy. Genovese hailed *Radical Paradoxes* as "easily the most important book on the American Left I know of." Clecak explains that his title refers to "the seemingly permanent separation of power and goodness in America" and, like Lasch, assumes the virtue of alienation and of distance from conventional politics. Although *Radical Paradoxes* continues the historiographical trend that began with *The New Radicalism in America*, perhaps the major intellectual influence on Clecak's view of totalitarianism is Sweezy,

who with Marcuse "was (alone among his generation) invited
to address students during the rebellion at Columbia in 1968."
Highly regarded abroad, Sweezy "has been eclipsed in his
native country by legions of less important social critics,"
which Clecak interprets as "but one sign of intellectual hard
times."[19] The justification for Sweezy's reputation may be
gauged from his political hegira. In the Thirties he condemned the Dewey Commission's investigation of the Moscow purge trials, and he offered critical support of the
Stalinist regime until 1956, when Sweezy, who was not a
quick student, announced that Russia had forfeited the
"moral leadership" of socialism. Thereafter he championed
Maoist China, moral leadership presumably devolving upon a
society even more closed than post-Stalinist Russia.

Clecak considers himself a democratic socialist but, like
Sweezy, would rather have socialism without democracy than
the other way around. Though critical of utopian extremism,
he seems to forget his own spirited defense of democratic
and liberal principles when actually faced with foreign dicta-
torships of the left. "Without authoritarian socialism as a
beginning point," he writes, "most nations of the Third
World will not have the opportunity to fashion even limited
modes of democracy and personal freedom that masses of
people can use." In support of this generalization, *Radical
Paradoxes* offers no comparative analysis of the economic
achievements of Third World countries, nor any convincing
explanation for the view that democrats should accept the
timetables of dictators for the introduction of freedom. The
echo of earlier apologetics for Stalinist tyranny, which Rahv
was among the first to condemn, is unmistakable, however.
Not that Clecak ignores Stalin's crimes, which are listed as
follows—"despotic rule, denial of basic freedoms, abrogation
of elementary legal guarantees, and severe restrictions on con-
sumption."[20] What is omitted from this catalog is the apparently minor detail that Stalin was also a mass murderer,
perhaps because Clecak is so anxious to insist that the Soviet
regime provided "food, clothing, housing, medical care, education, useful work, and moderate amounts of leisure . . .

China too has made spectacular beginnings." Similar claims could, of course, be made of many other states, including Fascist autocracies as well as regimes that have provided basic services without resort to "despotic rule." *Radical Paradoxes* concedes that Stalinism meant "the virtual absence of democracy" without explaining what that adjective means as a qualification. "Throughout Soviet history," Clecak continues, "political control has been exercised by a small minority, sometimes against the immediate wishes of a large majority, sometimes not."[21] How such popular consent could be ascertained Clecak does not explain—nor, as a defender of authoritarianism, should he be expected to. But ever since Lenin abolished the Constituent Assembly in 1918 (after the Bolsheviks lost the election to the Social Revolutionaries), free suffrage has not been permitted in the Soviet Union.

The mildness of criticism of Russian totalitarianism often coincides with exaggeration of the failures of American democracy, and *Radical Paradoxes* is no exception. While acknowledging the "preservation of a comparatively wide scope of personal and political freedom" in the United States, Clecak observes that in the Fifties "independent intellectuals . . . identified with the Communist Party faced prison and exile. With the sad exception of Julius and Ethel Rosenberg, however, most dissenters were not forced into silence by the threat of execution." No "independent intellectuals" are named, making the statement difficult to evaluate. The most eminent of those independent intellectuals was W. E. B. DuBois, who was indeed prosecuted in 1951 for failing to register as an "agent of a foreign principal" (the World Peace Council), despite Justice Department requests that he do so. DuBois' counsel served without fee, eight of the jurors were black, and the judge himself entered a verdict of acquittal. DuBois professed himself to be "puzzled by the fairness of the judge" who "held the scales of justice absolutely level."[22] And six years later Sweezy himself won a landmark Supreme Court case affirming his right to lecture at a state university. Exile was not enforced; what Communists and their sympathizers challenged in the Fifties was not expulsion but travel restrictions, which the State Department unjustly placed on Americans wishing to visit other countries. A jury decided that the Rosenbergs were guilty of espionage, not dissent; and whatever the unresolved mysteries of the case, Clecak should not have buried the assumption of their innocence so as to convey the impression that they were killed for engaging in political protest.

Amidst the resurgent radicalism of the Sixties, many writers went further than Clecak in subverting the paradigm of "totalitarianism" that was delineated in the mid-Thirties. As a term, as an idea, as a memory, totalitarianism was not minimized, nor dismissed as an historical episode that had been concluded. Nor was the anti-Communist component of American foreign policy compared to Nazi aggressiveness and left at that. Instead, American society was itself condemned for its systematic resemblance to earlier tyranny. In the 1930's Orwell wrote, "the sin of nearly all left-wingers" was to "have wanted to be anti-Fascist without being anti-totalitarian."[23] In the Sixties the tendency of the left was to have been against America without distinguishing it from totalitarianism.

Though Marcuse's influence on the New Left has been exaggerated, a former S.D.S. president commented in 1969, he was the chief theoretician of this attitude toward the United States; and he is therefore an inescapable part of the story of the transformation of "totalitarianism." In 1964 Marcuse defined the term as

not only a terroristic political coordination of society, but also a non-terroristic economic-technical coordination which operates through the manipulation of needs by vested interests. . . . Not only a specific form of government or party rule makes for totalitarianism, but also a specific system of production and distribution which may well be compatible with a "pluralism" of parties, newspapers, "countervailing powers," etc.

By reducing poverty without enhancing happiness, by abolishing toil without establishing peace, "totalitarian society brings the realm of freedom beyond the realm of necessity under its administration and fashions it after its own image." Industrialism is founded on technological rationality, which "reveals its political character as it becomes the great vehicle of better domination, creating a truly totalitarian universe in which society and nature, mind and body are kept in a state of permanent mobilization for the defense of this universe."[24]

Risking an oxymoron, Marcuse identified the phenomenon of "totalitarian democracy." Indeed, by preserving "the illusion of popular sovereignty," the democratic system could be considered "the most efficient system of domination," because it gilded the chains of its citizens. Terror, which Arendt deemed integral to totalitarianism, is hardly central to Marcuse's definition, which, following Mills, does stress the importance of militarism in the United States: "The essence of the established society [is] its innate need of expansion and aggression and the brutality of its fight against all liberation movements." Those liberation movements seem to have been what Marcuse had in mind in later aknowledging the "totalitarianism of the other side," which was "not expansive or aggressive and is still dictated by scarcity and poverty." Although a Russian critic of *Soviet Marxism* accused its author of having repeated "the old bourgeois lie about socialism being a rigorous totalitarian system based on universal oppression," the charge is not quite borne out in the text, which makes little mention of totalitarianism in the Soviet Union.[25] But the frequency with which the term appears in Marcuse's writings is not related to its clarity or its consistency. Totalitarianism is applied to the United States and Western Europe; it also may include the Soviet Union; it seems to embrace Third World Communist states. Totalitarianism can be both terroristic and tolerant, both expansionist and static, and compatible with both affluence and poverty. The term is therefore too grandly inclusive to have analytical merit, because it smothers serious and subtle distinctions, which is how—from the Socratic dialogues onward—thought is supposed to develop and render experience intelligible.

Marcuse's classification of democracy as totalitarian, and of America as a one-dimensional society, led him inexorably to the conclusion that "toleration" is fraudulent, "an instrument for the continuation of servitude." Since toleration requires the recognition of prevailing beliefs, no matter how dangerous, Marcuse therefore argued that such toleration be withdrawn whenever "the pacification of existence [and] freedom and happiness themselves are at stake: here, certain things cannot be said." Among those for whom the free exercise of speech and assembly would be prohibited were "groups and movements which promote aggressive policies, armament, chauvinism, discrimination on the grounds of race and religion, or which oppose the extension of public services, social security, medical care, etc." (That "etc." is priceless.) Who should administer such suppression? Not, obviously, the government but, presumably, an ill-defined "party of humanity." When is such suppression necessary? "The whole post-fascist period is one of clear and present danger. . . . I maintain that our society is in . . . an emergency situation, and that it has become the normal state of affairs."[26] Believers in private medical programs, opponents of affirmative action programs, advocates of military parity with the Soviet Union can't say they haven't been warned.

Buttressed with suitable quotations from John Stuart Mill, Marcuse's numerous critics have advanced cogent refutations of his essay, "Repressive Tolerance." But the inconsistency of that view of tolerance, when compared to *One-Dimensional Man*, has not yet been noticed. His book dismisses incremental reform because it only strengthens the existing framework of repression, because it makes the masters more attractive without abolishing the master-slave relationship. Yet in "Repressive Tolerance" freedom of speech and assembly is assured to those groups (civil rights workers, pacifists, proponents of national health insurance, etc.) whose activities by Marcuse's own analysis would strengthen the forces of domination. In fact his own advocacy of their cause therefore enhances the forces of repression. According to the principles of his essay, he himself should be suppressed for tolerating those groups whose reformism perpetuates totalitarian democracy. Marcuse's confusion can largely be traced to the recklessness of his use of the idea of totalitarianism.

The conceptual havoc Marcuse revealed did little to refine the radical critique of American society. Acting on Blake's principle that "the tigers of wrath are wiser than the horses of instruction," many New Leftists were drawn toward crude invective at the expense of subtle understanding. Their justified repugnance at many government policies, their valid objections to national failures and even to some national ideals, became coarsened by callous parallels to the totalitarian and especially to the Nazi experience. They condemned genuine injustices and drew attention to issues of conscience—but often in a manner that cheapened the almost ineffable suffering of the actual victims of totalitarianism. The consequence was not only to obscure the character of objectionable aspects of American policies and institutions, rendering some radical tactics dubious and making the eradication of evil and error more difficult. What was also striking about the Sixties was a style of political discourse which aimed at shocking the conscience but often succeeded only in insulting the intelligence.

Thus when some faculty members at Berkeley complained that campus radicals' "comparisons . . . of President Johnson with Hitler, or the present-day United States with Germany under the Nazis . . . constitutes a travesty of evident historical truth," David McReynolds of the War Resisters League was unruffled. War was launched and the Jews were persecuted, he replied, not in 1933 but after "several years had passed." McReynolds was patently wrong—a whole series of anti-Semitic laws were passed in 1933—but the conclusion was unaffected: "No, no of course one cannot compare Hitler with Johnson—Hitler moved more slowly toward murder." The Reichstag fire and subsequent Leipzig trial leaped to David Dellinger's mind after his indictment on conspiracy charges in Chicago. During that extraordinary trial in 1969, Dellinger complained that the U.S. attorneys had treated him and the other defendants "in a manner that reminds me of Prosecutor Vishinsky and the other Russian prosecutors in the time of the political purges in the Soviet Union in the Thirties." Perhaps realizing that the rambunctious conduct of the Chicago defendants would never be mistaken for the abject confessions of the victims in the purge trials, Dellinger dropped that analogy in favor of reminders of Nazism. Sentenced for contempt of court, he told Judge Hoffman: "You want us to be like good Germans supporting the evils of our decade and then when we refused to be good Germans and came to Chicago and demonstrated . . . now you want us to be like good Jews, going quietly and politely to the concentration camps while you and this court suppress freedom and truth." [27]

All convictions—for conspiracy, for crossing a state line with intent to start a riot, for contempt of court—were overturned or rendered moot, but that was no reason to repudiate Abbie Hoffman's remark at the end of the trial that "all we did is walk into the courtroom and the court system exposed itself as totalitarian." Instead for some radicals the word had to be more inclusive, had somehow to convey the horror of earlier tyranny without colliding with current evidence of effective opposition. Thus Paul Jacobs and Saul Landau, in their early book on the New Left, identified the enemy as "the broad liberal consensus that has developed present American society into the most 'flexible of totalitarianisms'"; and they warned that unless other Americans followed the prescriptions of the young radicals, a society would emerge "whose value system even George Orwell might not have imagined." Writing in *Studies on the Left*, Norman Fruchter amplified the altered meaning of the term, accusing Americans of participating "in the maintenance of a totalitarian state, because we allow and support our government's treatment of individuals as things . . . in all those countries whose inhabitants we see as ciphers in a political confrontation, and whose lives we threaten with nuclear annihilation. The implicit support . . . which we grant to our overt racists and the systems of inequality we perpetuate, increases the extent of a flaccid but pervasive American totalitarianism."[28]

If totalitarianism could be "non-terroristic," or "flexible," or "flaccid," it could mean almost anything. No wonder, then, that during the New Politics convention in Chicago in 1967 one reporter could ruefully observe that "the word 'genocide' began to be tossed about as though it could apply to acts of simple rudeness." Such debasement of the language, such spite toward the vanished and the forgotten, was not restricted to the radical young. The deaths of twenty-eight Black Panthers in 1968–69, Ralph Abernathy of the Southern Christian Leadership Conference charged, constituted "a calculated design of genocide in this country." Similar charges were repeated, although the figure of twenty-eight does not add up to "genocide" even if it were true, which it wasn't. Edward Jay Epstein's scrupulous investigation disclosed that Fred Hampton and Mark Clark were indeed tragically killed "as a direct result of a planned police raid." Other Panthers were killed in circumstances in which policemen had already been fired upon and wounded, or in which they could not have known that suspects or assailants were Black Panthers. Eighteen of the twenty-eight were not killed by police at all. Black militancy and police response present "basic issues of public policy," Epstein concluded, which "can be neither understood nor resolved in an atmosphere of exaggerated charges—whether of 'genocide' against the Panthers or of 'guerrilla warfare' against the police—that are repeated, unverified, in the press and in consequence widely believed by the public."[29]

A similar overheating of the emotional atmosphere occurred with the arrest of Angela Davis, who was charged with having purchased a shotgun with which a judge and others were killed in an escape attempt. A photograph of Davis handcuffed so shocked James Baldwin that he wrote her: "You look exceedingly alone—as alone, say, as the Jewish housewife in the boxcar headed for Dachau." No comparison could have been so inapposite. Davis' fate was the object of international sympathy and concern. Soviet observers were officially invited to her trial, in which she was effectively represented by counsel, acquitted, and freed. The "Jewish housewife" never made the cover of *Newsweek* (which is where Baldwin saw her photograph), was never tried, had no legal defense or rights and went to her death—not alone but in the anguished company of millions of non-Aryans. That is why the eloquent author of *Nobody Knows My Name* did not know the name of "the Jewish housewife," and that is why she should never have been compared to Angela Davis, to whom the publisher of her subsequent autobiography gave a "high six-figure" advance against royalties.[30]

Baldwin's unmindful comparison was hardly unique, however, for the Holocaust made available an exorbitant source of emotion to the artist as well as the historian, to the polemicist as well as the mourner. Amidst such complexities of feeling and taste, the possibilities of abuse are magnified. "In what sense," George Steiner therefore wondered, "does anyone, himself uninvolved and long after the event, commit a subtle larceny when he invokes the echoes and trappings of Auschwitz and appropriates an enormity of ready emotion to his private design?" The question becomes insistent in considering an honorable response to a poet like Sylvia Plath, who grew up in Wellesley and described her skin as "bright as a Nazi lampshade." In "Daddy," Plath imagined "an engine, an engine/Chuffing me off like a Jew./A Jew to Dachau, Auschwitz, Belsen./I began to talk like a Jew,/I think I may well be a Jew." The question is less urgent, because the answer is far easier, when confronting Erica Jong's second novel, in which the protagonist grotesquely compares the critical reception of her earlier novel to "Jews gassed at Auschwitz." Nor did Betty Friedan flinch from introducing a contradiction in terms by calling the American home a "comfortable concentration camp," in which "the women who 'adjust' as housewives . . . are in as much danger as the millions who walked to their own death in the concentration camp—and the millions more who refused to believe that the concentration camps existed."[31] Such parallels may not provide much illumination of private emotions and experiences in America, but they do degrade the martyrdom that is indelibly associated with totalitarianism. This flamboyant evocation of the victims of the Holocaust shows them little respect—and also suggests a lapse not only of historical sensitivity but of moral control.

Against the dissemination of faulty historical analogies, a genuine understanding of the past is the best weapon; and never were such discrimination and insight more required than in confronting Vietnam. If one error of the left in the Sixties was to depreciate the evil of Stalin, one error of the "hawks" was to generalize falsely from the aggression of Hitler. In itself the lesson drawn from the failure of appeasement, prior to the Second World War, does not account for the American commitment of lives, treasure, and prestige in the defense of the Republic of South Vietnam. But the folly of Neville Chamberlain's diplomacy was frequently interpreted as a validation of military intervention. The lesson of 1938 colored the debates over the necessity and morality of the war three decades later. It seemed to offer the warrant of history and, in affecting the policymakers, had political consequences. The memory of Munich was important because it was there, President Johnson announced, "we learned . . . that success only feeds the appetite of aggression. The battle would be renewed in one country and then another, bringing with it perhaps even larger and crueler conflict." He added the promise that "no man, whatever the pigmentation of their skins [*sic*], should ever be delivered over to totalitarianism."[32]

Such thinking surfaced at least as early as 1960, when Vice President Nixon, a Vietnam hawk even in 1954, denounced Senator Kennedy's reluctance to proclaim American willingness to defend Quemoy and Matsu. "We tried this with Hitler," Nixon warned in the third campaign debate, "and it didn't work." The Chinese Communists "don't just want Quemoy and Matsu; they don't just want Formosa; they want the world." His prophecy set the tone for much of the official analysis of Chinese intentions. In 1965, for example, Lin Piao, Peking's Minister of National Defense, published in the *People's Daily* what Ambassador at Large Averell Harriman labeled "the Chinese Communist doctrine of world revolution. Its significance is similar to that of *Mein Kampf.*" Oddly, the text that Harriman cited does not support his frenzied conclusion. On the contrary, as Theodore Draper pointed out, Lin Piao was telling the North Vietnamese that their revolutionary struggle would not be won with Chinese assistance ("it is imperative to adhere to the policy of self-reliance"). In that year, when North Vietnam was receiving over $200 million in aid from the Soviet Union and $35 million from China, Lin Piao was warning against fraternal relations with the Russians, and urged the North Vietnamese to "rely on the strength of the masses" rather than "wholly on foreign aid—even though this be aid from socialist countries."[33] That was hardly a blueprint for Chinese aggrandizement.

Nevertheless, as Senator McGovern complained a year later, "the Secretary of State continues to talk as though we were standing at Munich." Indeed Rusk told one reporter, somewhat testily: "I'm not the village idiot. I know Hitler was Austrian and Mao is Chinese. . . . But what is common between the two situations is the phenomenon of aggression."[34] The author of *The Origins of Totalitarianism* was therefore correct in noting that "this parallel business . . . runs like a red thread through the justification of American policy in Vietnam," and she considered the parallel an "absurdity." Arendt speculated: "It is as if France or England would have tried to stop Hitler, not by making war on him, but by making war on Slovakia as being somehow in collusion with the Nazi government against the Czech government. They would have started bombing Bratislava and intervening in what could only have been a civil war in Czechoslovakia. If anyone in 1938 had thought that this would have helped to stop Hitler, he would not have been very realistic." In 1954, when the Eisenhower administration asked the British government to help stave off a Viet Minh victory, no support could be mustered even from Prime Minister Churchill, who was not exactly ignorant on the subject of Munich. The Chinese, Arthur Schlesinger suggested, "have neither the overwhelmingly military power nor the timetable of aggression nor, apparently, the pent-up mania for instant expansion which would justify the parallel." Howard Zinn specified another difference: "The Czech government . . . was a strong, effective, prosperous, democratic government . . . The South Vietnamese government which we support is a hollow shell of a government, unstable, unpopular, corrupt, a dictatorship of bullies and torturers" whose national elections were "totalitarian-type."[35]

Given the fragility of the equation of Nazi and Maoist ambitions, a variant was introduced to salvage the lesson of appeasement. A Citizens Committee for Peace with Freedom in Vietnam, which included political scientists Ithiel de Sola Pool and Milton Sacks, claimed to speak for "understanding, independent and responsible men and women who have consistently opposed rewarding international aggressors from Adolf Hitler to Mao Tse-tung." It warned that if the United States were to jettison its commitments in Vietnam, "Peking and Hanoi, flushed with success, [would] continue their expansionist policy through many other 'wars of liberation.'"[36] The historic resistance of the Vietnamese to Chinese hegemony is simply ignored in the assumed identity of interest in expansion.

Others justified American intervention as a specific response not to the Chinese but to the North Vietnamese. Graham Martin, the last American ambassador to our client Republic of South Vietnam, warned in 1974 that Hanoi wanted "to bring the people of South Vietnam under a regime so totalitarian that, in comparison, Solzhenitsyn's *Gulag Archipelago* describes a moderate and liberal regime." More measured in his judgment, John P. Roche condemned North Vietnam for its "aggressive totalitarianism" and thus favored preserving "the integrity of the Saigon Government from Communist aggression masked as 'civil war.'" Roche altered the Munich analogy by comparing South Vietnam to the fascist regime in Poland before the Second World War: "Poland was the symbolic break in the policy of appeasement, the place where the line was drawn. . . . South Vietnam, which is certainly not a fascist state, has today the same sort of symbolic significance"—the place, in effect, where the lie had to be fought in the name of a partial truth.[37]

These arguments only heightened the confusion, for it is difficult to see what was misleading about the designation of the conflict in Vietnam as a civil war. The demilitarized zone established in the Final Declaration of the Geneva Accords was not intended to be a territorial or political boundary nor anything more permanent than a military demarcation line. Pham Van Dong, the premier of North Vietnam, was a Southerner by background; Saigon's Marshal Nguyen Cao Ky was a Northerner. The Viet Cong were overwhelmingly Southerners; even the Department of Defense claimed that only about a battalion of North Vietnamese regular troops were in the South when the systematic bombing of North Vietnam began in February 1965.[38] Since the intervention of Italian ground troops and the German Condor Legion did not mean that the Spanish civil war ceased to be Spanish, it is unclear what additional criteria would have satisfied the definition of a civil war in Vietnam. Since no analyst claimed that the North Vietnamese Workers Party (Lao Dong) had territorial ambitions beyond Indochina, it made no sense to enunciate the symbolic need to end the policy of appeasement as though Ho were Hitler.

Those who supported American intervention, Arthur Waskow explained, "were deeply and permanently scarred by the emergence of Hitler and Stalin, into the belief that Totalitarianism had a capital T, was unchangeable and diabolical . . . a belief which ratifies the assumption that Vietnam is the same situation as that of Czechoslovakia." This explanation is incomplete, for many intellectuals who were scarred by totalitarianism—Arendt, Macdonald, Lippmann, Niebuhr, Irving Howe, Schlesinger after 1965, among those discussed in this essay—did not believe that their memories of Hitler and Stalin dictated military intervention in Indochina. Others opposed the war precisely because in part they feared the growth of the totalitarian spirit in the United States. Rebutting Justice Fortas' pamphlet against civil disobedience, Zinn warned against undue deference to authority: "To exalt the rule of law as an absolute is the mark of totalitarianism, and it is possible to have an atmosphere of totalitarianism in a society which has many of the attributes of democracy." The psychologist Stanley Milgram drew a similar implication from what was nicknamed "the Eichmann experiment" in his analysis of American military conduct in Vietnam. Noam Chomsky also speculated that war in Asia might result in "a growing totalitarian menace" at home, and so scarred was he by the earlier European experience that he wondered "whether what is needed in the United States is dissent—or denazification. . . . To me it seems that what is needed is a kind of denazification." To Chomsky the Munich analogy made sense only if Johnson were cast in the role of Hitler, thus adding to the case against the war the weight of the most frightening and complicated memories.[39] That weight was not evenly distributed, for Chomsky did not accept the obligation to distinguish the motives and effects of two disastrous wars. For both hawks and doves, the legacy of totalitarianism continued to reverberate in diverse but discernible ways; and the efforts to combat it necessarily tinctured American political culture.

Despite the residual power of "totalitarianism" in general discourse in the Sixties and thereafter, the idea was not sustained in scholarly and theoretical literature. One instance of this decline was Merle Fainsod's standard text, *How Russia Is Ruled.* Positing the continuity of Soviet totalitarianism, the 1953 edition concluded with the generalization that "the totalitarian regime does not shed its police-state characteristics; it dies when power is wrenched from its hands." This rigid conclusion did not reappear in the 1963 edition. Other leading practitioners of Soviet studies also discarded the totalitarian model by the early Sixties as "ahistorical" and "historically limited." It was therefore possible for Michael Curtis to insist that "it does not serve the cause of comparative political analysis or of political understanding to cling to the concept of totalitarianism."[40]

Even the historical value of the idea—not merely its current applicability—came into question. To classify the Soviet regime of the Sixties as no longer totalitarian was of course quite different from insisting that it had never been so. Yet that was the form that revisionism took in the historiography of modern Germany. The editors of an important collection of Nazi documents announced that "the conventional view of the Third Reich as a monolithic totalitarian state, a view perpetuated by numerous popular accounts of the regime . . . bear[s] little resemblance to reality." And Geoffrey Barraclough's review of the historical literature on Nazism also claimed that the Third Reich was so anarchic and inefficient as to constitute "almost a 'caricature' of a totalitarian state."[41] Was there a definition precise enough to convince intellectuals for whom totalitarianism meant almost everything and compelling enough to instruct those for whom totalitarianism meant nothing?

Despite the revisionism and skepticism of scholarly discourse, the value of the concept of totalitarianism, however limited, still needs to be asserted as a formulation of what is most painful about the twentieth century past. Though the idea is without current applicability in comparative political analysis, it can still help to illuminate—even if it cannot dispel—the historical darkness. Above all, Irving Howe has concluded, the theory "has helped us to maintain a moral response." The characteristic studies of Arendt and Orwell, "whatever their faults and 'exaggerations,' did us a moral and intellectual service by insisting that totalitarianism was not merely an extension of monopoly capitalism, Russian expansionism, Leninist dictatorship, man's inherent sinfulness, or anything else."[42] The concept of a tyrannical rule unprecedented in its scope and capacity for evil has not been superseded, for no other framework has been found within which to assimilate all the reports which "describe something beyond the imagination of mankind."

In the same essay Howe suspected that totalitarianism had not been extinguished in the West, that "impulses in the direction of totalitarianism, or at least authoritarianism," could be located in America as well. Because Howe's suspicion represents a measured and more reasonable version of the radical denunciation of American society, because his fear of domestic totalitarianism indicates the resonance of the idea in the Sixties, some confrontation with this view is obligatory. "This process," Howe suggested, "which is as difficult to label as it is easy to observe, involves the increasing helplessness of individual man, the loss of energy and direction among traditional social movements, the lessening of distinctions between political and economic power, the triumph of the state in every area of economics and culture, the 'machinization' of life." This trend, in reducing the pressure of material need, might result in a "usually nonterroristic yet essentially unfree authoritarianism, a society that might provide men with food, television, and houses of a kind but would not permit or encourage them to achieve true human status." He hoped, rather nervously, that "this is merely a bad dream of my own."[43]

Such anxiety, it is apparent, was not unique to Howe, whose image of the future is akin not only to the present one-dimensional society of Marcuse but also suggestive of the "mild tyranny" that Tocqueville dreaded as a possible culmination of American democracy. Volume II, chapter 6, of his 1840 classic imagines a society that would keep its citizens "in perpetual childhood. . . . It provides for their security, foresees and supplies their necessities, facilitates their pleasures [and] manages their principal concerns. . . . Thus it every day renders the exercise of the free agency of man less useful and less frequent." Such a dream cannot be utterly discounted, for not all the precincts have reported that it can't happen here; but so far it is a bad dream from which all of us should have awakened.

To lament, for example, the present "helplessness of individual man" is to be burdened with a useless abstraction. Only if it is specified which sorts of men and women, of which class and occupation, of which race and religion and region, of what age and belief and purpose, can such a problem be analyzed. Even in the turbulence of the Sixties, much evidence could have been marshaled against the fear of impending authoritarianism. Blacks had never been more successful in the active pursuit of their constitutional rights and of their just place in American life. Young people had never been more aggressive or free. The feminist movement was also reborn in the Sixties; and its impact in enhancing women's sense of autonomy has been incalculable as an antidote to the feeling of individual helplessness. The socialist movement indeed lost its energy and direction; some of its panaceas were, in however desultory a fashion, enacted as the buccaneer capitalism of the nineteenth century was transformed into the welfare state. Certainly the labor movement has lost much of its élan, though hardly its clout or its impulse to increase the benefits of that state.

Furthermore, the view that the representatives of political and economic power have never been chummier is ahistorical. Even if a socialist cannot tell the difference between Democrats and Republicans and the constituencies to which they have appealed, it would be difficult to miss, say, the tenacity with which all the instruments of the state were used to crush labor in the late nineteenth century, or the cohesiveness of class rule in the 1920's. Nor has the state triumphed "in every area of economics and culture." The problem with the mass media is not that they are politicized but that they are commercialized; and prestigious sectors of the academy are, though not inviolate, largely independent of political control. State intervention, while no unmixed blessing, has commonly emerged in opposition to often pernicious business power, not upon the ruins of freedom. And while it is not enviable to have to advocate the mechanization of life, for most of history the absence of machines has meant toil of the most brutal and degrading kind, not the alternative of arcadia.

In describing the postwar trend of diminished freedom, it is curious that Howe failed to discuss state intervention under the aegis of the judiciary, which has resulted in an extraordinary extension of civil liberty. The increased respect for individual rights in a Constitutional system is utterly incompatible with totalitarianism, as literary evidence makes plain. Falsely accused of treason, Ivan Denisovich Shukhov yields to compulsory self-incrimination. "The way he figured," Solzhenitsyn writes, "it was very simple. If he didn't sign, he was as good as buried. But if he did, he'd still go on living for a while. So he signed." Even more stark is the title story of Jakov Lind's collection of Holocaust stories, *Soul of Wood*, which opens as follows: "Those who had no papers entitling them to live lined up to die." That is the essence of totalitarianism.

The recognition that American experience has been different may not offer much consolation, since it is impossible to ignore the tangle of injustice and pain in which our history has been enmeshed. Those evils have been genuine, but they must not be complicated and obscured by parallels which can neither hasten the removal of our own discontents nor inspire fidelity to the mute agony of the victims of totalitarianism. A balanced sense of history is more than a corrective to the illusions of sentimentality, to the assumption that past societies were more conducive to liberty. The historical sense can also guard against unwarranted pessimism, against the fear that the experience of European tyranny is about to repeat itself. Nazism and Stalinism are likely to remain elusive in important respects, not quite within the capacity of the sensible intelligence to absorb. Nevertheless the effort to assimilate the meaning of unparalleled disaster must be made, as the sense of human solidarity and continuity requires. But Hawthorne's admonition ought to guide the struggle to comprehend totalitarianism: "Keep the imagination sane."

Notes

1. George Orwell, *My Country Right or Left, 1940–1943,* ed. Sonia

Orwell and Ian Angus (New York: Harcourt Brace Jovanovich, 1968), p. 256. Herbert Marcuse, *Negations: Essays in Critical Theory* (Boston: Beacon, 1968), p. xv.

2. Leonard Schapiro, *Totalitarianism* (New York: Praeger, 1972), pp. 13-14. Giovanni Gentile, "The Philosophic Basis of Fascism," *Foreign Affairs*, 6 (January 1928), 299, 301. Franz Neumann, *Behemoth: The Structure and Practice of National Socialism, 1933-1944* (New York: Oxford University Press, 1944), pp. 48-49. Leon Trotsky, *The Revolution Betrayed* (New York: Pioneer, 1945), p. 279.

3. "Editorial Statement," *Partisan Review*, 4 (December 1937), 3. Philip Rahv, "Trials of the Mind," ibid., 4 (April 1938), 7.

4. Rahv, "Disillusionment and Partial Answers," ibid., 15 (May 1948), 528. William Phillips, "The Politics of Desperation," ibid., 15 (April 1948), 452.

5. George F. Kennan, *Memoirs, 1950-1963* (Boston: Atlantic, Little Brown, 1972), pp. 90, 92. Kennan, "Totalitarianism in the Modern World," in Carl J. Friedrich, ed., *Totalitarianism* (Cambridge: Harvard University Press, 1954), p. 17.

6. Daniel J. Boorstin, *The Genius of American Politics* (Chicago: University of Chicago Press, 1953), p. 3. Boorstin, *The Americans: The Colonial Experience* (New York: Random House, 1958), p. 154. Will Herberg, "McCarthy and Hitler: A Delusive Parallel," *New Republic*, 131 (August 23, 1954), 14.

7. Alfred Kazin, in "Outstanding Books, 1931-1961," *American Scholar*, 30 (Winter 1961), p. 612.

8. Quoted in Alfred Kazin, *Bright Book of Life: American Novelists and Storytellers from Hemingway to Mailer* (New York: Dell, 1973), p. 81. Robert Conquest, "Evolution of an Exile: *Gulag Archipelago*," in Kathryn Feuer, ed., *Solzhenitsyn* (Englewood Cliffs, New Jersey: Prentice-Hall, 1976), p. 95. H. Stuart Hughes, *The Sea Change: The Migration of Social Thought, 1930-1965* (New York: Harper and Row, 1975), pp. 120, 121, 123.

9. Hughes, *Sea Change*, p. 125. Arthur Koestler, *The Yogi and the Commissar* (New York: Macmillan, 1945), p. 100.

10. H. Stuart Hughes, *An Approach to Peace* (New York: Atheneum, 1962), pp. ix, 70, 76.

11. C. Wright Mills, *The Power Elite* (New York: Oxford University Press, 1956), p. 126n. Mills, *The Causes of World War III* (New York: Simon and Schuster, 1958), pp. 46, 77, 78.

12. Mills, *World War III*, p. 108.

13. Christopher Lasch, *The New Radicalism in America, 1889-1963: The Intellectual as a Social Type* (New York: Knopf, 1965), pp. 300, 301, 308, 331.

14. Howard Zinn, *Postwar America: 1945-1971* (Indianapolis: Bobbs-Merrill, 1973), p. 35. Zinn, *The Politics of History* (Boston: Beacon, 1970), p. 219.

15. Robert Conquest, *The Nation Killers: The Soviet Deportation of Nationalities* (New York: Macmillan, 1970), pp. 11-12. Trotsky, *Revolution Betrayed*, p. 113.

16. Richard J. Barnet, *Roots of War* (Baltimore: Penguin, 1973), p. 253. Earl Warren, *The Memoirs of Chief Justice Earl Warren* (Garden City, New York: Doubleday, 1977), pp. 5-6.

17. Warren Susman, "The Radicalism of Exposure," *Studies on the Left*, 3 (Winter 1963), 72-73.

18. Eugene D. Genovese, *In Red and Black: Marxian Explorations in Southern and Afro-American History* (New York: Vintage, 1972), p. 371.

19. Peter Clecak, *Radical Paradoxes: Dilemmas of the American Left, 1945-1970* (New York: Harper and Row, 1973), pp. vii, 321.

20. Ibid., pp. 26, 292.

21. Ibid., pp. 26, 85, 281.

22. Ibid., p. 16. Francis L. Broderick, *W. E. B. DuBois: Negro Leader in a Time of Crisis* (Stanford: Stanford University Press, 1959), pp. 218, 223.

23. George Orwell, *As I Please, 1943-1945*, ed. Sonia Orwell and Ian Angus (New York: Harcourt Brace Jovanovich, 1968), p. 236.

24. Carl Oglesby, ed., *The New Left Reader* (New York: Grove, 1969), p. 32. Herbert Marcuse, *One-Dimensional Man; Studies in the Ideology of Advanced Industrial Society* (Boston: Beacon, 1964), pp. 3, 18. Marcuse, *Negations*, p. xx.

25. Marcuse, *One-Dimensional Man*, p. 52. Marcuse, *Five Lectures* (Boston: Beacon, 1970), pp. 86, 94. Marcuse, *Soviet Marxism: A Critical Analysis* (New York: Vintage, 1961), pp. v, 96.

26. Herbert Marcuse, "Repressive Tolerance," in Robert Paul Wolff et al., *A Critique of Pure Tolerance* (Boston: Beacon, 1965), pp. 85, 88, 100, 109-110.

27. "Open Letter to Faculty Participants in the Vietnam Day Committee," and David McReynolds, "Comment," *Liberation*, 10 (November 1965), 20, 29. Dave Dellinger, *Revolutionary Nonviolence* (Garden City, New York: Doubleday Anchor, 1971),

pp. 480-482, 487-488. Mark L. Levine et al., eds., *The Tales of Hoffman* (New York: Bantam, 1970), p. 262.

28. Levine, *Tales of Hoffman*, p. 286; Paul Jacobs and Saul Landau, *The New Radicals* (New York: Vintage, 1966), pp. 36-37, 85. Norman Fruchter, "Arendt's Eichmann and Jewish Identity," in James Weinstein and David W. Eakins, eds., *For a New America: Essays in History and Politics from "Studies on the Left"* (New York: Vintage, 1970), pp. 428-429.

29. Renata Adler, *Toward a Radical Middle* (New York: Dutton, 1971), p. 241. Edward Jay Epstein, *Between Fact and Fiction: The Problem of Journalism* (New York: Vintage, 1975), pp. 35, 52, 76-77.

30. James Baldwin, "An Open Letter to my Sister, Miss Angela Davis," *New York Review of Books*, 15 (January 7, 1971), 15. Shlomo Katz, "An Open Letter to James Baldwin," *Midstream*, 17 (April 1971), 3-5. "Bernard Geis and Bantam Books Sign Angela Davis," *Publishers Weekly*, 202 (October 30, 1972), 36.

31. Irving Howe, *The Critical Point: On Literature and Culture* (New York: Horizon, 1973), pp. 164, 166. Betty Friedan, *The Feminine Mystique* (New York: Norton, 1963), pp. 305-308, 309.

32. *New York Times*, July 29, 1965, 12; October 26, 1967, 10.

33. Quoted in Robert A. Divine, *Foreign Policy and U. S. Presidential Elections, 1952-1960* (New York: Franklin Watts, 1974), p. 263. Theodore Draper, *Abuse of Power* (New York: Viking, 1967), pp. 141-142. Arthur M. Schlesinger, Jr., *The Bitter Heritage: Vietnam and American Democracy, 1941-1966* (New York: Fawcett Crest, 1967), p. 82.

34. George McGovern, in "Containing China," *Commentary*, 41 (May 1966), 36. Schlesinger, *Bitter Heritage*, pp. 80-81.

35. Hannah Arendt, in "Containing China," *Commentary*, 41 (May 1966), 34. Schlesinger, *Bitter Heritage*, pp. 81-82. Howard Zinn, *Vietnam: The Logic of Withdrawal* (Boston: Beacon, 1967), p. 87.

36. Quoted in Noam Chomsky, *American Power and the New Mandarins* (New York: Vintage, 1969), pp. 51-52.

37. Quoted in William Shawcross, "How Thieu Hangs On," *New York Review of Books*, 21 (July 18, 1974), 16. John P. Roche, *Sentenced to Life: Reflections on Politics, Education, and Law* (New York: Macmillan, 1974), pp. 62, 63, 66, 67.

38. Frances FitzGerald, *Fire in the Lake: The Vietnamese and the Americans in Vietnam* (New York: Vintage, 1973), p. 90. Draper, *Abuse of Power*, pp. 75-82.

39. Arthur I. Waskow, "The New Student Movement," *Dissent*, 12 (Autumn 1965), 491. Howard Zinn, *Disobedience and Democracy: Nine Fallacies on Law and Order* (New York: Vintage, 1968), p. 120. Stanley Milgram, *Obedience to Authority* (New York: Harper and Row, 1974), pp. 180-183, 210-211. Noam Chomsky, *At War with Asia* (New York: Vintage, 1970), p. 159. Chomsky, *New Mandarins*, pp. 16, 262, 353.

40. Stephen F. Cohen, "Bolshevism and Stalinism," in Robert C. Tucker, *Stalinism: Essays in Historical Interpretation* (New York: Norton, 1977), pp. 10, 24. Michael Curtis, "Retreat from Totalitarianism," in Carl J. Friedrich, et al., *Totalitarianism in Perspective: Three Views* (New York: Praeger, 1969), p. 116.

41. Jeremy Noakes and Geoffrey Pridham, eds., *Documents on Nazism, 1919-1945* (New York: Viking, 1974), p. 9. Geoffrey Barraclough, "Farewell to Hitler," *New York Review of Books*, 22 (April 3, 1975), 16.

42. Irving Howe, *Steady Work: Essays in the Politics of Democratic Radicalism, 1953-1966* (New York: Harcourt, Brace and World, 1966), pp. 240, 241.

43. Ibid., pp. 242-243.

Part II

The Politics of Literature

and Language

Chapter 3

Mimesis and the Motive for Fiction

Robert Alter

If you suggest some fresh and more ingenious reason for doubting that the author meant what he said, or that what he said had any truth-content of the remotest kind, you win ten points by the rules of the modern-critical game; you lose ten points if you suggest he said it because he meant it, and twenty if you suggest he said it because it was true.
—George Watson, "Literary Research: Thoughts for an Agenda," *Times Literary Supplement*, February 25, 1977

Mimesis, which for so long has seemed the very touchstone of the Western literary enterprise, and which only a generation ago served as the grandly resonant title for one of our century's masterworks of criticism, appears to have fallen on evil days. The current objections to the idea that literary works might be thought to *represent* the real world were first generally articulated, with formidable dialectical subtlety, in France in the mid-1960's. By the end of the decade, Structuralism and its various metaphysical and psychoanalytic deviations had come to dominate literary discourse in France, with strong waves of influence radiating out to neighboring countries and across the Channel to England. In America the tide of Structuralism began to rise in the early 1970's, and it would be foolhardy to predict when it is likely to ebb. Handbooks to explain the movement, dictated both by the intrinsic difficulty of the primary texts and by the monolingualism of most American literary intellectuals, appear every few months; new journals of semiotics sprout like mushrooms; and it is hard to find a doctoral dissertation in literary studies these days that does not bristle with Roland Barthes, Gérard Genette, Jacques Lacan, Michel Foucault, Tzvetan Todorov, Jacques Dérrida, and their confrères.

Criticism, like any other cultural activity, has its social and political contexts, and I think we can make some sense of the current vogue of Structuralism in America if we consider what was happening in this country in the Sixties together with the mixed legacy of the previous generation of American criticism. We have come to think of the 1940's, with some overlap from the preceding and subsequent decades, as our Great Age of Criticism. It is important to keep in mind, however, that most of the influential critics of this period were divided, roughly speaking, into two groups of opposing tendencies. The New Critics, of course, were politically and culturally conservative, agrarian in background and allegiance, and characteristically devoted their subtle attention to the lyric poem, which they tended to imagine as a world in itself detached from history, an intricate structure of paradox and irony at once immeasurably denser and finer in substance than the crude stuff of extraliterary reality. On the other side of the cultural divide, in that age of little magazines, stood the *Partisan Review* critics, whose values were urban and cosmopolitan, whose politics ran from left-liberal to Trotskyist, who were anxiously concerned with how imaginative literature reflected historical forces or provided a critical perspective on them, and who therefore chose the novel as their favored genre of discussion, with particular emphasis on the nineteenth and early twentieth century.

All this is familiar enough, but what I should like to stress is that the New Critics provided a method, while the New York critics suggested a stance, and that difference had large consequences in the kind of influence exerted by the two groups. Lionel Trilling, Philip Rahv, Irving Howe, Alfred Kazin, and others of the New York circle projected an image of the critic addressing himself with boldness and discrimination to the great social and political issues through an intel-

lectually vigorous engagement with literature. By doing
so they inspired a whole generation of students of literature
with the idea of the engaged critic, but beyond that idea
they offered no system or set of operations that could be
seized on by followers, and as the American political mood
swung through the quiescence of the Eisenhower years to
the militant activism of the 1960's, the idea itself came to
seem progressively more difficult to emulate. In any case,
when it came to imitating a stance, if you were not Trilling,
with his native subtlety and his intellectual breadth, you
might easily be reduced to an inadvertent parody of Trilling's
mannerisms, and such hollow performances grew less and less
tenable with the passage of time. The *Partisan Review* critics,
then, have scarcely had any significant disciples. By contrast,
Cleanth Brooks and Robert Penn Warren alone taught two
generations how to read poetry because their New Critical
approach was above all a highly teachable method of close
reading. My guess is that even at this late date, most of our
college English classes, outside a score or more prestige-
conscious institutions swaying in the winds of intellectual
change, still use what is basically a New Critical method in
presenting literary texts to students.

Against this whole background, the campus protests and
the fierce energies of politicization in the late Sixties had a
particularly disruptive effect on professional morale. It
seemed painfully pointless or, as the cant of those years put
it, irrelevant, to be tracing the ingenious shifts of diction in a
lyric by Donne or the sound patterns in Hopkins at a time
when American planes were raining napalm on Asian peasants
and our universities themselves were held to be part of a
conspiratorial network of the military-industrial complex.
Some younger literary scholars became militant Marxists,
at their vulgar worst proposing that literature classes should
be converted into coaching sessions for agitprop or exercises
in the adversary analysis of advertising jingles and other instances of capitalist discourse. Here and there members of
this generation, finding no credible way of bringing their
academic activity into phase with the disturbing realm

of history in the making, simply dropped out of the profession.

By the early Seventies the waves of political turbulence had generally subsided, and most of the literary scholars who had been at all caught up in this experience now found themselves high and dry, still drawing their university paychecks but without much sense of purpose in what they were doing. It was then that the *Nouvelle Critique,* or whatever could be gleaned of it from the immense cultural distance of an American vantage point, seemed to many to open up new vistas. Despite the Marxism or Maoism of some of its French proponents, it was as disengaged from history as the New Criticism had been, though on "scientific" rather than aesthetic grounds; and so it provided an attractive retreat from history after the disorienting involvements of the Vietnam years. By insisting, moreover, on the place of literary studies among the "human sciences," concerned with the structuring functions of the mind and with the interlocking systems of communication that constitute culture, it appeared to be offering the gravely challenged discipline an objective grounding. Concentrating on a series of complex taxonomic operations and on the definition of formal relations within literary works and in the corpus of literary discourse, with linguistics as its model, it swept away all the essayistic concerns of the New York critics—like politics, history, ethics, even psychology (in any guise except a metaphysicalized, Lacanian one which displaces discussion from individual personages to abstract systems).

This general approach, precisely because it is so alien to the customary Anglo-American habits of thinking about literature, seems to have a magnetic appeal for many American intellectuals at this moment in history. Disappointed with the inherited notions of literature as uniquely privileged discourse or as a profound expression of social and moral values, they are braced by the Cartesian spirit of the new French criticism. There is something satisfying in the idea that literature, for which such excessive claims had been made, can be pulled down to the level of all other modes of discourse; and, even more important, the prospect of a value-free study of literature is positively consoling after the apparent failure of engaged criticism as an ideal. The formidable intellectual apparatus of Structuralism, moreover, lends it a particularly powerful attraction as a method of studying literature without the old embarrassing concerns of value; for it offers the literary intelligentsia what any professional or priestly caste needs in order to maintain its own coherence and morale—an esoteric language, a set of elaborate procedures that can be performed only by the initiate, and the conviction that the specialized rituals of the caste have universal efficacy, or at least universal applicability.

If Structuralism, as it is understood in this country, is thus a wonderfully apt solution to the professional malaise of literary studies, it may also be, in a longer historical perspective, the appropriate response to the needs of a new kind of reader. Such judgments are bound to be highly conjectural, but one may wonder whether there might be a growing number of readers, in any case at our universities, who prefer their reading to be as free as possible from emotional involvement with the material read. For them the novel would not be, as Stendhal once put it in a flamboyant metaphor, a violin whose sounding box is the reader's soul, but rather an elaborate puzzle or game with which the author confronts the reader. This might in part explain the popularity, in some circles, of fictional gamesmen who are, in a double sense, "cool" writers, like Donald Barthelme and John Barth. It might also be a further reason for the appeal of Structuralism as a way of talking about literature. Some Structuralist theory acutely perceives how readers' emotions are manipulated by literary texts, but Structuralist *discourse* about literature is, by the necessities of its nature and as a matter of principle, peculiarly affectless. A semiotic analysis of a joke or of a disastrous reversal of fortune may explain all its ramified functions in the narrative economy, but with a strict dissociation from the actual feelings which the narrative material is meant to elicit. This disjuncture between analysis and affect may be precisely what is attractive to many readers.

The ultimate direction of this whole movement was brought home to me strikingly a couple of years ago in a friendly conversation with a young scholar who has established himself as one of the leading American proponents of Structuralism. Having just read a critical piece of mine, he observed, "You make your argument with a certain elegance, but the trouble with it is that you base your assessment of novels on *experience*, and we have demonstrated that there is no such thing." I think I understand the remark better now than I did at the time, and it is worth pondering; for the attack on mimesis ultimately depends on defining experience out of existence, and that in turn, as I shall argue, leads to a misreading of whole categories of literary works.

In the Structuralist view, *homo sapiens* is effectively replaced by what Jonathan Culler has aptly called "*homo significans*, maker and reader of signs."[1] The epistemological shift is crucial: in this approach there are no discernible "objects" of knowledge in human experience, only signs to be interpreted, and hence man can no longer be defined as the knower. What immediately follows from this assumption is a global expansion of the concept of *text*. Where previous epistemologies talked about data of experience or objects of knowledge, Structuralist man encounters nothing but texts wherever he looks. From actual written texts set on the elaborate grid of literary conventions, to fashions in clothing, restaurant menus, sexual mores, and the most unmeditated gestures of social intercourse, all life in culture is an endless series of encoded meanings that need constant decoding.

If texts are ubiquitous, *intertextuality* becomes the essential aspect of existence, or rather of communication, for all texts. In the case of literary texts, this means first of all a heightened awareness of how any given text may operate in a complex, dynamic interrelation with several or many antecedent texts and with the generic norms they embody. Intertextuality in this sense was extensively explored by certain American critics before the advent of Structuralism—most sweepingly by Northrop Frye, most sensibly by Harry Levin—but the Structuralist perspective involves a new acute consciousness of the pervasive artifices of writing and of reading, and that is its one major contribution to the understanding of literature, just as a cultivation of the skills of close reading was the one signal contribution of the New Criticism. Many Structuralists, however, are inclined to extend the concept of intertextuality beyond the realm of allusion and genre, using it to replace the old-fashioned notion of verisimilitude. For if the real world is altogether something we construe, a shifting constellation of texts we decode, then the relation, say, of *The Rape of the Lock* to the realm of eighteenth-century English society in which the poem's action is set is as intertextual as the relation of *The Rape of the Lock* to the *Iliad*.

This absolutist extension of intertextuality strikes me as an ultimately casuistic piece of ingenuity, because it does considerable violence both to our perceptions as readers and to our sense of the differential quality of different modes of experience, literary and extraliterary. It is possible to argue that a lover's intimate caress is every bit as "semiotic" as a traffic light or an image in a sonnet by Baudelaire, each being a signifier that we have to relate to a signified, but in point of experiential fact we make sharp qualitative distinctions among the three. When, for example, a caress is evoked in an erotic poem by Judah Halevi through the allusion to a verse in the Song of Songs (6:2)—"my hands went grazing in your garden"—the reader clearly and automatically distinguishes between the relation of Halevi's line to its biblical source, which is properly intertextual, and its relation to an actual lover's tender touch, which is something known from extraliterary experience and perceived as the referential object of the poetic image.

There seem to be two complementary strategies for dissolving the connection between literature and the real world. One, as we have just observed, is to exorcise the other-than-literary presence of the real world by reducing everything to text. The other is to emphasize the nature of the literary text as a collocation of arbitrary linguistic signs that can be joined together only on the basis of internal principles of coherence even as they pretend to be determined by objects outside themselves to which they supposedly refer. In this view, reality, whatever it may be, is inaccessible to the literary text because of the text's very constitution. This is how Gérard Genette argues the case in his influential essay, *"Vraisemblance et motivation"*: "The linguistic sign is also arbitrary in the sense that it is justified solely by its function, and it is well known that from the linguistic standpoint the motivation of the sign, and particularly of the 'word,' is a typical case of realist illusion. The term motivation (*motivacija*), then, has been happily introduced into modern literary theory by the Russian Formalists to designate the way in which the [purely internal] functionality of narrative elements masquerades under a façade of causal determinism: thus the 'content' [of any narrative] can only be a motivation, i.e., an *a posteriori* justification of the form which, in fact, determines it."[2] In other words, if the Princesse de Clèves confesses to her husband that another man is in love with her, we would be naïve to inquire, as many French critics in the past have done, whether such a woman would really make such an avowal to her husband. Mme. de Clèves, after all, is merely an arbitrary configuration of arbitrary linguistic signs, and her confession is in fact dictated by dramatic considerations of the narrative moment and by larger structural necessities of the plot as a whole; and these determinants of internal functionality are "motivated" by what is only an illusory correspondence to anything outside the novel.

The either-or rigidity of this formulation is a little perplexing. For it is by no means clear why the choice of details in a fictional narrative cannot be dictated simultaneously by principles of internal coherence and by the writer's sense of a just, plausible correspondence to the social, moral, psychological facts of real existence as he understands them. Indeed that is precisely what happens in most of the great realist novels, why they seem both artistically satisfying narrative wholes and probing visions of their time and place. Genette himself admits to an internal overdetermination of narrative data (several different considerations of narrative form may lead a writer to introduce the same single detail), but he is unwilling to grant the possibility that the details of the narrative might be overdetermined in another sense, both by the formal needs of the narrative and by the nature of the world it represents. I suspect that his one-sidedness on this issue is a result of the way he presses the analogy between language and literature, and that analogy is worth pursuing for a moment, because what we may call the *linguistic fallacy*—as even a sympathetic expositor, Jonathan Culler, has tended to show—is at the root of certain confusions in Structuralist thinking about literature.

Let us go back to Genette's example of the individual word (*mot*). It is of course true that the relation between the word "tiger," for example, and the real striped beast in the jungle is purely conventional and therefore arbitrary. We know, however, that there are real tigers, which are not in themselves texts, although references to them can be manipulated into texts. Once a writer uses the agreed-upon sign "tiger" in a story or poem or play, the relationship between verbal reference and beast referred to is no longer completely arbitrary: we judge what kind of statement is being made by certain objective information we possess about extraverbal tigers. A narrative which began "The tiger flew over the moon" would not, we grasp at once, be a realistic narrative. It might be treating the materials of reality with fantastic arbitrariness; it might perhaps have a nonrealistic logic of its own as part, let us say, of a Malaysian nursery rhyme. On the other hand, were we to encounter a narrative that began, "The tiger crouched in the bamboo thicket," we would recognize an attempt to make the verbal construct match what we know of zoological reality. Every feature of the sentence might also be formally determined by what followed it in the story, but the effort to show fidelity to the real world would be palpable in the choice of the verb for the subject and of the prepositional phrase to modify that verb — in every detail the sentence presented.

In Jorge Luis Borge's great poem "The Other Tiger," the

poet recognizes, as the Structuralists often warn, that by naming the tiger he is constantly converting it into "a tiger of symbols . . . a string of labored tropes," but he makes his medium strain, in a fever of mimesis, at catching something of the flowing, deadly beauty of the beast that is a real presence out there, tantalizing the poet into the effort of representation. "Among the bamboo's slanting stripes I glimpse / The tiger's stripes and sense the bony frame / Under the splendid, quivering cover of skin."[3] Such lines are brilliantly evocative, not only because they are perfectly justified by the formal necessities of the poem but because there is a rightness of matching between the images, the setting, the rhythmic movement of the language, the viewer's visual standpoint, and our knowledge and imaginings of the life and look of a real tiger.

To be sure, my experience-doubting Structuralist friend would object that all this is based on unacceptably simplistic epistemological premises. Does it make any sense to speak of a real tiger? Even if we go to a zoo to look at one, we cannot "experience" the tiger directly. Rather, from a shower of sensory impressions, we discriminate certain patterns of color, texture, outline, dimension, and so forth, and these in turn are transmitted from the retina to the brain, there to be sorted, correlated with various kinds of stored information, and interpreted. What we call, by convention, seeing the tiger is really decoding it and, as such, is not different in kind from what we would do when confronted with the signals indicating a tiger in a painting, film, story, or poem. Indeed, one might even say that any assertion we make about the tiger we have seen is, inescapably, a narrative (*récit*), not, as we naïvely imagine, a factual report.

The flaw in this argument is its assumption that the presence of a common denominator in different activities implies virtual equivalency among them. All perception is of course mediated by the physical apparatus and the cognitive processes with which we perceive, but that hardly leads to a necessary conclusion that there is no ultimate qualitative difference between our perception of a painted tiger and a tiger in the zoo. However sophisticated we may become about cognition, indispensable common sense tells us that the real tiger exists—quite terrifically, as the poet knows—apart from our cognition. We are free to decenter, deconstruct, decode, re-encode a tiger in a text, but even the hardiest Structuralist would not step inside the cage with the real beast, whose fangs and claws, after all, are more than a semiotic pattern.

The tendency to see literature as closed-circuit poesis rather than mimesis leads to especially problematic consequences when the genre under discussion is the novel. No other form in Western literary history has served so often and so well as a reader's vehicle for vicarious experience. From embarrassingly naïve readers like the kind fictionally represented in Emma Bovary to the most sophisticated intellectuals, we have overwhelmingly persisted, from the seventeenth century to the present, in "entering into" the experience of fictional characters in teeming thousands of novels, exchanging lives with them, testing our perceptions of reality against the absorbing details of their invented worlds. This predilection may say a good deal about the psychological quandaries and sociological situations of modern readers, but it also surely suggests that we generally perceive a high degree of effective mimesis in novels or we would not be so prepared to accept the novelistic world as a credible equivalent of our own.

Structuralist readings of novels, on the other hand, especially in their recent American distillations, reverse the common actual experience of novel readers by insisting, for book after book, that the novel is a self-referential system of signs in which the real interest is in the way language calls attention to its own predicaments, making us aware of the eternal gap between the signifier and the signified. One may grant that this emphasis has the advantage of alerting us to an important dimension of many fictional works that in the past has been slighted by Anglo-American criticism; but it also tends to make all novels, from *Eugénie Grandet* to *A Hundred Years of Solitude*, sound tediously alike, and it fails to account adequately for other aspects of novels to which large numbers of readers seem to be responding.

Against this view, I would argue that all novels are in fact mimetic, though they exhibit, broadly speaking, two basically different modes of mimesis. Words and things, to be sure, are radically different in kind, and so mimesis is never a direct reproduction of reality but rather a way of eliciting in the mind of the reader—through complex chains of verbal indicators—the illusion of persons, places, situations, events, and institutions convincingly like the ones we encounter outside the sphere of reading. The mimetic process has been succinctly described with beautiful precision by E. H. Gombrich in commenting on an illusionist painting of a lightning-riven landscape by Cuyp: "[It is] not a transcript, of course . . . but a configuration which, in context, became the valid cryptogram of that unpaintable glare."[4] Not, we should note, the cryptogram of itself, or the cryptogram of another cryptogram, but the cryptogram of an unpaintable glare we have seen in the real world, and against which we measure the validity of the mimetic effort.

There are very few novels that really surrender the commitment to create through configurations of language—drawing on inherited verbal schemata as Gombrich shows painters must use visual schemata—valid cryptograms of things outside themselves. I have proposed elsewhere[5] that the history of the novel may be thought of as a dialectic between two traditions, one self-conscious and the other realist. Some critics, breathing the heady air of the current intellectual climate, seized on this notion of self-consciousness with an enthusiasm I would not have anticipated, and questioned my equivocality, wanting to know why I had not simply said that the novel *was* a self-conscious genre. The distinction between the two kinds of novel still seems to me important to maintain if we are to have some way of distinguishing between the kind of experience we undergo, say, in reading *The French Lieutenant's Woman*, on the one hand, and *Nana*, on the other.

A self-conscious novel is one that systematically flaunts its own necessary condition of artifice, and that by so doing probes into the problematic relationship between real-seeming artifice and reality. In Gombrich's terms, the self-conscious novelist is acutely aware that he is manipulating schemata, devising ingenious cryptograms, and he constantly invents narrative strategies for sharing this awareness with us, so that he simultaneously, or alternately, creates the illusion of reality and shatters it. The realist novel, by contrast, seeks to maintain a relatively consistent illusion of reality. Thus Richardson's epistolary novels, with their pseudodocumentary form, clearly contribute to the establishment of a realist tradition in England, while Fielding's novels, with their flaunted contrivances of plot and nomenclature, their coyly obtrusive narrators, their discursive explorations of the theory of fiction, are eminently self-conscious. Not all novels, of course, will be so easy to categorize. Some by design are rich mixtures of the two kinds—*Ulysses* is probably the most memorable instance of this sort—and along a broad spectrum from self-conscious to realist there will be some novels in the ambiguous middle sector about which readers may not agree. Nevertheless, I think the two terms usefully designate two perceptibly different modes of fiction, each constituting a discernible tradition. For those who are uncomfortable with so problematic a label as realist, I would suggest that the two types of fiction could also be described as consistently illusionist and intermittently illusionist.

Let me comment briefly on that intermittence because it illustrates how central and durable the mimetic function of the novel remains. The self-conscious novel, which has become fashionable and at times facile in the practice of contemporary writers, was never meant to be an abandonment of mimesis, but rather an enormous complication and sophistication of it: mimesis is enacted as its problematics are explored. *Tristram Shandy*, in many ways the ultimate self-conscious novel and certainly the paradigmatic one, provides the most vivid illustration of this essential point. It continually evinces a three-tiered attitude toward the representation of reality in fiction: to begin with, a hyperconsciousness of the sheer arbitrariness and conventionality of all literary means, from typography and chapter divisions to character and plot; at the same time a paradoxical demonstration, perhaps especially manifest in Sterne's brilliant stylistic improvisations, of the illusionist power of fictional representations of reality; and, finally, a constant implication of the reader in the arbitrary structure-making functions of the mind, which themselves, as our most intimately familiar mental experience, become part of the reality represented in the novel. It will be seen that the third tier is only the mimetic obverse of the critical exposure of mimesis observable on the first tier. As modern readers, we are of course closely attuned to all the cunning convolutions of Sterne's fictional self-consciousness, but it is well to keep in mind that his novel managed to enjoy considerable popularity throughout the age of realism of the nineteenth century—where its sexual indecencies did not shock—because of the convincing mimesis it produces through its maze of flaunted artifice (the bizarre, touching character of the two Shandy brothers, Trim's tender sensibilities, the vivid comic images of domestic and provincial life, and so forth).

In order to make the validity of these two categories of fiction clearer, and to demonstrate the persistent power of mimesis even in "postmodern" writing, I would like to juxtapose two striking novels of the early seventies, both involving elaborate artifice but one clearly a self-conscious fiction and the other a realist one. The two novels I have in mind are Nabokov's *Transparent Things* (1972) and the third novel of the gifted new Argentine writer, Manuel Puig, *The Buenos Aires Affair* (1973).

Transparent Things is a beautifully controlled short novel in which Nabokov develops new modalities of self-consciousness for new expressive purposes—exactly the opposite of what happens in his subsequent book, *Look at the Harlequins* (1974), where he tends to do what his detractors often accuse him of: slipping into coy self-citation and a facile rehearsal of old themes, situations, and devices. The self-conscious mode is pervasive and systematic, from the very title of the novel to the naming of its characters and places, the narrative technique that constantly comments on itself, and the deployment of fictions within fictions. Things turn transparent as they become objects of the narrator's "act of attention": consciousness dissolves the seeming solidity of surfaces and the bounded determinacy of objects, plunging into the history of things, their transformation through time, the myriad filaments of causation, analogy, and metonymy that bind any given object to a swarm of other objects. The title, then, explicated by a brilliant set piece in the first two chapters, at once introduces us to a practical and epistemological difficulty of mimesis: how is one credibly and effectively to *narrate* anything that seems real when everything, by virtue of being an object of consciousness, threatens to be infinitely unstable, infinitely filiated with other things for which there is no room in the narrative?

The protagonist of *Transparent Things* is called Hugh Person (actually pronounced "You Person" by another character), and this designation obviously presents him as a kind of conventional fictional hypothesis to be worked with—not a verisimilar personage with a name that might appear in the civic registry, but Hugh/You, this Person, the focus of certain contractual assumptions between writer and reader around which a narrative can be constructed. Yet it is one of the book's essential paradoxes that Hugh Person is given convincing mimetic specificity as a particular kind of gangling New England man—perhaps even with a parodistic allusion to certain male figures in Henry James—whose character reflects his class and family backgrounds and cultural biases, who has his own plausible neuroses, his own sexual difficulties, and so forth.

The novel's 104 pages offer a crammed repertory of self-conscious devices. The plot incorporates exercises in proofreading which draw our attention to the typographic conventions of the medium. Vladimir Nabokov, in the Hitchcock effect so familiar in his novels, makes strategic walk-on appearances—first in a satirically distorted self-portrait as the novelist Baron R., a morally dubious English-language writer residing in Switzerland who is known for his "luxuriant and bastard style . . . at its best . . . diabolically evocative";[6] then, in an anagrammatic signature, as Adam von Librikov, a minor character in a novel by Baron R. Most of the self-conscious ploys have the double effect, like the treatment of Hugh Person, of laying bare the artifice and at the same time using the artifice to create a heightened sense of mimesis. The style, for example, which tends to be more ironically astringent, less lush than that of earlier Nabokov novels, manages in fact to be "diabolically evocative" even as it repeatedly makes us aware that it is, like all literary language, merely a redeployment of linguistic conventions. Here is a very simple example that illustrates the principle operating in more elaborate passages as well: "Hugh retraced his steps, which was once a trim metaphor" (page 14). The second half of the sentence brings us up short, calling attention to the cliché that has been used and thus moving us, in an antimimetic direction, from the event narrated to the verbal medium itself. Yet by reviving the dead metaphor buried in the cliché, the second clause also forces us to do a kind of double take, back to the narrated event, and we vividly see the character not just turning around but literally "retracing" his steps. Indeed, the concluding segment of the whole plot is implicated in this oddly overfocused action, for Hugh Person will try to recuperate the past by repeating it literally step by step, going back to the same Swiss resort where he had been with his late wife eight years earlier, staying in the same hotel room, following the same sequence of actions. This internal consistency between local statement and narrative structure is simultaneously justified—and not just arbitrarily "motivated"—by considerations of psychological verisimilitude, for the presence of such a repetition compulsion is what we might plausibly expect in such a person—small p now—in reality.

So far, we have observed the first two tiers of the three-tiered self-conscious approach to the literary representation of experience. The third tier, however, is the thematically decisive one in *Transparent Things*. For the narrator, through his constant attentiveness to the ways in which the mind transforms what it contemplates, involves us in the life of consciousness, and in the epistemological anxieties of the life of consciousness, which is our most immediate human reality. Mimesis here is focused not on an object, place, or kind of person but on a set of cognitive processes, on the mental relation of time-bound self to other. Just before the fatal conclusion of what is called the "pilgrimage" of Hugh Person to his conjugal past, the narrator is led through a reflection on the semantic limitations of conventional typefaces and punctuation to a remark on children's books, and through that to a general comment on the human condition:

Human life can be compared to a person dancing in a variety of forms around his own self: thus the vegetable of our first picture book encircled a boy in his dream—green cucumber, blue eggplant, red beet, Potato père, Potato fils, a girly asparagus, and, oh, many more, their spinning ronde *going faster and faster and gradually forming a transparent ring of banded colors around a dead person or planet.*

Another thing we are not supposed to do is to explain the inexplicable. Men have learned to live with a black burden, a huge aching hump: the supposition that "reality" may be only a "dream." How much more dreadful it would be if the very awareness of your being aware of reality's dreamlike nature were also a dream, a built-in hallucination! One should bear in mind, however, that there is no mirage without a vanishing point, just as there is no lake without a closed circle of reliable land. (Pages 92-93)

The ache of contradiction between the lively, restless movement of consciousness and the finality of death has long been a preoccupation of Nabokov's, but his particular deployment of self-conscious strategies in *Transparent Things* brings him closer to a direct imaginative confrontation with the prospect of his own death than in any of his other books. That event is adumbrated at a remove in the death of the old novelist, Baron R., then imagined from within in the last sentences of the novel, as Hugh Person perishes in a hotel fire. Here the narrator passes on to the protagonist his own image of an illustration from a child's book as a telescoped version of a man's life: "Rings of blurred colors circled around him, reminding him briefly of a childhood picture in a frightening book about triumphant vegetables whirling faster and faster around a nightshirted boy trying desperately to awake from the iridescent dizziness of dream life." The awakening will be the escape from hallucination, the terra firma beyond the mirage, promised at the end of the earlier passage. "Its [presumably, dream life's] ultimate vision was the incandescence of a book or a box grown completely transparent and hollow." The self-conscious writer ingeniously makes us see, in this final perception of the protagonist, the book which we are holding in our hands and which we are about to finish, but the exposed artifice is no less the vehicle for a serious moment of vision, located with verisimilar conviction in the last living moment of a fictional personage. For the pressingly urgent motive behind Nabokov's playfulness in this book is to try to intimate some conceivable persistence of consciousness beyond that condition "blocked by masses of rubbish" which he identifies with death. And so the virtuoso demonstration throughout the book of how consciousness produces transparency all around it is made in this ultimate moment to prefigure the operation of consciousness beyond the realm of earthly mimesis, which is the sphere of the novel: "This is, I believe, *it*: not the crude anguish of physical death but the incomparable pangs of the mysterious mental maneuver needed to pass from one state of being to another." (Page 104)

Behind Nabokov's whole enterprise are Gogol's fantastic grotesquerie and playfulness, the ideal of perfectly wrought craftsmanship in Flaubert, Biely's exploration of the artifices of consciousness, the elaborate formalism and the stylistic high jinks of Joyce, Proust's rendering of the ambiguous dialectic between art and life. What would seem to be the decisive influences on Manuel Puig are the realist aspects of Joyce and Faulkner and, most particularly, their experiments with multiple techniques for representing inner life and for showing how consciousness and character are enmeshed in the minutiae of cultural milieu. In all three of his novels, Puig exhibits a zest for exploring the possibilities of technique that is not easy to find anywhere these days except in Latin America.

There are, by my count, at least seventeen distinct narrative points of view deployed through the sixteen chapters of *The Buenos Aires Affair.*[7] The novel begins with a traditional omniscient narrator who makes generous use of *style indirect libre* to report the consciousness of one character. After this we encounter: chronological dossier accounts of the two protagonists; a first-person narration; an experiment in obtruded omniscience where only overfocused sensory details are reported; several different renderings of the characters' fantasy life, from a fantasy interview of the heroine, as she lies beside her lover, with the fashion magazine *Elle* (!), to a slow-motion cinematic version of the chain of fantasies experienced by three different personages in a climactic scene of threatened violence and bizarre sexuality. Perhaps most strategically, Puig provides several inventive varieties of occluded narrative, where as we read we have to struggle to fill in gaping lacunae, the most extreme instance being a scrambled elliptic stenographic record, made by a police sergeant, of a phone call about a murderer (we are never allowed to hear the actual voice at the other end of the wire).

Even from this brief summary, it should be clear that novelistic artifice in *The Buenos Aires Affair* is pervasively conspicuous, but this high degree of visibility does not make the artifice self-conscious in the sense I have proposed. As sophisticated readers, we are of course free to *infer*, from the novelist's elaborate manipulation of formal possibilities in his medium, certain ideas about the essential arbitrariness of all techniques of representation. The book is not, however, a series of "Exercises in Style," like the Raymond Queneau experiment bearing that title which is directed entirely toward the narrative medium, its anecdotal kernel being merely an excuse for exploring different narrative strategies. On the contrary, what urgently engages Puig is the nature and fate of two verisimilar personages—Leo Druscovich, a Buenos Aires art critic tormented by guilt and sexual insecurity, and Gladys Hebe D'Onofrio, a painter of uncertain talents, seemingly defeated by life, desperate for some viable human relationship. Through all the novel's shifting points of view, there is no suggestion that Gladys and Leo are merely arbitrary constructs, no intimation of epistemological quandaries in the relation of the literary representation to its objects. Instead, the multiplicity of points of view is dictated by the multiplex nature of its human subjects, its basic justification being mimetic rather than formal. The novelist's ability to know his lifelike personages is never at issue, and such knowledge, as he concieves it, involves seeing them physically, relationally, chronologically, professionally, from the outside and through their own consciousness and their fantasies. In the case of Leo, who is killed just before the conclusion of the novel, even the icily clinical terms of a coroner's report are deemed necessary—the mind and body that were seen in the novel as a seething center of anguished experience are envisaged at the end, under the objective of the microscope, as an inert conglomeration of deteriorating cells.

The tools of novelistic realism, to be sure, are inevitably literary. The novelist's primary guides, that is, in how to represent reality are bound to be other novelists. Puig's hyper-lucid rendering of Leo's decomposing body in fact is intended formally to emulate the hauntingly distanced effect Joyce achieves through the peculiar narrative mode of catechism in the penultimate section of *Ulysses*. Puig, then, is keenly aware of the indispensability of artful patterning and of the pressure of literary tradition, but he chooses patterns and models from the tradition that will best serve his own mimetic ends.

The only novels in which narrative convention may perhaps be effectively camouflaged are those cast in pseudo-documentary form (the epistolary novel, the fictitious journal, certain kinds of first-person confessional narratives). It is hard for a third-person fictional narration to escape somehow foregrounding its novelistic artifice, but the category of novel which I would persist in calling *realist* operates with a tacit agreement between author and audience that these artifices are the necessary and efficacious vehicle for conveying the truth about the characters, and that they are to be assumed as a transparent medium even in their conspicuousness; for our chief interest is in the personages and events they convey to us, not in the nature and status of the artifices. This, it seems to me, roughly describes the way the common reader, from Dr. Johnson's day to our own, has actually been accustomed to experience realist fiction. I was recently impressed, however, by the different habits of reading that certain professionals have been cultivating in the current intellectual climate when I read an unpublished critical piece on *The Buenos Aires Affair*. This Structuralist reading of Puig by an obviously intelligent young literary scholar could easily have its counterparts in a score of American departments of Spanish or comparative literature, if one may judge by the latest products of our more prestigious graduate schools.

In this approach, the key to the structure and purpose of *The Buenos Aires Affair* is its subtitle, "A Detective Novel." That, of course, invokes a genre, and so what we must attend to before all else is the tracing and replacing of generic conventions in the narrative. The detective novel, fortunately, exhibits a highly conventionalized set of formal devices, and so it has been dealt with in detail by the *Nouvelle Critique.* The general rules of the genre as defined by Tzvetan Todorov can thus be conveniently cited, and the permutations they supposedly undergo here can be presented as the real argument of the novel.

In the generically regulated whodunit, we look for the corpse and then try to ascertain which character is responsible for it. Puig, so this argument runs, has created a novel in which the whodunit is made to turn back on its own constitutive rules as a genre. At the outset, with the appropriate techniques of suspense, we are given exactly the kind of clues we have learned to read elsewhere: an unexplained kidnapping, a gagged and chloroformed victim, an ominous lingering description of a hypodermic needle, a knife, a loaded revolver. But the promised act of violence never materializes, and as we work our way into the novel, it emerges that the only corpse here may be simply a figment of Leo Druscovich's imagination—an unknown stranger whom once he laid low with a brick in a chance homosexual encounter in a vacant lot, and who may or may not have died from the blow. Leo, in any case, is pursued by his own private conviction that he is guilty of homicide, and years later, when a police patrol tries to stop him for speeding, he jams down the accelerator of his car, certain that the authorities have at last tracked him down for the murder, and careens over a curve to his death. In a careful formal design, the hypothetical corpse that never appeared in the narrative is replaced by the corpse that Leo has finally made out of himself, and the structure of the novel as a whole thus comes to encode another one of those ubiquitous Derridean ideas about the inevitable absence of presence, the gap between the signifier and the signified which is the ineluctable fate of language and of fictions.

This fashionable method of reading is nothing if not ingenious, but what it happens to neglect in the case of *The Buenos Aires Affair* is the essential experience of the novel. For the most salient feature of the book is clearly not any concern with narrative codes but the compelling psychological reality of the two principal characters. Puig calls it "A Detective Novel" and makes certain parodistic allusions to that genre in order to suggest that the really interesting work of detection for a novelist and for his readers is psychological—a ferreting-out of the cadaver that is buried, not in the garden or the garage, but in the protagonist's consciousness. The use of varying strategies of occluded narrative powerfully reinforces the difficulty in getting at the tangled facts of any human character or relationship. In this, Puig seems to follow the model of works by Faulkner like *Absalom, Absalom!* and the general mimetic tradition of the impressionist novel, in which narratives are made baffling and circuitous in order to simulate the processes by which we discover things in reality. There is, moreover, one prominent formal device in *The Buenos Aires Affair* that has nothing to do with the detective novel: each chapter is set off by a piece of dialogue from an old Hollywood film, usually from the thirties and forties. These movie epigraphs serve a double mimetic function: they help characterize the deluded inner world of the protagonists, who have grown up in a culture suffused with this kind of media-fostered debased romanticism; and, in their patent contrivances and sentimental clichés, the epigraphs also act as a foil to the sharply realistic textures of Puig's own writing.

Instructively, the Structuralist reading of *The Buenos Aires Affair* stops two chapters before the end, where the idea of the absent corpse is supposedly completed in the death of Leo Druscovich. The crucial fact, however, is that the significant conclusion of the novel takes place in the two chapters after Leo's death. For this is a tale of deprivation and renewal—deprivation without reprieve for Leo, who has lost his mother in infancy, and a final possibility of hope for Gladys, herself emotionally maimed by a narcissistic mother. At the end of the book, Gladys, alone late at night in Leo's apartment, barely pulls herself back from the brink of suicide. The couple next door has been audibly making love; then the husband leaves. The young wife, going out onto her balcony, strikes up a conversation with Gladys on the adjacent balcony, eventually inviting her obviously troubled neighbor to come and keep her company.

In bare summary, the details of the last pages may sound schematically contrived: the young wife, who is busy taking care of her baby, offers Gladys a glass of milk and some cake, then actually encourages her exhausted visitor to rest in bed with her and the child. At the very end we find the wife, still recollecting the warmth of her husband's body, wondering whether the seed of another life has just been implanted in her. In context, I think Puig introduces these symbolic details with an inventive subtlety that makes them seem plausible, but in any case the emotional direction he wants to intimate at the end of the novel is clear. Gladys discovers, in this archetypal relation of mother and child, the possibility of simple human compassion and finds courage to try to live her life again. The novel, then, engages verisimilar imaginary personages in a complex plot in order to imitate convincingly a recurrent rhythm of human life which most of us, in one way or another, have at least glimpsed. Without a sense in readers that something in their experience was being confirmed or perhaps even illuminated, the novel's chief effect would be lost.

The last decade of developments in literary theory has surely taught us that the relation of *verba* and *res*, book and world, is a good deal more problematic and more essentially ambiguous than was allowed for by the sturdy moral realism of Anglo-American novel criticism, from James to Leavis to Ian Watt. We seem now, however, to run some danger of being directed by the theoreticians to read in a way that real readers, on land or sea, have never read. If one insists on seeing all novels as congeries of semiotic systems intricately functioning in a pure state of self-referentiality, one loses the fine edge of responsiveness to the urgent human predicaments that novels seek to articulate. The greatness of the genre, both in its realist and in its self-conscious modes, has been to present to us—through the most inventive variety of artifice, whether disguised or manifest—lives that might seem like our lives, minds like our minds, desires like our own desires. That has been what most novelists quite clearly have tried to accomplish in their writing, and that is what still makes the reading of novels for most people, intellectuals included, one of the perennially absorbing activities of modern culture.

Notes

This chapter was originally published in *Triquarterly*, 42 (1978), 228-249. Copyright © 1978 by Robert Alter.
1. Jonathan Culler, *Structuralist Poetics* (Ithaca: Cornell University Press, 1975), p. 130.

2. Gérard Genette, *Figures II* (Paris: Editions de Seuil, 1969), pp. 71–99. The translation is mine.

3. *Entre las rayas del bambú descrifo / Sus rayas y presiento la osatura / Bajo la piel esplendida que vibra*. The fine translation is by Norman Thomas di Giovanni.

4. E. H. Gombrich, *Art and Illusion* (New York: Pantheon, 1960), pp. 319–20.

5. Robert Alter, *Partial Magic: The Novel as a Self-Conscious Genre* (Berkeley and Los Angeles: University of California Press, 1975).

6. Vladimir Nabokov, *Transparent Things* (New York: McGraw-Hill, 1972), p. 75.

7. Manuel Puig, *The Buenos Aires Affair*, translated by Suzanne Jill Levine (New York: E. P. Dutton, 1976).

Chapter 4

The Difficulties of Modernism and

the Modernism of Difficulty

Richard Poirier

On every side, these days, there is talk of modernism—what was it? what is it? when did it happen?—and partly because these questions have been voluminously but not satisfactorily answered, the modernist period threatens to stretch into a century, or, for some people, into two. Literary history has never allowed such longevity, and the prospect raises a number of embarrassing questions. During this whole time, has there been so little change in the cultural and social conditions which supposedly begat modernism that there has been no occasion for a radical change in literary consciousness? Or could it be said that poets and novelists have either been unresponsive to upheavals in the culture or that they have been able to respond only by modifications of Joyce, Eliot, and Pound—or, stretching it a bit, of Hawthorne, Melville, and James? Or perhaps we should ask if there has been a wholly uncharacteristic failure on the part of literary historians to make those discriminations of periods which keep them busy. They have proposed subdivisions like neomodernism, paleomodernism, or postmodernism, which only serve to illustrate the problem.

In fact, modernism in literature has become so amorphous that it is possible to be half persuaded by Harold Bloom when he says that "modernism has not passed; rather it is exposed as never having been there." While this seems in no way a satisfactory solution, it is generated by a healthy and beneficial contempt for the kind of thinking that has encumbered attempts to locate the specific cultural anxiety we call modernism. For it is not cultural anxiety itself, scarcely the sole privilege of the twentieth century, but a peculiar form of it that needs to be diagnosed. We can begin simply by noting that modernism is associated with being unhappy. It is associated with being burdened by the very materials, the beliefs, institutions, and forms of language, that are also our source of support as we labor under the burden. To be happy in the twentieth century is to see no burden *in* these supports; it is to be trivial. Modernism carries a very learned but always a very long face. I recall in college hearing an unusually beautiful and vibrant young woman from Smith murmur to herself in the middle of a party, "I have measured out my life in coffee spoons." Obviously, at eighteen or nineteen, she was boasting. Nowadays she would probably say, "Keep cool, but care," and while this might register an advance in social amiability, it would not be an advance for literary criticism, which has found it more or less impossible not to take everything in modernist texts seriously. Or perhaps seriously is the wrong word. It finds it impossible not to take everything solemnly.

The phenomenon of grim reading—that is what I would like to offer as my initial definition of modernism. Modernism happened when reading got to be grim. I locate modernism, that is, in a kind of reading habit or reading necessity. I am concerned with the degree to which modernist texts—and it should be remembered that in the annals of twentieth-century literature these texts are by no means in the majority— mostly prevent our asking questions about any spontaneous act of reading, even when it is accompanied by a high degree of learned competence. Modernism in literature can be measured by the degree of textual intimidation felt in the act of reading. That act can become, especially in the classroom, a frightened and unhappy experience in which we are made to feel not only inferior to the author but, in the face of constant reminders that he is himself dissatisfied with what he has just managed to put before us, totally uncritical.

There are almost no critical as distinguished from interpretive readers of the twentieth-century classics. Speaking only of English and American literature, but knowing of a similar but more politicized argument made by Leo Bersani with respect to French literature as exemplified in Malarmé, it can be said that modernism is to be located not in ideas about cultural institutions or about the structures of life in or outside literary texts. It is to be found, rather, in two related and historically verifiable developments: first, in the promotion, by a particular faction of writers, of the virtues and necessities of difficulty and, second, in the complicity by a faction of readers who assent to the proposition that the act of reading should entail difficulties analogous to those registered in the act of writing.

Modernism is an attempt to perpetuate the power of literature as a privileged form of discourse. By its difficulty it tries, paradoxically, to reinvoke the connections, severed more or less by the growth of mass culture, between the artist and the audience. Since this special connection is no longer based on inherited class, as it was up to the Restoration, and since there is no provision for a Spenser, a Milton, a Marvell—great writers who were also members of a governing class for whom they wrote—a corresponding community of writer and reader has to be created. To this end they are asked to participate in a shared text from which others are to be excluded. This may sound as if modernism were a snob's game. It certainly was and is just that, despite all the middle-class keys and guides to the club. It was and is, of course, much more. Significantly, modernism in English literature is nearly exclusively the result of American and Irish—Pound, Eliot, Joyce, Yeats—rather than of English writers and, as I have argued elsewhere, Melville and Hawthorne are, in what they require of the reader, modernist in theory and practice. (It took the inculcation of "difficulty-as-a-virtue" in this century before either of these writers began to be read properly.) Obviously involved here is a colonialist protest on the part of these writers against the shapes the language had assumed as it came forth from England, the seat of cultural and political authority. More importantly, the protest occurred when English literature had itself begun, in the novel and in the great popular poets of the nineteenth century, to cater to the ethos of the so-called common man or common reader. It was to escape incorporation in the ethos that modernist writers turned to the City, with its sharpened social and cultural discriminations, to ancient myth and its hierarchies, to the coteries of French literature, and to English literature of the seventeenth century, a literature of privilege. It is consistent with all this that the two great twentieth-century writers who often seem comparatively easy, Lawrence and Frost, were charged by their modernist contemporaries with being relatively deficient in the sophistications of culture as embodied in the university and the modern city.

Modernism can be thought of as a period when, more than in any other, readers were induced to think of literary texts as necessarily and rewardingly complicated. It represents a demand made upon readers not by anything called twentieth-century literature but by a few peculiarly demanding texts which were promoted as central during this century. In most cases the authors were also remarkably persuasive as literary critics, both in their poems and novels and also in critical writing itself. They rewrote literary history from the retrospect of their own preeminence, expected or achieved. So successful were they in doing this that only in about the past fifteen years has it become possible to bring to vividness on the map of English literature those areas left rather dingy since the advent of modernism as a *critical* fashion. If, through the preeminence of Eliot early in the century, it became necessary to give prominence to Donne and Marvell, it is because of the later eminence of Stevens that Wordsworth has recently been seen for an ever more strange and wonderful poet, just as it is thanks to Frost and Stevens together that the extraordinary importance of Emerson has still to be coped with.

Literary history is to so great an extent the product of such tactical moves and thrusts for power that I cannot agree with the argument offered by Robert Adams in his essay "What

Was Modernism." Of the term itself, Adams writes that "one odd if forceful proof of its reality is that we've so far been unable to write a coherent history of modern English literature." No one can argue with this proposition, but it is possible to take it as a case for celebration rather than bewilderment, and certainly not as an occasion for holding one's breath. A major achievement of recent criticism has been the effort to break down the coherencies that have passed for literary history and to invalidate the principles on which that coherency has traditionally depended. It is possible now to see that the very cult of modernism is in itself a demonstration of the arbitrariness and impertinence by which literary history gets made and remade. Fortunately there is no longer a "coherent history" of English poetry to replace the one which could claim coherence only by reading Shelley out of the line of succession and by trying to dislodge Milton from it. Nor is there a coherent history of American literature, since it has in the past been so often only a history of the Northeast. The coherencies that may ultimately be found will have less to do with chronology, or with periods, or so I hope and expect, than with habits of reading, and related fashions in classroom pedagogy.

Modernism, then, is not an idea or a social condition. The ideas usually associated with it are in themselves not unique to any historical period. It is, rather, the proffered experience which, in its intensity, is unique to this century. Thus, some of the ideas ascribed to Eliot or Joyce or Faulkner belong just as much to Matthew Arnold or to Diderot; they can be extrapolated from Shakespeare, especially from *Troilus and Cressida*, or from the tragedies of Seneca. But none of these is a modernist writer. No one of them has written a book that asks to be read with the kind of attention—unique in the history of literature—required by Eliot or Joyce or Faulkner. It is through Joyce and Eliot especially, and the works published roughly between 1914 and 1925, that most people have learned about modernism, learned to think of it as a phenomenon of the first half of this century, and learned also that it is supposed to entail great difficulties, both for the writer and for the reader.

The peculiar and contradictory nature of that difficulty is the subject to which I can now turn. The necessity of difficulty was put in an unabashedly intimidating way by Eliot in an essay of 1921, "The Metaphysical Poets." "We can only say," he writes, "that it appears likely that poets in our civilization, as it exists at present, must be *difficult*. Our civilization comprehends great variety and complexity, and this variety and complexity, playing upon a refined sensibility, must produce various and complex results. The poet must become more and more comprehensive, more allusive, more indirect, in order to force, to dislocate if necessary, language into his meaning." There is a most unappealing quality in Eliot's prose when he is in this particular mood, a Brahmin indirection, as of a fastidious gentility reluctantly, but no less arrogantly, taking on the whole of the twentieth century. "We can only say that it appears likely that poets in our civilization, as it exists at present . . ."

But Eliot's statement is only arrogant on the face of it. His explanation of why modern poetry is of necessity "difficult" is in fact a self-protective, reductive, and defensive apology for "difficulty." The passage translates difficulty into social and historical causes which in themselves were not at all as peculiar to "our civilization" as he makes them out to be. It is an attempt, that is, actually to vulgarize the necessity for "difficulty," and it might make us wonder how much of his difficulty derived from causes more intimately personal and sexual. Self-serving or not, the representative importance of this insistence on the necessary difficulty of poetry and prose in the twentieth century—Eliot makes even more pointed remarks on the subject in his essay on *Ulysses*—ought to be apparent. It became the bedrock of literary criticism and the study of literature from about 1930 onward. No one can object to difficulty or to any effort to cope with it. At issue are the implications that the difficulty was something only the poet could confront *for* us, and that the reader should be selfless and humble and thankful for the poet's having done this.

It has been said that modernist texts have been misread in the interests of making them more available, more rationally organized, more socially and historically referential than they truly are, and that instead of demystifying these texts, criticism ought to protect their inherent mysteriousness and their irreducible power to baffle. But can it not also be claimed that one reason for the kind of reductive misreadings and interpretations that modernist texts have received lies *in* the works and the writers themselves? Modernist texts make grim readers of us all, that is, by the claim that most people are inadequate to them. We are met with inducements to tidy things up, to locate principles of order and structure beneath a fragmentary surface. We work very hard at it. And then we are told that in fact we have been acting in a witless and heavy-handed fashion, embarrassingly deficient of aristocratic ease. We should have let things be, problematic and unresolved, the meanings perpetually in abeyance. This may seem like a contradiction, but in fact there is not even a choice. We are left precisely within the alternatives, and honestly to recognize this situation as our own allows us, at last, to recognize the writer as being in a situation not very different. It encourages us to humanize the work, the industry of modernist writing, to locate a self and a personality in it. Against Eliot's dictum, it is time to insist that the man who writes is also the man who suffers. In this view, the modernist writer is working within the same contradictions as the reader. The text becomes a drama wherein the culturally or biologically determined human taste for structure or for structuring is continually being excited into activity, and just as continually being frustrated. Each thrust toward order proves no more than another example of the urgency to achieve it.

Modernist literature is tough going, and there is no point in deluding ourselves, and especially our students, with talk, too slowly going out of fashion, of "an erotics of reading," or an escapade of reading, for claims for the sheer fun that awaits us in the pages of Pound or Pynchon. In an engaging book on Ezra Pound, for example, Donald Davie proposes that the

best way to read the *Cantos* is to read them "many at a time
and fast":

*This indeed is what irritates so many readers and fascinates
an elect few—that the* Cantos, *erudite though they are,
consistently frustrate the sort of reading that is synonymous
with "study," reading such as goes on in the seminar room
or the discussion group. It is hopeless to get at them cannily,
not moving on to line three until one is sure of line two.
They must be taken in big gulps or not at all. Does this mean
reading without comprehension? Yes, if by comprehension
we mean a set of propositions that can be laid end to end. . . .
Which is not to deny that some teasing out of quite short
excerpts, even some hunting up of sources and allusions, is
profitable at some stage. For the* Cantos *are a poem to be
lived with, over years. Yet after many years, each new reading—if it is reading of many pages at a time, as it should be—is
a new bewilderment. So it should be, for so it was meant to
be. After all, some kinds of bewilderment are fruitful. To one
such kind we give the name "awe"—not awe at the poet's
accomplishment, his energy, or his erudition but awe at the
energies, some human and some non-human, which interact,
climb, spiral, reverse themselves, and disperse, in the forming
and reforming spectacles which the poet's art presents to us
or reminds us of.*

This is a charming prescription with which I am anxious to
agree, and it is impossible to live up to. It is impossible
because Pound has made it so, just as have Eliot and Joyce,
Beckett and Pynchon.

These writers lent themselves to and *encouraged* a programmed and widespread misreading. For reasons to be
argued later, the notion that every reading is a misreading
seems to me theoretically acceptable if you wish to quibble
but wrong and misleading when it gets down to specific cases.
The misreading in question—with its emphasis on order and
design—is demonstrably less synchronized with the "work"
than are misreadings that like to play fast and loose. That

most readers were led away from the nerve centers of these books by the stimulations of merely external design cannot be explained by claims that for historical reasons literature "must be difficult" in this century. There has been instead, on the part of the writers themselves, a curious *will* to reduce and impoverish what the texts potentially offer. The kinds of clues supplied by Eliot's famous *Notes*, Joyce's handouts, Yeats's system, Faulkner's Christian symbolism—all tended to nullify a reading experience which was in itself meant to mock the efficacy of such clues. As a result, there have been for most readers at least two texts of works like *The Waste Land* or *Ulysses*. One is full of marginalia by which the work is translated into something orderly, fit for class discussion, lectures and articles; while the other is remembered with fondness for all sorts of fragmentary pleasures. There has been almost no critical acknowledgment that these works are a sort of battleground: the flow of material wars against a technology which, however determined, is inadequate to the task of controlling the material. This imbalance is, of course, a contrived one, meant to demonstrate the breakdown of any technique or technology in the face of contemporary life, and it received its most articulate expression first, I think, not in Henry Adams but in Henry James, when in *The American Scene*, he remarks that "The reflecting surfaces, of the ironic, of the epic order, suspended in the New York atmosphere, have yet to show symptoms of shining out, and the monstrous phenomena themselves, meanwhile, strike me as having, with their intense momentum, got the start, got ahead of . . . any possibility of poetic, of dramatic capture."

Pynchon is a remarkable instance of a writer who uses literary technique as an analogue to all other kinds of technology, and does so in order to show that where technique or technology work, it is always at the expense of the material it processes. He seems to call for a labor of exegesis and to encourage the illusion that he will be best understood by those who bone up on entropy or quantum theory or theories of paranoic closure. In fact, his works can best be appreciated by those who can, like Davie's supposititious reader, take his arcane knowledge for granted and be in no way confused by the elaborateness of his "plotting," treating it not as a puzzle to be solved but as a literary symptom of social, historical, economic plotting, an image of the so-called network. But, again, no such reader exists, and it is of no practical use to badger ourselves into thinking that we might become wholly adequate to a text like *Gravity's Rainbow*. It is absurd to posit ideal readers—a favorite exercise of literary criticism—in instances where there cannot be one. But this is where our reverential concessions to literary difficulty have led us. No one *can* be the right kind of reader for books of this sort—open, excited, titillated, knowing, taking all the curves without a map. Some of the exhortations to do this in critical writing smack of high cultural fantasy, the aristocratic pretension that one can be at the same time casual and encyclopedic.

Let us try to tell the truth: writers as well as readers of twentieth-century classics have to do more book work than writers or readers have ever had to do before in history. Why is this the case, even for people from educated households? And why have so many assented to its being necessarily the case? At issue is not the basic difficulty of gaining the competence to read almost anything that is fully aware of the resources of its own language—Shakespeare or Spenser, Milton or Marvell, Wordsworth or Frost. For all the learning and allusiveness in such writers, they only infrequently exhibit the particular kinds of difficulty encountered in what I would call modernist literature. Granting Eliot's proposition—that "our civilization at present" requires a "difficult" kind of writing—why need that difficulty register itself as at once compendiously learned and disjointed, at once schematic in its disposal of allusions and blurred in the uses to which it puts them?

There is a clue, curiously enough, in that plainest of all modernists, Hemingway. Hemingway is not a difficult writer; to read him requires no special knowledge and a familiarity with only a limited repertoire of vocal tones, of sentence sounds. So the connection is made with the proviso that only after the difficult bookishness of Joyce or Eliot has been mastered, if it ever can be, can the reader then fully appreciate their sensuous and rhythmic pleasures. Ideally, that is, the apparatus of Eliot or Joyce functions the way bull fighting or boxing functions metaphorically in Hemingway, and the apparatus therefore probably deserves, though still on the other side of a bookishness Hemingway does not require, the same kind of response from the reader. The learning, the cultural displays, the mechanics of structuring, are forms of partial discipline, of willful signification in a situation where it is being admitted that acts of signification refer themselves to no authority other than the will. They offer an opportunity for making a kind of form which is effective precisely because it is temporary, satisfying only because it is allowed to remain local and finite. It is appropriate to invoke the great William James here, and to use, rather freely, a passage from his "Humanism and Truth." We might say that form in modernist literature is imagined as "the advancing front of experience." And as James so beautifully puts it

Why may not the advancing front of experience, carrying its immanent satisfactions and dissatisfactions, cut against the black inane as the luminous orb of the moon cuts a caerulean abyss? Why should anywhere in the world be absolutely fixed and finished? And if reality genuinely grows, why may it not grow in these very determinations which here and now are made?

Any "form," in a memorable phrase of Robert Frost, our most William Jamesian poet, is no more than "a momentary stay against confusion." And how momentary some of these can be is evidenced in Eliot's *Notes* where he is not giving the reader much of anything except an example of how he can cheer himself up with bits and pieces: "The interior of St. Magnus Martyr is to my mind one of the finest of Wren's interiors. See *The Proposed Demolition among Nineteen City Churches:* (P. S. King & Son, Ltd.)." Thus also the relish of Joyce in lists, parodies, schemes. The best way to read such persistent schematization is as an *act*, an action, something a writer is *doing* in a posited situation; and the posited situation, conceived by Joyce and Eliot as being more unique to their historical moment than either William James or Frost would have allowed, is one in which all more encompassing orders have become as arbitrary and as subject to deterioration as any they are themselves proposing. It is not, to repeat, so much the substance as the act of allusiveness or of schematization which should occupy the reader. In general it can be said that middle-class anxieties about culture and about some possibly terminal and encompassing acts of interpretation, both fostered by the mythologies of general education, were only further increased by the often trivial or boned-up cultural erudition of the middle class "great" writers of the twentieth century, with their religious and cultural nostalgias.

Eliot and Joyce are not romantic writers; they are not classical writers either. In Eliot's telling phrase about Joyce, they are "classical in tendency." "Tendency"—they are what they are *in* an action, and by virtue of a kind of self-monitoring by which a writer interprets the forms he has just offered up for interpretation. It is said, with no embarrassment about being obvious, that the reader helps in the creation of the text and therefore functions, in his reading, like a poet. It can be said, less obviously, that Eliot and Joyce must be classified as readers of the text they are writing. Critical reading, that is, is simultaneously a part of the performance of writing, and to some degree it always has been. At the outset of "Tradition and the Individual Talent" Eliot remarks that "criticism is as inevitable as breathing, and that we should be none the worse for articulating what passes in our minds as we read a book and feel an emotion about it, for criticising our own minds in their work of criticism." This is precisely what he does in his poems.

In thus suggesting the kinetic, the volatile nature of both the reading and the writing, Eliot calls our attention to an active authorial presence even while forswearing it. That presence is supposed to be notoriously hard to find, according to him; it does not have a "voice" even in the great varieties of style displayed in modernist writing. But it can be found, if not in any of the styles, then in the mode of variations among them. It is to be found not in any place, despite all the formal placements made available, but in the acts of *dis*placement by which one form is relinquished for another. Recall how Faulkner described the reading-writing experience that gave us *The Sound and the Fury*. He wanted to tell a story that occurred to him when he saw a girl with dirty panties in a tree. He told it from a point of view that proved inadequate. So he told it again from another point of view, and on reading the second version he found that it, too, was inadequate; so he told it a third time from yet another, and when that did not satisfy him, he told it in more or less his own voice. That, too, was unsatisfactory, but the whole thing, the four versions, constituted the novel as we have it, a novel made from Faulkner's having read what he had written as a source of what he would then write. Apropos of this is an offhand remark by Gore Vidal which is altogether more useful than his considered and therefore superstitious observations on contemporary fiction: "In a way I have nothing to say but a great deal to add."

Eliot is so much a poet of probing additions, additions seeking a destination, that he could easily accept most deletions and abridgments made by Pound in *The Waste Land*. The penultimate admission in "Preludes" that "I am moved by fancies that are curled / Around these images, and cling: / The notion of some infinitely gentle / Infinitely suffering thing" comes from a poet for whom narrativity—with a destination—would have been an act of presumption. He can never take anything in stride; he moves, falteringly, toward the formation of images and concepts which dissolve as soon as he has reached them. The indecisiveness was as pronounced after as it was before his religious conversion. In the later poetry of *The Quartets*, as Leavis shows, the reader is not invited to translate abstract concepts about "time present and time past" but rather to witness and participate in the intensity of Eliot's personal engagement as he tries to arrive at some security, never actually achieved, about such abstractions and the feelings engendered by his use of them. Eliot became a poet precisely because he embraced those conditions which prevent others from becoming one—of being "moved" by something even while not knowing what to make of it. Writing for him was more or less indistinguishable from a critical reading that was all but crippling.

For Eliot's use of images that remain at once evocative and random there are well documented poetic precedents in Laforgue and others. But the images do not refer only to other images; they refer us also to a man named T. S. Eliot and to a feeling in him—we are allowed only faintly to sense it—that is close to an envy of natures more masculine, or should we say more operatically masculine, than his own. It is as if he imagines that for some other man the images in a poem like "La Filia ché Piange" would not remain transient and painful. They would instead initiate and sustain a plot. Eliot is someone—man as well as poet—incapable of initiating a plot within which the images could be secured and pacified.

Joyce exhibits, flamboyantly, altogether more psychological, sexual assurance. It is a commonplace that the Joycean hero is customarily on the fringe of activities—a game, a dance, a family dinner, a boisterous conversation. Other people can take pleasure in these activities unconscious or careless of what the hero knows about them: that they are bound by sometimes deadening rules and clichés, that the activities are programmed and encoded without consultation with the participants. Privileged consciousness, as Poulet would have it, is not at the center but on the circumference of the area of inhabited space, and it is ready to move still further out into abstractions, as at the end of "The Dead." But Stephen is no more his hero than Gabriel is, and no one can read him with a deserved relish without feeling that the true hero of Joyce's writing has been identified by those who say it is Joyce himself. He took a kind of pleasure—to call it sadomasochistic is to be obvious—in the fact that a Stephen or a Gabriel is forced to confront, to be intimidated by, the power, the exuberance, the virtuosity, however prefabricated, that is emplanted *in* the programmed or encoded life, in codes which only a genius can release onto the page. Joyce exulted in the evidence that he was master of the codes, master of the techniques, the revelry of forms. All writers are cold and calculating, but no one more brazenly celebrates his own arbitrariness. He is unlike Eliot in the delight he takes in *not* feeling put upon or anguished by what he has just written. Joyce is the quintessential celebrant of literary technology.

All literature is to some extent aware of itself as a technology. But literary modernism thrusts this awareness upon us, and to an unprecedented degree asks us to experience the enormous difficulties of mastering a technology. It is this matter of degree which allows us to distinguish literary modernism from the sort of literary self-consciousness which may be exhibited by any text in any period. Modernism manifests itself whenever a text chooses to demonstrate that one of its primary purposes is to expose the factitiousness of its own local procedures. In order to do this, it must make the experience of reading in some way almost directly analagous to the experience of writing. It can be said that modernist texts are about the corrosive effect of reading, by author and reader, upon what has just been shaped by the writing.

Modernist writers, to put it too simply, keep on with the writing of a text because in reading what they are writing they find only the provocation to alternatives. "To begin to begin again," as Gertrude Stein once said. If the texts are mimetic in that they simulate simultaneously the reading/writing activity, then *that* is the meaning of the text. The meaning resides in the performance of writing and reading, of reading in the act of writing. This is emphatically the reverse of saying, as part of a rear-guard perpetuation of humanism, that these texts are subject to multiple interpretations. Rather, their capacity to mean different things, to take different shapes, is in itself their meaning.

It is important to insist on this as against the fashion that imposes an infinite variety of possible readings. In that proposition is one evidence of a kind of ahistoricism in contemporary theory importantly different from the kind with which this essay might be charged. Modernist texts are of enormous historical consequence as *texts*. They are of consequence to the extent that their meaning resides in an induced habit of reading, using that word in the broadest sense, a habit finally of analysis that can be exercised outside the literary text on social and economic structures.

Modernist texts are important less for any commentary they offer on contemporary life than for the degree that they empower us, by the strenuous demands made upon our capacities for attention, to make our own commentaries.

To say that modernist poetry and fiction exists also and simultaneously as works of literary criticism is therefore to say that literary criticism can be a unique schooling in the workings of structures, techniques, codes, stylizations that shape the structured world around us.

Of course it could be argued that the plays of Shakespeare or the poetry of Wordsworth also exist as works of literary criticism. And where Shakespeare in *Troilus and Cressida* or Wordsworth in his shapings and reshapings of *The Prelude* reveal an extraordinary degree of self-consciousness about being critics of their own creation, they too are modernists. But it is well to remember that they become available to us *as* such only by virtue of what we have learned about the strains and difficulties of literature from Eliot, Joyce, and the like.

Modernism exists predominantly in the twentieth century only because it is predominantly there that we have been forced to become what I have called "grim readers." Modernism does not occur, that is, whenever a work addresses itself to literary traditions, the genres or tropes or topics which it shares with other poems and novels. Modernist texts include such allusiveness but are also consciously occupied with the nature of reading and writing then and there going on and with the relation between these two acts.

Modernism enters history not with a mirror, not even with a lamp, but with instruments by which to measure the hidden structure of things and the tactics of their movement. It enters history as a mode of experience, a way of reading, a way of being with great difficulty conscious of structures, techniques, codes, and stylizations. In modernist works the revealed inadequacy of forms or structures or styles to the life they propose to explain or include is meant in itself to be a matter of historical importance, regardless of whether the material is historically accredited. Our training in this could begin as easily with Melville as with Joyce. Modernist texts teach us to *face* the failure of technology in that version of it which we call literary technique—the failure significantly to account for all that we think technology should account for. In that sense, the reader of these works is made conscious, in Hawthorne's phrase, of "what prisoners we are," and this could be a discovery of great spiritual as well as cultural importance.

Chapter 5

The Crack in the Chimney: Reflections

on Contemporary American Playwriting

Robert Brustein

In the second act of Ibsen's *The Master Builder*, Halvard Solness endeavors to explain to his young admirer, Hilda Wangel, the origin of his peculiarly lucky career as a builder. It had all begun with a fire in his own house, a fire that caused the death of his children and turned his wife into a living corpse, but which also gave him his first chance to exercise his building talents. The curious thing about this scene is the manner in which Solness describes the cause of that fatal blaze.

> You see, the whole business revolves around little more than a crack in a chimney.
> *Hilda.* Nothing else?
> *Solness.* No; at least not at the start. . . . I'd noticed that tiny opening in the flue long before the fire. Every time I wanted to start repairing it, it was exactly as if a hand was there, holding me back. So nothing came of it.
> *Hilda.* But why did you keep postponing?
> *Solness.* Because I went on thinking, through that little black opening, I could force my way to success—as a builder.

So far, one finds nothing unusual. The passage looks like a perfectly conventional piece of exposition, with the playwright demonstrating how the past influences the present—

how Solness began his career and developed his guilty conscience. A crack in the chimney, leading to a dreadful fire. An opportunity to subdivide the burnt-out area into building lots. A new reputation as a builder of suburban homes.

But then something extraordinary happens in the scene, as Ibsen proceeds to annihilate his own, very carefully fashioned causal construction.

> *Hilda.* But wait a minute, Mr. Solness—how can you
> be so sure the fire started from that little crack
> in the chimney?
> *Solness.* I can't, not at all. In fact, I'm absolutely certain
> it had nothing whatever to do with the fire. . . .
> *Hilda. What?*
> *Solness.* It's been proved without a shadow of a doubt
> that the fire broke out in a clothes closet, in
> quite another part of the house.

Hilda's exclamation of astonishment could be joined by a chorus of readers and spectators, for the play seems to have taken a very mischievous turn. But Ibsen is not intending to be perverse here. Quite the contrary, what he is suggesting is entirely consistent with his poetic apprehension of reality and with the metaphysical impulse animating all his plays, including his so-called "social-realistic" drama. The determination of guilt and its expiation may still constitute the moral quest of his characters, but Ibsen obviously believes that the sources of this guilt are not very easily accessible to the inquiring mind.

What Ibsen is anticipating, in this passage, is the significant turn that the theatre was to take some time around the end of the nineteenth century, in common with similar developments in science, philosophy, and literature—the artistic departure which was responsible, in part, for the movement called modernism, and which influenced the work of a number of major European dramatists, among them Strindberg, Pirandello, Beckett, Ionesco, and Handke.

For Ibsen has quietly proceeded to undermine a basic

assumption of the naturalist universe—namely, that cause A precedes consequence B, which in turn is responsible for the catastrophe, C. Isn't it possible, he suggests, that A has nothing whatever to do with B, much less with C, regardless of the apparent evidence? Isn't it possible that events are so multiple and complex that the human intelligence may never be able to comprehend the full set of causes preceding any situation, consequence, or feeling? Ibsen, in short, is attempting to repeal the simple, fundamental law of cause and effect which has been an unquestioned statute at least since the Enlightenment—the law that ruled the linear, logical, rationalistic world of literature, and, in particular, the Western literature of guilt. In its place, Ibsen is reconfirming the unknowable, ineffable secrets underlying the will of Nature.

All of Ibsen's plays contain religious elements, but *The Master Builder* is clearly his most religious play since *Brand*. What the playwright is trying to do through the character of his ruthless, guilty hero, Solness, is to challenge the orthodox pieties at the same time that he is preserving the romantic mysteries. The purpose of the universe, the structure of character, the nature of sin—all are beyond the reach of traditional concepts; they can be determined only through the artist's intuition, and then only darkly. And the task of the modern artist is to help humankind move beyond the sterile cycle of guilt and expiation, which is one of the offshoots of cause-and-effect thinking. Hilda exhorts Solness to challenge God by developing a robust Viking conscience. Ibsen exhorts us to become gods by transcending our sense of guilt, through a gargantuan effort of the will and the inspired intelligence. Whether this is finally possible is open to serious doubt. But one thing is certain: The old rationalistic assumptions will no longer serve the modern understanding. Indeed, they can only compound ignorance and point us toward false paths.

Although Ibsen's proposals were at the time revolutionary, challenging not only conventional theatre but also conventional religion, conventional psychology, and conventional social theory they were actually a return to the assumptions of an earlier age of mystery, which held sway before the advent of Newtonian physics, Cartesian logic, and behavioral psychology. The drama of the Greeks and Elizabethans, for example, is rarely causal in our modern sense. Human motives are sometimes so numerous that latter-day commentators find it hard to give the characters credibility. Clytemnestra offers not one but five or six reasons for killing Agamemnon; Iago mentions so many motives for hating Othello that Coleridge was led to speak of the senseless motive-hunting of a "motiveless malignity"; and T. S. Eliot criticized Shakespeare for failing to give Hamlet an "objective correlative," meaning simply that he found Hamlet's feelings to be in excess of his situation.

While contemporary social scientists are busy rooting around in search of clear explanations of poverty, crime, neurosis, and madness, great artists have traditionally understood that the true explanations *are* beyond concepts, to be reached only through the intuition, and then only darkly. As Shakespeare's Edmund puts it, "This is the excellent foppery of the world, that, when we are sick in fortune—often the surfeit of our own behavior—we make guilty of our disasters the sun, the moon, and the stars. . . . Pfut! I should have been that I am, had the maidenliest star in the firmament twinkled on my bastardizing."

European drama has recaptured this understanding also, at least since the middle of the last century, when Ibsen—along with Nietzsche and Kierkegaard—threw down a gauntlet not only before orthodox religion but before the prevailing liberal ideology of the nineteenth and twentieth centuries, meanwhile reducing the middle-class living room to a pile of rubble and exposing domestic realism as a cardboard illusion.

A quick look at the history of our own theatre reveals that American drama has been very slow in rising to this challenge, or even in revealing any awareness of it. Just as the dominant strain of our religious life has been a form of Judaeo-Christian Puritanism, and the dominant strain of our politics a form of liberal reform democracy, so the dominant strain of our stage has been social, domestic, psychological, and realistic—which is to say, *causal*—and its dominant theme, the excavation, exposure, and expiation of guilt. The fires that burn through most American plays have been caused by that crack in the chimney, and the guilty conscience of our theatrical characters can usually be traced to a single, recognizable event. This is particularly striking when one considers how many playwrights in the mainstream of American drama have thought themselves to be writing consciously in an Ibsenite tradition. And I speak now not just of the dramatists of the pre-World War II period—such social-minded writers as Clifford Odets, Sidney Howard, Maxwell Anderson, Robert Sherwood, Lillian Hellman, Irwin Shaw, and John Steinbeck—but also of the postwar "mood" playwrights—including such psychological writers as Tennessee Williams, Arthur Miller, William Inge, Paddy Chayefsky, William Gibson, Frank Gilroy, and, more recently, Lanford Wilson, Mark Medoff, Paul Zindel, Michael Cristofer, and David Rabe.

Even the progenitor of our drama, Eugene O'Neill—though he began writing under the strict influence of Nietzsche and Strindberg—became a causal dramatist in his last plays, when he was writing under the influence of Ibsen. In his greatest play, indeed the greatest play ever written by an American, *A Long Day's Journey into Night*, O'Neill proceeds to weave a close fabric of causality; every character in the play is suffering pangs of remorse and every character is trying to determine the root cause of his guilt. If the blighted house of Tyrone is misbegotten, then every one of the family is implicated in the other's hell. Each separate action radiates outward into myriad branches of effects, and characters interlock, imprisoned in each other's fate. The miserliness of the elder Tyrone is the cause of his wife's addiction, since it was the quack doctor he hired who first introduced her to drugs, and Edmund's tuberculosis accounts for his mother's resumption of her habit, since she cannot face the fact of his bad health. Jamie is plagued by the very existence of Edmund, since his brother's literary gifts inspire him with envy and a sense of failure; and his mother's inability to shake her habit has made him lose faith in his own capacity for regeneration. Even the comic elements are structured causally: Tyrone is too cheap to burn lights in the parlor, so Edmund bangs his knee on a hatstand, and Jamie stumbles on the steps.

My point reflects not on the quality of this play, which is a masterpiece, but rather on the fact that *A Long Day's Journey into Night* is remorselessly American in its concentration on the sources of guilt, and on the painful confrontations between parents and their children. These emphases are also evident in the work of an even more conscientious disciple of Ibsen—Arthur Miller—who, along with Tennessee Williams, has been the most celebrated postwar American dramatist and the strongest influence on the American realist theatre. Miller first broke upon the contemporary consciousness, in fact, with a play that draws heavily from such middle Ibsen works as *The Wild Duck, Pillars of Society*, and *An Enemy of The People*—namely, *All My Sons.* Located in a middle-class living room around the end of World War II, this play had the task of identifying the guilt and establishing the responsibility of its elder protagonist, a wealthy manufacturer named Joe Keller.

Keller has served a short time in the penitentiary, having been convicted of increasing his profits by manufacturing faulty cylinder heads for aircraft engines; these have caused the deaths of a number of American fighter pilots. Keller's older son, Larry, is missing in action and, at one point, the characters consider the possibility that the same faulty parts may have been responsible for his death as well. By the play's end, we learn that the causal connection exists, but in indirect form: upon discovering that his father was responsible for the deaths of his comrades, Larry committed suicide by purposely crashing his plane. After a confrontation with his surviving son, Chris, Keller is forced to recognize that he is responsible not only for the lives of his immediate family but for "all my sons." He expiates his guilt through his own suicide.

It is easy enough to score points on Miller's dramaturgy, which often seems as faulty as Joe Keller's airplane parts. But my quarrel is not with the far-fetched plotting of a young and relatively inexperienced writer; his work is to grow considerably more convincing as his career progresses. The point is, rather, that *All My Sons* is based on assumptions and conventions which, regardless of how the playwright matures, remain central to all his work, as well as to most mainstream American drama—assumptions and conventions which are virtually anathema to Ibsen. For Miller is firmly wedded to simple theatrical causality, whether the sequential links are direct or indirect, and his plays never outgrow the kind of connection he establishes, in *All My Sons*, between Joe Keller's crime and Larry Keller's aircrash. The action A precedes the consequence B, which leads inevitably to the guilty catastrophe C.

And the catalyst in this chemical mixture is almost invariably the protagonist's son, who manages to bring the plot from a simmer to a boil. In fact, the typical Miller drama has a code that might be deciphered: The son exposes the father's guilt and shows him the way to moral action and sometimes, inadvertently, to suicide. Take Miller's most famous play—often called the finest tragedy of modern times—*Death of a Salesman*. The familiar main plot concerns the false values of Willy Loman, but the character who confronts Willy with the fraudulence of his life is Biff, Willy's older son. Once extremely close to his father, Biff has now grown estranged from Willy, for reasons that Miller chooses to keep hidden until the end of the play. Something has happened between them, something which has affected not only their relationship, but Biff's entire mature life; he has broken off a promising high school career and drifted aimlessly around the country. This, in turn, has had a powerful influence on Willy's life, since Biff once represented his main hope for the future. Ineluctably, the play brings us toward the revelation buried inside this family mystery: Coming to visit his father in Boston one day, Biff discovers that Willy has a woman in his room.

Clearly, Miller is willing to risk a great deal of credibility in order to establish a moral showdown between father and son.

Consider how much of the plot, theme, and character development hinge on this one climactic hotel-room encounter. *Death of a Salesman* purports to be about false American values of success, but beneath the sociological surface lies the real drama—a family drama of guilt and blame. The source of Biff's hero worship, the model for his own life and behavior, has been discovered in Boston being unfaithful to Mom.

In short, the premises underlying Miller's themes and actions are not Ibsenite in the least. They belong to the eighteenth century, which is to say the age of Newton, rather than to the twentieth, the age of Einstein. And Miller's theatrical Newtonianism remains an essential condition of his style, whether he is writing about the Salem witch hunts, the guilt and responsibility of those implicated in the Nazi crimes, self destructive glamour queens, or East European dissidents. In each of Miller's plays—indeed, in most of the plays of his contemporaries and disciples—every dramatic action has an equal and opposite reaction. It is the crack in the chimney that sends the house up in flames.

So prevalent is this pattern in mainstream American drama that even now, toward the end of the 1970's, our most highly acclaimed playwrights are still shaping their works to sequential diagrams. The style of our drama has admittedly undergone something of an exterior change; its causal pattern is occasionally more elliptical than in Miller's work; and the familiar fourth-wall realism is occasionally broken by stylistic devices. But these are changes touching the surface rather than the hearts of these plays. More often than not, American mainstream dramatists continue to explore the causes behind their effects; the event to be excavated is still the guilt of the (generally older generation) protagonists; and the drama retains the air of a courtroom, complete with arraignments, investigations, condemnations, indictments, and punishments.

Take David Rabe, perhaps the most typical and the most highly esteemed of the younger generation playwrights. Rabe has been called the likely successor to Eugene O'Neill—but a perfunctory glance at his accomplishments soon reveals that he has a closer relative in Arthur Miller. Like Miller, Rabe is fundamentally a social dramatist, fashioning vague attacks on the system; like Miller, he identifies the nexus of corruption in the heart of the family; and like Miller, he will occasionally make modest departures from domestic realism in order to indict his middle-class characters for the crimes of the nation at large.

In Rabe's case these crimes are almost invariably linked with the Vietnam War, an event that continues to obsess him—not surprisingly, since he is a veteran of that war. In *Sticks and Bones*, for example, he sketches a semisurrealist portrait of middle-class guilt, pitting a returning blind soldier (also named David) against the members of his immediate family: Ozzie, his father, Harriet, his mother, and Rickie, his guitar-playing brother. These names, recognizable from a popular sit-com series, promise a satire on TV—but Rabe is more interested in savaging the people who watch it. In the background, visible only to the blind son throughout most of the play, is Zung, a Vietnamese woman with whom David had lived during his service abroad.

Rabe's larger purpose depends on our believing that Ozzie, Harriet, and Rick represent a typical American family, but before long, Ozzie is strangling Zung, outraged by her sexual relationship with David; Harriet is revealing a callous cruelty that belies her pose of maternal self-sacrifice; and Rickie is helping David to cut his wrists in full view of his approving parents. What Rabe is attempting to symbolize is the hatred and savagery that middle-class Americans feel not only toward foreigners but toward members of their immediate families, in order to identify racism as the fundamental cause of the Vietnam War.

Rabe's "poetic" and "surrealist" devices are actually only stratagems, permitting him to generalize about his characters and his themes, while his political concerns seem to have less inner importance for him than his domestic interests. What he has actually created is a relatively straightforward family drama about the confrontation between an indignant radical young man and his unfeeling conservative parents, with a crisis not very different from the climactic scenes in *All My Sons* and *Death of a Salesman*. A son uncovers the source of his father's guilt and thereupon proceeds to lecture him about his past and present errors, and, by extension, the errors of the country he represents.

The idea that the young have more insight than their elders and are therefore in a position to teach them wisdom is not a notion that Orientals would find very easy to understand. But it seems fundamental to the progressive beliefs of our stage, not to mention the liberal philosophy of our country, where each generation is expected to improve upon the previous generation until Utopia is inexorably achieved. Rabe's work suggests some of the reasons why this Utopia has not yet materialized. David may be superior to his parents, but he surpasses them primarily in self-righteousness. The strain of violence in *Sticks and Bones*—it dominates other Rabe plays as well, like *Pavlo Hummel* and *Streamers*—is more of a reflection than an indictment of this central American problem; and the crude caricaturing of Ozzie and Harriet at the same time that David and Zung are drawn as sanctified victims suggests that the tolerance and compassion called for in the play are not always felt by the author himself.

What is remarkable is the way in which American audiences have sat still for *their* portion of guilt, not only failing to rise to these baited challenges but conferring fame, fortune, and Pulitzer Prizes on the writers who savage them most. At least one member of this audience, however—a young writer named Christopher Durang—has refused Rabe's indictment. In parodying the Western theatre of guilt, Durang has hinted at one of the directions our drama might take, were that crack in the chimney ever to be repaired. Durang's play is entitled *The Vietnamization of New Jersey*, and it is a satire of such ferocity that it runs roughshod not only through the conventions of *Sticks and Bones* but through some of our most cherished liberal illusions.

Durang is a lineal descendant of Lenny Bruce, which is to say he is always trespassing on forbidden ground, skirting perilously close to nihilism. Still, Durang's nihilism is earned;

like Bruce, he obviously suffers for it. The satire in *The Vietnamization of New Jersey* has been called collegiate, but it is rarely facile, and never self-righteous. Durang's comedy, at its best, has deep roots in a controlled anger, which can only be expressed and purged through a comedy of the absurd.

The Vietnamization of New Jersey is set in a suburban American living room, piled high to the ceiling with the detritus of our consumer culture: two hair dryers, three TV sets, an outsize roto-grill, sculptured ducks in flight over the fireplace. Seated at the breakfast table are Rabe's benighted family, now renamed Ozzie Ann, Harry, and Et, their teenage delinquent son. Et is pouring cornflakes down his trousers and eating his breakfast out of his crotch. Hazel, the black maid, clears the table by ripping off the cloth, dropping coffee, toast, and cereal into the laps of her employers whom she proceeds to indict as malignant symbols of white America.

Into this disaster area comes David, home from the war, with his Vietnamese wife, Liat. Both are blind, which David demonstrates by walking into the refrigerator. Et moralizes: "The fact that they're blind literally in a way points to the fact that we and the American people are blind literally. We suffer, I think, a moral and philosophical blindness." Liat has married David because he is "the best damn stick man in the U.S. Army"—as a result, she can't remember if his name is Cholly or Joe. When they both fall into the family septic tank, Et draws the inevitable political conclusion that this symbolizes the way America is mired in the Vietnam War. Eventually, we learn that Liat is actually a girl named Maureen O'Hara from Schenectady, who went to Vietnam because she wanted to break into American musicals like *The King and I*.

David suffers a nervous breakdown when he learns that he can no longer use Liat to excoriate his parents' guilt, and spends the next four years hiding under the breakfast table. The coming of inflation reduces the family's fortunes: for Thanksgiving they can only afford Campbell's Chunky Soup. Creditors repossess not only the furniture, but the walls of the set as well. Harry loses his job and shoots himself, ruining

Ozzie Ann's nice new rug. The family is saved by Harry's brother, Larry, a Mafia hit man, who is also a sergeant in the Army reserves. Dressed like General Patton in jodphurs and a bright chrome helmet, Larry brings order back into the household, teaching the family discipline, seducing Liat with chocolates and nylons, and catching David in a bear trap. At the end of the play, with everything having returned to normalcy, David decides to burn himself to death, and while Hazel regales the audience with ludicrous Bicentennial Minutes, the family admires the lovely orange glow that David is making in the sky.

Durang owes a certain debt to Ionesco in his manipulation of the absurd, but his style is peculiarly American. What he is obviously satirizing here is the heavy-handed symbolism, the fake piety, the smug self-satisfaction, the ponderous confrontations, and the cut-rate merchandising of guilt and indignation that pervade so much linear American drama, at the same time that he is demolishing the clichés about the Vietnam War expressed by both the right and the left. With *The Vietnamization of New Jersey*, Durang has declared a separate peace, and as far as American culture is concerned he has finally brought the Vietnam War to a close.

Insofar as Durang belongs to a previous Absurd tradition, however, he breaks no new formal ground. One dramatist who is beginning to turn over the theatrical topsoil is Sam Shepard, a writer with an unusually large body of mythic material, considering his comparative youth. In common with a number of young playwrights today, Shepard is exploring ways to shortcut the habitual terrain of plot, character, and theme, primarily through the use of legendary material, borrowed from Western myths and myths of the movies, including gangster films, horror films, and science fiction. By bringing recognizable figures onto the stage from popular culture, Shepard and his followers are able to dispense with illusionary settings and obligatory exposition, fashioning instead a drama that is metaphorical and mysterious, with the ambiguous reverberations of poetry.

In one of his more recent plays, *Suicide in B Flat*, Shepard goes one step further, attempting to achieve the condition of music—particularly the spacey effects of progressive jazz. Jazz of this kind is, in fact, played throughout the evening, by a pianist who sits on the stage with his back to the audience, accompanying the actors. The play takes the form of an improvisation, within the genre of pulp fiction. Two detectives, with mysterious links to government agencies, are trying to solve a mystery regarding Niles, a celebrated jazz composer, whose corpse has been found in his room. Was his death the result of murder or suicide? The gumshoes cannot decide, and the chalked outline of his body on the floor does not reveal the secret. When these conventional-minded working stiffs are joined by a suicidal female bass player and a skinny spaced-out saxophonist who blows soundless music (Niles' jazz is so advanced that even dogs can't hear it), the whole business begins to get beyond them. One of the detectives starts wrestling with his own hand which, having developed a life of its own, is trying to stab him with a knife. The other grows increasingly paralyzed as the sax player sits on his lap and tortures him with his protruding bones.

Niles appears, invisible to all except a nervous young groupie who accompanies him. He may be dead, or, perhaps the same thing, he may have gone over into another space-time dimension—Shepard never tells us. But before Niles can rest, he must annihilate a series of identities that prevent him from achieving authenticity. His girl companion dresses him in a child's cowboy costume and shoots him with a bow and arrow; one of the detectives receives the arrow in *his* back. The girl fits him out as a concert conductor, in white tie and tails, and shoots him with a revolver; the other detective receives the bullet in *his* gut. Neither detective is actually wounded, but both are so disoriented that they will never be "normal" again. By the end of the play, Niles has walked through the walls of his room to accept the guilt for his own death. As the detectives lead him away in handcuffs, the upstage pianist concludes with the haunting strains of his own jazz.

Like much of Shepard's work, the play is a hallucination

and therefore not readily available to logical explanation. Still, the themes curl up like vapor from the performance: the problems caused by celebrity in America, the necessity to transcend despair, the need of the artist to break down false self-images in order to create a genuine vision. And it is interesting that, in the act of disintegrating the causal conventions of realistic theatre, Shepard has also managed to reinterpret the conventional drama of guilt. For *Suicide in B Flat* is a self-accusation, rather than an indictment, in which guilt becomes the price we pay for being alive.

With Sam Shepard, the American theatre takes a step beyond the Newtonian universe into a world of dream, myth, and inner space. With Robert Wilson it leaps into the universe of Einstein, developing new dimensions of outer space and fractured time.

My reference to Einstein's universe is not gratuitous. All of Wilson's bizarre theatre pieces involve a relativity-influenced temporal and spatial sense, and his recent work—a dance-opera-drama created in collaboration with the composer Philip Glass—is actually entitled *Einstein on the Beach*.

This five-hour meditation shows the influence of Einstein both in its physics and its spirit. In fact, every one of the actors has been made up to resemble Albert Einstein (they are dressed in suspenders, grey pants, and tennis shoes), and the principal soloist, like Einstein a violinist, wears a flowing white wig and a bushy white moustache.

The opera brings us from the world of the locomotive, which is to say the machinery of the Industrial Revolution, to the world of the space ship, which is Einstein's culminating gift to the twentieth century. Built around three separate settings—a train, a trial, and a field—connected by little dialogues in front of the curtain called "knee plays," the work dramatizes (so subtly one absorbs it through the imagination rather than the mind) the change in perception—especially perception of time—that accompanied this technological development. The interminable length of the performance, therefore, becomes a condition of its theme, as do the strange, schematic settings, the vertical and horizontal shafts of lights, and the apparently meaningless snatches of dialogue.

The train scene at the beginning of the play gives some sense of its style. A little boy stands atop a crane, throwing paper airplanes into the air every five or ten minutes; a woman dances diagonally back and forth the length of the stage, spasmodically waving her arms. Two people create and examine a triangle made of string. A man listens to the sound of a seashell. A huge locomotive cut-out, manned by an engineer with a pipe, inches forward, disappears in a blackout, then appears a little further forward, always preceded by billows of smoke. The scene takes over an hour to perform.

Other episodes include the trial of a woman, presumably Patty Hearst, who is condemned and sentenced by a robot jury, and by two bewigged judges (an old black man and a child), a dance sequence in a field culminating with the appearance of a space ship model on a string sliding across the upper proscenium, and a second train scene, this time with the caboose facing the audience, involving some inexplicable conflict between a man and a woman. The final big scene provides the most striking effect of the evening: the stage is converted into the huge interior of a space ship, propelled by the entire cast, in which plastic capsules containing human bodies move laterally across the length of the stage, and the statistics of the Hiroshima disaster are projected on a scrim. We have been involved in a progress from locomotion to rocket propulsion, from paper airplanes to space travel, from firecrackers to nuclear explosions. And yet, as the final knee play demonstrates—bringing a bus cut-out into view, driven by a man who tonelessly recites the lyrics of a romantic song—our language for love has remained essentially the same.

Some of this seems irritatingly self-indulgent; but most of it is extremely evocative for those who have the patience to receive its images. Wilson is beginning to fashion some very powerful visual metaphors which have been surpassed, I believe, only in the movie that obviously influenced *Einstein on the Beach*—namely, Stanley Kubrick's *2001*. It is true that the visual effects are the most dazzling and original aspects of the work: Wilson is essentially a painter who paints in motion. But with this work he is launching the theatre into the unknown and the unknowable, in a way that makes our contemporary domestic plays look like ancient artifacts of a forgotten age.

These three playwrights, then, have virtually demolished the "tasteless parlor" of the illusionistic theatre, and not simply through the let's-pretend devices associated with, say, the theatre of Thornton Wilder. Durang, in an excess of satiric rage, literally knocks down the walls of the family home; Shepard walks his characters through those walls, like poltergeists from another space-time continuum; and Wilson is beginning to investigate the outer reaches of the expanding universe. By leaping beyond the physical confines of the kitchen, the bedroom, and the living room, these writers are transcending the thematic limitations imposed by those rooms as well. Artists working in other forms have been responsive to the kinds of discoveries now affecting the modern consciousness—relativity theory, black holes, quasars, bends in time, antimatter, ESP, and the like. Now the theatre is showing some sign that it has not remained impassive before the liberating new possibilities of the imagination.

And that has been the destiny of all great art—theatrical, literary, visual, or musical; ancient or modern—to expand rather than to limit the structure of imagination. The strict laws governing so much modern drama provide an atmosphere of safety and predictability, but only at the cost of severe restrictions on the possibilities of creation. To live in uncertainty in such insecure, inchoate times as ours is to live in fear and trembling. But what the poet Keats called the "negative capability"—meaning our capacity to function with doubts and ambiguities—remains an essential condition of the poetic imagination. We are beginning to discover that we have been speaking bourgeois prose all our lives—and we have been listening to too much of it. But the nonlinear theatre fulfills some of the conditions of poetry by introducing us to the unexpected, and bringing us beyond the prosaic formulas of our social-psychological universe.

For it is constructed on metaphor, the channel through which artists find their way to a hidden reality inaccessible to barren explanations and causal links. I hope it is obvious that I am not arguing here for obfuscation or obscurantism. If excessive rationalizing is the bane of modern theatre, then there is an equal problem in formulating mystery for its own sake, as I believe Edward Albee and Harold Pinter are sometimes prone to do. The true dramatic poet understands that metaphor is a tool with which to reveal rather than to obscure, a key to turn those locks that remain impervious to conceptual thought.

And, finally, this metaphorical theatre will help to free us from the facile guilt-mongering of our accusatory playwrights. Rhetoric—as Yeats told us in a famous passage—proceeds from the quarrel with others, poetry from the quarrel with ourselves. The rhetorical indignation so familiar to twentieth-century drama is a result of a failure to understand that the accusing finger may not belong to a blameless hand. Master Builder Solness denounced himself for failing to repair that crack in the chimney, even though he knew full well it had nothing to do with the fire that destroyed his house. Thus he accepted his own guilt, a condition of being human—and thus he transcended it, a condition of being an artist. Only through this double responsibility could he preserve the mysteries without losing his humanity, and go on to create a penetrating new art.

Chapter 6

The First County of Places

Howard Nemerov

Rhapsodical Prelude

Grown-ups, maybe the hardest thing to believe about us is that we used to be children. Is it true? Can it possibly be true? There is a great deal of evidence to say so, but it is all circumstantial evidence, dusty accumulations tending to establish a fact—which is, however, not a state of mind, and thus remains somewhat inert and unconvincing.

And if we were children, where can they have gone? Were they someone else, someone now outlawed, or expired owing to some sublime statute of limitations? Or do we carry them around within our present lives, delicate explosive charges of unexpiated innocence? Again, a great deal of evidence favors the latter assertion—where else, after all, can they have gone? — and it is even said that by a species of "dreaming back" one can arrive for a moment where one first began, after the ignoble and happy collapse of the monumental false front with its file of old license plates and walletful of inapplicable identities, that Maginot Line bypassed by the Hitler Jugend in their field-grey diapers. . . . But not the couch, not this time; not even the lion-headed couch of Thebes, where the embalmers wait with our mature and perfectly adult eternity.

Poetry and Childhood

On a recent occasion, when I was invited to reflect on a subject of which I know so little—the subject, very roughly, of

Poetry and Childhood—I was given certain materials descriptive of what is actually done in schools, and, more to my fascination, a list of topics and questions on the subject. One of the questions in particular seems to give me an access to the theme, and it is this:

How can we understand children enough to help them put their wisdom into words?

I am far from being able to answer, but then it is not the business of poets to give answers. If a poet can help at all, it will be by doing what he usually does, that is, tease out the sense of things by finding ways in which they might be said so as to yield their fullest (and strangest) possibility. This I shall proceed to attempt with reference to the question, which has several assumptions in it.

1. That children have wisdom.
2. That words are not wisdom, but a something instrumental to the expression of wisdom.
3. That we—grown-ups—are able to help the children to help us by making their wisdom available, and that we shall do this by providing the children with language. Our language.
4. That we should be able to recognize wisdom if only it were put into proper language. Again, our language.
5. That so desirable a result would come about could we but understand the children.

When I unfold the question so, I can see that it gives expression to some very profound thoughts about the nature of experience and about the nature of language, and that these thoughts are also somewhat entangled, as profound thoughts have a way of being and perhaps must necessarily be. There are circularities in the questions, for example, and in the arguments behind the question, or to which the question leads.

1. The first assumption—that children have wisdom—must be allowed to stand as the very basis of any argument whatever; if we do not believe that children have wisdom, then we do not wish to provide them with language for the expression of whatever else it is they may be thought to have instead, and our education of them will strenuously attempt to replace whatever else they have instead with our wisdom—something rather close, we may suspect, to what in fact happens in schools. Let us allow, then, that children have wisdom just as they also have folly, that they have love and that they have hatred, that in fact they rather resemble ourselves in these respects, with perhaps a couple of important differences: they have these things more purely and more intensely (and more temporarily) than we do; and they do not have the full resources of language for expressing any of them.

2. That words are not wisdom themselves, but a sort of tool making possible the expression of wisdom, and its communication to others. Here I grow full of doubt. Of course, if words were wisdom there could be no foolish statement, and we have ample evidence that foolish statements do occur, having made so many ourselves. But if I try the opposite tack, try to remove the words from around whatever wisdom, or folly, or thought of any kind whatever I may happen to believe I have, then I don't get very far either. It appeals to me to say that words are related to thoughts, not as a suit or a dress is related to the body, but rather as the body is related to the spirit, and to infer from this that language—the great dictionary—contains the possibilities of the human spirit's expressing itself in the world, moving through the world, transforming the world, transforming itself; and, further, that language in this respect much resembles what I said of children; it too contains wisdom and folly, love and hatred, and while it lies silent in the dictionary it has these things more purely and more intensely, but less expressively, than it has these things when it gets out into the world, in the mouths and, presumably, minds of men and women.

But if words are the incarnation of thoughts whether wise or foolish, and not merely the clothing of thoughts—the party dresses, the rags, the mink coats, the tuxedos, the sweatshirts, the brassieres, the uniforms (maybe above all the uniforms) of thoughts—there occurs a serious discontinuity and perhaps contradiction in the course of the argument about children and language. This possible reversal comes up dramatically when we consider the third and fourth assumptions of the question:

3. That grown-ups provide the children with language for the expression of the children's wisdom.

4. That grown-ups will understand the wisdom when the children assert it in grown-up language, provided by education.

Within these assumptions are implicit two more: first, that we recognize wisdom when we hear it, which is questionable but has to be allowed to pass for the moment because without it the argument immediately ends; second, that our test of wisdom is its making sense to us, and that cannot so easily be allowed to pass without question.

I have had the opportunity of observing but one child's relation to language; many of you will have a much richer experience. But I do happen to remember three things that child said between the ages of five and seven. They are as follows.

1. When I was thirty-five and *you* were five, we lived in New Hampshire. Mummy hadn't been bored yet.
2. (During a trip in a car). The earth is the moon, and we live on a map.
3. (With oracular solemnity). In the first country of places, there are no requests.

Let me for a moment beg the question of whether these statements are or represent wisdom. I think I remembered them for their extreme strangeness, and because they are poetically rather striking in their way of putting things together. Probably I remember all three together because they share a certain character; different as they are one from another, all of them are about another sort of world.

Now it becomes the object of my discourse to say something about the possible, whether probable or improbable, responses a grown-up might make to these three statements, and to decide whether they have any relation at all to wisdom, and, if they do, to see if I am able to understand them. But before I can do any of that, I have to lay it on the line by saying what I believe wisdom to be.

Wisdom is characteristically cryptic, far out, and impractical. An ancient said already of the oracle at Delphi that it could not have lasted ten minutes if it ever gave you a straight answer; and I shall have to stand by a statement I made in a poem: "The first thing to learn about wisdom is / This, that you can't do anything with it." The voice of wisdom is described by Franz Kafka in his parable "On Parables," which is too long to retell here but may be summarized for the sake of its ending. A man complains that the words of the wise are always parables; if the wise tell you that you must cross over you will look in vain for a real bridge to a real place, etc. Another man says:

Why don't you turn into parables, and with that
be rid of all your cares?
The first replies: I bet that is also a parable.
You have won your bet.
Unfortunately, only in parable.
No, in reality. In parable you have lost.

Here are a few examples of statements by grown-ups that I have cherished as being wise.

A painter said: You have to learn to live with
your own crumminess.
A musician said: If you strike the note exactly
on time, you have eternity to play it in.
A poet wrote: We were born to marry strangers.
A poet said: Our sacred books have sacred
misprints in them.

A philosopher said: The last Christian died
  on the Cross.
St. John said: And the light shineth in
  darkness, and the darkness comprehended
  it not.
Concerning this, a poet said: The one thing
  you are able to see in darkness is a light.

And so on, endlessly, and to what avail? Wisdom is a com-
fort to us, and a consolation; it is not a proverb such as Cast
no clout / Till May be out; it is not a moral instruction nor
even a commandment; it is, perhaps, a description of what is.
As such, it merely asserts, it does not apologize, does not
explain, does not say "under certain conditions" or "other
things being equal"; it says, and it shuts its mouth. Or, as a
great poet put it, Wisdom wants nothing more. That may be
why wisdom has so little share in the running of the world.

Returning now to consider the three statements made by
that child: my wife looked over my shoulder and said a couple
of things about them. First, she said, a child beginning to talk
talks about experience that preexisted his being able to talk.
Second, she said, the child has an arbitrarily or capriciously
limited vocabulary, so he uses words hard. These sayings were
something of an illumination to me. The first one says how
marvelous is the child's subject matter—he is speaking of
something we have forgotten and that he too must presently
forget; upon this something he is our *only* source of intelligence. And the second one says how marvelous is the child's
poetic technique, a triumph born of limitation; for what is
poetry but using words hard? so hard that they are compelled
to mean at least twice what they would have meant in prose?

That child's statements participate in the nature of wisdom
as I have in my perhaps partisan way defined it: they are
cryptic, far out, impractical, and unaccompanied by any
explanation, context, or book of instructions for their proper
use, they just are. How then should a grown-up treat them,
what are the ranges of his response, and especially how does

the grown-up deal with this sort of thing in his quality of teacher? I shall present a small sampling of the possibilities, or impossibilities.

You might say, Those statements are not factually true. For instance, there never was a time when you were thirty-five and I was five. And we never did live in New Hampshire. I am trying to imagine a grown-up who would say that to a child, but my heart isn't with it.

A grown-up who was an amateur psychiatrist (and this may even hold of some professional psychiatrists) might say, That child betrays a dangerous degree of alienation from reality. Normal children do not believe that the earth is the moon. And so on. I hope he wouldn't, but suspect he might.

You might say, Yes, dear, and then, later on, to your wife, Wasn't that cute? Brr.

What a teacher said would probably depend on the nature of the instruction at that time being imparted. In an arithmetic class, the statement that the earth is the moon and we live on a map would get nowhere fast, while in a geography class it would have to be denied as positively harmful, and detrimental to the group understanding. In a grammar class, a teacher would be responsible for saying that the proper form is "born" not "bored"—though the child's grammar does open up some remarkable territories that the correct grammar wouldn't touch; and though the child's grammar is no worse than that of St. John in the remark previously quoted—the light shineth in darkness, and the darkness comprehended it not—which is probably passed because it is the grammar given in the King James bible, and not for the true reason that St. John is expressing eternity in the first clause but time in the second, and therefore has to dislocate the tenses some.

In fact, I do not know of any class in the curriculum whose work it would be to entertain, in a manner both serious and humorous, statements of that sort made by the children. And I am sorry not to know of such a class. Maybe there's one at Summerhill.

But supposing we were to imagine a class in which remarks

at random were encouraged and, when made, a little considered and their sense teased out? It would not be a class in poetry, for in that class the teacher would in great probability neglect or even quell the statement that in the first country of places there are no requests, and get the children instead to recite the Midnight Ride of Paul Revere or some other equally egregious example of serious imaginative deficiency, in which patriotism, devotion, or inspirational thought replaces the power of the imagination.

I shall try to suggest what might be the preoccupations of such a class, of the teacher of such a class, and what the teacher's thoughts might appropriately be about the three statements I have made my examples.

All three of them have the charm of strangeness and the not quite predictable, yet they are not altogether without reference to the predictable. In the first, for instance, there is an exchange between thirty-five and five, in the second between the earth and the moon. All three of them express the conditions under which life is lived in a world different from ours, a world called The First Country of Places. Our job, let us say, is to find out from the three statements all we can about that world, no matter if it is a silly world, no matter if it happens not to exist. We can receive no help from that child, who is near being grown up himself by now and talks of the nearer realities of football, grades, dates, and so on. We shall have to interpret the surviving evidence archaeologically, so to say, or poetically.

The first statement—When I was thirty-five and *you* were five, we lived in New Hampshire. Mummy hadn't been bored yet.—is not by any means inert; it expresses a reciprocal rela tionship not at all unknown to philosophy and poetry, and is quite recognizable in, for example, the Heraclitian saying that all things die each other's life and live each other's death; it echoes Wordsworth's "The child is father to the man," about which Gerard Manley Hopkins made the mar velous dead-pan parody:

"The child is father to the man."

How can he be? The words are wild.
Suck any sense from that who can:
"The child is father to the man."
No; what the poet did write ran,
"The man is father to the child."
"The child is father to the man!"
How can *he be? The words are wild.*

The bit about New Hampshire is not interpretable to me,* nor is the bit about Mummy, though I can half catch the logic of a time arrangement in which a mother five years younger than the father could not quite have been born under the circumstances as given. But it is at least interesting that a child should come up with so bold a metaphysical speculation about the chance and change of things.

The second statement—The earth is the moon, and we live on a map.—poignantly expresses the child's beginning perception of distance and separation, his perhaps partly reluctant new understanding that words, which largely express invisible things—that is, relations—are henceforth going to govern more and more of his life in this new world. The sentence is his myth about the expulsion from Eden, and grimly correct in its poetic penetration to the truth that we live on a map. If you don't believe it, try throwing the map away next time you drive through a strange city; and then consider how to generalize out the reference of maps, as two-dimensional representations, to the reality they are said to represent, that great exchange (also shown in the myth of the Fall of Man) whereby we get power over the environment by abstracting from it every local peculiarity of sense and individual being: a numerical world that we can handle, instead of a real one we can't. Tragedy. The earth is henceforth the moon, perhaps because the moon looks a little map-like; you can see the whole of it, it is small and distant. But I should read the line further, to say that from now on, the world of experience,

*But we did live in Vermont, which is as it were the twin and inverse of New Hampshire—which equals the inversion of 35 and 5?

for the child, is going to grow small, hard, white, cold, and distant as the moon, and that the child is quite simply saying so.

The third statement—In the first country of places there are no requests.—is a mysterious talisman. I have said it over to myself, especially in difficult circumstances, for many years. The psychiatrist would say—wisely, perhaps—Aha! the security of the womb! and doubtless that does play into the symbolism. But if we are not to prejudge that country by the conditions of our present experience, it might equally well be a wistful representation of the esoteric reading of the myth of the Fall, that it was in the first place the fall of the spirit into matter, which we are told came about because of desire, and that in its primal condition the spirit had no requests, that is, no wish to be embodied and suffer pain, individuation, death. Wisdom wants nothing more. The myth is tremendously old, and has many expressions, but here is a modern one: Proust writing of the death of Bergotte:

there is, in the conditions of our life here, no reason which should make us believe ourselves obliged to do good, to be fastidious or even polite. . . . All such obligations, which have no sanction in our present life, seem to belong to a different world based on goodness, consideration and sacrifice, a world altogether different from this one, and from which we emerge to be born on this earth, before perhaps returning there to live under the rule of those unknown laws which we have obeyed because we carry their teaching within us, though unaware who traced it there—those laws to which every profound work of the intelligence tends to reconcile us, and which are invisible only—and forever!—to fools.

What I have been saying may very probably seem, with reference to the very grave problems of education, cryptic, far out, and impractical. Could there ever be such a class? What would be the curriculum? What textbooks would you use? Was there ever such a class?

Yes, it happens that there was once such a class. It worked out about the way we should expect, as it is narrated to us by one who says to begin with that he has had perfect understanding of all things from the very first:

And when they found him not, they turned back again to Jerusalem, seeking him.

And it came to pass, that after three days they found him in the temple, sitting in the midst of the doctors, both hearing them and asking them questions.

And all that heard him were astonished at his understanding and answers.

And when they saw him, they were amazed: and his mother said unto him, Son, why hast thou thus dealt with us? Behold, thy father and I have sought thee sorrowing.

And he said unto them, How is it that ye sought me? wist ye not that I must be about my Father's business?

And they understood not the saying which he spake unto them.   Luke 2:45–50

So it would seem, to remember at the end the profound question that was our beginning, that we cannot, in the terms of our life and the conditions of our schools, understand children enough to help them put their wisdom into words. Or that we will not. I hear as I write this the imperfectly remembered echo of something about becoming as a child again, but neither has that instruction been found practicable.

Part III

Philip Rahv: The Critic

and The Man

Chapter 7

Philip Rahv

Milton Hindus

Rahv's vision originated in what he described as his "sixth" sense about literature, explaining the term as Nietzsche did to denote a powerful awareness of the historical dimension of reality which is peculiarly modern. This historical sense, which may have been awakened initially in him by Marxism, survived when the special theory that had given rise to it lost its hold on his mind. It was inseparable from his omnivorous reading, not only of books but of newspapers, and from the massive, sturdy common sense which gave him an extraordinary insight into the logistics of reality, both in life and in literature. It is the notable quality of his common sense that gives some point to the comparison sometimes suggested between him and Samuel Johnson. Both were talkers even more than writers, and one can imagine Rahv attempting to refute the idealistic philosophy of Berkeley by kicking a stone. He was unusually responsive to the stubborn inertness of the matter of fact, and it was this awareness of reality which provided him with insight into unfolding historical events and into the substantiality (or lack of it) of imaginative writing. He was giving expression to an idea that was axiomatic to him when he wrote in 1950: "In art nothing speaks to our mind which does not simultaneously engage our senses."

It is his unshakable insistence upon this view that keeps him from being taken in by "words, words, words." Somewhere along the line, he had learned the lesson that Gertrude Stein had once tried to teach young Hemingway when she insisted on the distinction between journalism and literature:

"If you keep on doing newspaper work you will never see things, you will only see words and that will not do, that is of course if you intend to be a writer." Rahv was keenly aware of the difference between words and things, and of the fact that *things* were what words sought to express. It is Rahv's receptivity to the heightened reality of literature that makes him impatient of academic critics who appear to him to be little better than word-mongers. When he lays about him with his polemical broadsword on occasion, he is like Gulliver among the Lilliputians. In such an essay as "Fiction and the Criticism of Fiction," he reduces the once fashionable symbol-hunting of Robert W. Stallman in the works of Stephen Crane to absurdity by showing that Stallman has abandoned the ground of common sense without knowing it. For all his love of intellectual generalizations, Rahv instinctively abhorred nothing so much as empty abstraction, and it is empty abstraction that he found in many academic critics. He comes close to summing up his view in a single sentence when he writes: "Literature relates itself to life through experience and only secondarily through ideas."

It is literature's fidelity to experience which, for Rahv, creates the disparity between the writer's intended message and the actual one that reaches his readers, between what a writer thinks his work means or wishes it to mean and what it really means. An Indian saying is that "A work of art has many faces." But fashionable hobby-horses of interpretation are not what is wanted, as his caustic comment on one unfortunate academician indicates: "The payoff of the rage for symbolism is surely Mr. Charles Feidelson's recent book, *Symbolism and American Literature* . . . In this curious work the interest in symbolism has quite literally consumed the interest in literature."

Rahv's comments on Dostoievski's *The Possessed* indicates how well he learned from D. H. Lawrence to trust the tale rather than the teller of it:

Setting out to report on the moral depravity of the revolution, Dostoievski was nevertheless objective enough to

*demonstrate that Russia could not escape it . . . Dostoievski
was a reactionary, but never a conservative; and with the
other great cultural reactionaries of the bourgeois epoch he
shared the insight into the corruption of modern society
which at several points relates them to revolutionary thought
. . . Reactionary in its abstract content, in its aspect as a system of ideas, his art is radical in sensibility and subversive in
performance . . .*

To appreciate what Rahv was trying to do, we might examine his writings over a period of about thirty years on Henry
James. James is the central subject of his essays "The Heiress
of All the Ages," "Attitudes Toward Henry James," "Pulling
Down the Shrine," and the uncollected essay-review of Leon
Edel published in *The New York Review of Books* a few
years before his death, "Henry James and His Cult." James
also enters importantly into the essay "The Cult of Experience in American Writing," and he is treated more glancingly
elsewhere—for example, in the essay "Paleface and Redskin,"
and in the 1957 Preface to Rahv's collection of essays entitled
Image and Idea.

The search everywhere in these writings is for a stance of
judicious balance with regard to James. Rahv's quest is for a
via media, not because he is a cautious trimmer but because
he thinks the middle way is the way to the truth about his
subject. Rahv became one of the leaders in the revival of
interest in James which occurred toward the end of World
War II. In 1944 there appeared two new and influential
anthologies of James's fiction; Rahv edited one of them. The
initial resistance to the appeal of James that he set himself
to overcome was from political radicals like himself, who had
continued earlier attitudes established by progressive, popu-
list, social-minded historians, critics, and educators who had
been repelled by the expatriation of James, by his doubtful
national loyalties, by the refinement of his aestheticism and
his ironies, by the increasing complexity, obscurity, and
ambiguity of his later literary style, by his affectations and
social snobbery.

Expatriates have rarely found favor with their countrymen even when, as in Tsarist Russia and other dictatorial regimes, they had the excuse of escaping from political repression. Democracies, in which tyranny is exercised by public opinion, are even less tolerant to defectors than other polities. Earlier American writers had often lived abroad for extensive periods and some of them had represented their country diplomatically, but no one had carried the matter to the length that James did when he renounced his American citizenship completely in 1915, a year before he died. The reciprocal American attitude to him for a long time was expressed in a passage Rahv quoted from a textbook used in the 1940's, *The College Book of American Literature*, gravely informing students that "it is not certain that Henry James really belongs to American literature, for he was critical of America and admired Europe." Rahv's initial target was this kind of simple-minded nationalism as well as the type of progressivism represented by Vernon Parrington, who rejected James because his snobbish social attitudes seemed clearly at odds with the democratic ethos.

On the most primitive level of the case, James was a casualty of the struggle between Anglophiles and the nativist Anglophobes in American literature. When the latter became increasingly powerful in the closing decades of the nineteenth century and triumphed unquestionably in the twentieth, and James was contemptuously rejected by its *chefs d'école* (Whitman and Twain), the effect upon his American reputation was bound to be devastating. But even the Anglophiles could not defend him wholeheartedly for a long time, since his expatriation had a quality of alienation from his native land which made his loyalty deeply suspect. For a time, the only Americans who sided with him openly and without qualms were expatriates like himself. It is curious to note the extent to which the Rahv of 1940 in his essay on "The Cult of Experience in American Writing" is indebted for his conception of James to a famous synoptic essay on the subject published by Ezra Pound in 1918. This is clear if we compare two passages from their essays. Rahv tells us that

James's attitude toward experience is sometimes overlooked by readers excessively impressed (or depressed) by his oblique methods and effects of remoteness and ambiguity. Actually, from the standpoint of the history of the national letters, the lesson he taught in The Ambassadors, *as in many of his other works, must be understood as no less than a revolutionary appeal. It is a veritable declaration of the rights of man—not, to be sure, of the rights of the public, of the social man, but of the rights of the private man, of the rights of personality, whose openness to experience provides the sole effective guaranty of its development. Already in one of his earliest stories we find the observation that "in this country, the people have rights but the person has none." And in so far as any artist can be said to have had a mission, his manifestly was to brace the American individual in his moral struggle to gain for his personal and subjective life that measure of freedom which, as a citizen of a prosperous and democratic community, he had long been enjoying in the sphere of material and political relations.*

Pound, too, begins by dismissing questions of difficulty of style as secondary considerations and concentrates his attention upon what James *represents* to him:

I am tired of hearing pettiness talked about Henry James's style. The subject has been discussed enough in good conscience, along with the minor James. Yet I have heard no word of the major James, of the hater of tyranny, book after early book against oppression, against all the sordid personal crushing oppression, the domination of modern life . . . The outbursts in The Tragic Muse, *the whole of* The Turn of the Screw, *human liberty, personal liberty, the rights of the individual against all sorts of intangible bondage! (Note: This holds, despite anything that may be said of his fuss about social order, social tone . . . What he fights is "influence," the impinging of one personality on another; all of them in highest degree damn'd, loathsome and detestable. Respect for the peripheries of the individual may be, however, a*

*discovery of our generation; I doubt it, but it seems to have
been at low ebb in some districts . . . for some time.)*

The coincidence of Rahv's and Pound's views of James,
which emphasize his insistence on an uncompromising
individualism as the essence of his ineradicable Americanism,
is interesting. It is not at all a usual view of the matter. It is
in some ways a European view, a view of men who are themselves sufficiently detached from American convention and
hostile to the usual American conformities to sympathize
deeply with James on these grounds. In Rahv's case it must
be related to his break four or five years earlier with the
Communist movement. It was the stubborn individualism of
James that may have drawn Rahv's sympathies originally to
his work, just as it was an individualism of a different kind
that drew him to Dostoievski, about whom he wrote very
nearly as much as he did about James.

But it would not be fair to leave the impression that his
interest in James and Dostoievski was due solely to the challenge of their individualistic "ideology" in a collectivistic,
totalitarian age. His writings show a profound sensitivity and
responsiveness to their more purely literary and intellectual
qualities. Rahv was a man who loved literature deeply, and he
respected those who had written it too much to reduce them
to a formula or to fit them to the requirements of a theory,
even one which he regarded as valid. Marx and Freud were at
various times theoretical guides to him, but he was not ready,
as other Marxists or Freudians were, to use their theories in
Procrustean fashion upon literary artifacts. His real love of
literature and respect for its autonomy are among the most
important things that give authority to what he has to say
about it.

Still, this love is not to be confused with infatuation. Rahv
denied the imputation of Maxwell Geismar that he had ever
become part of a Henry James "cult." His motivation initially
had been to see to it that James received his due as a writer.
But the dimensions of the success of the publishing enterprise exceeded all expectations, and in a Foreword to an

enlarged edition in 1957 of his collection of essays *Image and Idea* Rahv wrote: "I was quite as surprised as anyone else . . . by the collapse of the resistance to [James's] appeal in some of the literary and academic circles . . . But it may well be that his apotheosis is not quite what was wanted. For it seems that the long-standing prejudice against him has now given way to an uncritical adulation which, in a different way, is perhaps quite as retarding to a sound appraisal of his achievement." It is from this passage that Rahv quotes, in 1963 in his answer to Geismar's blanket indictment of the "cult" in *Henry James and the Jacobites.*

In the early 1970's, not long before he died, Rahv was moved to utter a protest against the lengths to which adulation of James had been carried by Leon Edel in his five-volume biography of "the master." In a review of the final volume, Rahv wrote:

That Edel makes too much of James, that he overestimates his importance in the most extravagant manner possible, that he is much too expansive, even rapturous, about him has been evident all along . . . The excessive length of this biography is explained by its glut of detail of which much is only of minor interest. No wonder that the effect of far too many pages is that of supersaturation . . . After all, we are interested not in every casual person who came [James's] way, but only in his principal literary and social relationships. Moreover, the few happenings that might be regarded as "events" in his life are treated at inordinate length . . . Edel describes the failure of the play Guy Domville, *James's only strenuous theatrical venture, at such length and in such detail as to make one think that he is recounting an event comparable, say, to Napoleon's retreat from Moscow.*

Rahv's final view of James did not differ markedly from the one he had expressed earlier about Hawthorne, namely that there was a difference between the way he appeared in a purely American cultural context and his measure on a world scale. Commenting on a comparison made by

Q. D. Leavis between *The Scarlet Letter* and *Anna Karenina*, Rahv had written: "No doubt *The Scarlet Letter* is in its way a masterpiece, though only if measured on a strictly national if not provincial scale, whereas *Anna Karenina* is one of the four or five great novels of the world, incomparably superior, in its total vision as in its creative resources, to anything that Hawthorne, with his fear of life induced by bare and crabbed circumstances and his obsessive memories of the past, could have possibly produced." In the same vein, he writes of Edel's biography:

If James is a great writer and I believe he is one it is strictly on a national scale that he can be most highly appreciated. In the literature of the world he is not a figure of the first order. European readers lacking a deep background in American or at least Anglo-Saxon culture of the Victorian age make very little of him. He is one of those writers, like the Russian novelist and story-teller Nikolai Leskov, the Austrian novelist Adalbert Stifter, and the Swiss Gottfried Keller, who have proven themselves incapable of readily crossing their own language frontiers. Indeed, nearly every literature counts among its luminaries writers of this special type. Though some of the works of Leskov, Keller and Stifter are available in English, the response has been inconsiderable. The same can be said of the attempted translations of James, who is indissolubly at one not only with his language, but with the determinate circumstances of his culture and background . . . Whereas American writers like Melville, Whitman, Poe, Faulkner, and Hemingway, have attained international renown, James remains only a "name" even to the most cultivated Europeans, in spite of the best efforts of many foreign specialists in American letters.

This passage probably sounds more patronizing than it was meant to be to those who have not read Rahv on a writer like Leskov and do not realize how he savored Leskov's particular literary and linguistic excellence. Rahv's view of literature is similar to that expressed by Malraux concerning art after he was taken on an extensive tour of The National Gallery in Washington. Asked to express his opinion concerning what he had seen, he said diplomatically that some of the treasures belonged to America while others just as clearly belonged to the world. Rahv, like Arnold whom he admired, believed in a cosmopolitan scale of aesthetic and intellectual measurements and resolutely set his face against provincialism, not because he did not recognize its charms but because he did not overestimate them.

At his best, the profundity of his observations and the manner in which he expresses them remind one of Francis Bacon's differentiation of various kinds of reading: some books are to be tasted, some quickly swallowed, a few carefully chewed and digested. Rahv's criticism is often of this last, challenging kind. I have read much on the meaning of literary naturalism but little that goes so deep or is as memorable as a passage in Rahv's essay entitled "Notes on the Decline of Naturalism:"

I would classify as naturalistic that type of realism in which the individual is portrayed not merely as subordinate to his background but as wholly determined by it—that type of realism, in other words, in which the environment displaces its inhabitants in the role of the hero. Theodore Dreiser, for example, comes as close as any American writer to plotting the careers of his characters strictly within a determinative process. The financier Frank Cowperwood masters his world and emerges as its hero, while the "little man" Clyde Griffiths is the victim whom it grinds to pieces; yet hero and victim alike are essentially implements of environmental force, the carriers of its contradictions upon whom it stamps success or failure—not entirely at will, to be sure, for people are marked biologically from birth—but with a sufficient autonomy to shape their fate.

This generalization is balanced by an appreciation of Dreiser which is instructive and which indicates that Rahv was no less sensitive to the virtues of Dreiser than he was to those of Henry James:

Dreiser is still unsurpassed so far as American naturalism
goes, though just at present he may very well be the least
readable. He has traits that make for survival—a Balzacian
grip on the machinery of money and power; a prosiness
so primary in texture that if taken in bulk it affects us as a
kind of poetry of the commonplace and ill-favored; and
an emphatic eroticism which is the real climate of exis-
tence in his fictions—Eros hovering over the shambles . . .

Rahv's search for precision and balance in his assessment
of contemporary literary phenomena is illustrated by his
comment in 1952 on the publication of Hemingway's
book *The Old Man and the Sea:*

. . . free as this latest work is of the faults of the preceding
one [Across the River and into the Trees], *it is still by no*
means the masterpiece which the nationwide publicity set
off by its publication in Life *magazine has made it out to be.*
Publicity is the reward as well as the nemesis of celebrities,
but it has nothing in common with judgment. Though the
merit of this new story is incontestable, so are its limitations.
I do not believe that it will eventually be placed among
Hemingway's major writings . . . At its core it is actually
little more than a fishing anecdote . . . To be sure, if one is
to judge by what some of the reviewers have been saying and
by the talk heard among literary people, the meaning of
The Old Man and the Sea *is to be sought in its deep sym-*
bolism. It may be that the symbolism is really there, though
I for one have been unable to locate it. I suspect that here
again the characteristic attempt of the present literary pe-
riod is being made to overcome the reality of the felt
experience of art by converting it to some moral or
spiritual platitude. It goes without saying that the platitude
is invariably sublimated through the newly modish terms of
myth and symbolism . . . Hemingway's big marlin is no Moby
Dick, and his fisherman is not Captain Ahab nor was meant
to be. It is enough praise to say that their existence is real

and that their encounter is described in a language at once
relaxed and disciplined which is a source of pleasure . . .

The appeal from nebulous speculation to common sense is
characteristic of Rahv, and after more than a quarter of a
century his judicious assessment, giving Hemingway his due
but refusing to exaggerate or be swept away, requires no
apology. He was "narrow" enough not to be satisfied with
anything less than the highest excellence from a writer he
thought capable of it.

John Steinbeck, on the other hand, did not seem to him
to be in that class at all, and we look in vain for approval of
any of his works in Rahv. Steinbeck, it has been said, is a
borderline literary case. Certainly he had literary apologists,
and his humanitarian sympathies were not alien to Rahv, but
it may be that these facts only contributed to the hardness
of Rahv's judgment upon him. In an essay on another subject
he remarks in passing: "If one says of a novel by Steinbeck
that it is without appreciable literary merit, one is actually
dismissing it *in toto*, for it certainly offers us nothing else by
way of intelligence and relevant meaning." Of Steinbeck's
greatest and most popular work, Rahv writes: "What does a
radical novel like *The Grapes of Wrath* contain, from an
ideological point of view, that agitational journalism cannot
communicate with equal heat and facility? Surely its vogue
cannot be explained by its radicalism. Its real attraction for
the millions who read it lies elsewhere—perhaps in its vivid
recreation of a 'slice of life' so horridly unfamiliar that it can
be made to yield an exotic interest."

I have an anecdote that bears on this point. On November
24, 1962, a historic date in the midst of the Cuban missile
crisis when it was not yet clear that the Soviet ships approaching the coast of Cuba would respect the American
blockade of the island and turn back at the last moment, the
news on the radio was obsessively centered on this international crisis which threatened nuclear war, but toward the
end of one broadcast there was relief in the announcement

that the Nobel Prize in Literature had just been awarded to John Steinbeck. I heard this news while driving to work in the morning, and when I reached Brandeis and met Rahv my natural impulse was to share it with him because my own reaction was as negative as I knew his would be. But when I called out to him, "Phil, have you heard the news?" he evidently thought that it was something to do with the movements of the Russian fleet and gasped, "No!", almost falling headlong down the flight of steps on which he was walking. I hastened to complete my message: "Steinbeck has just won the Nobel Prize!" "Oh," said Rahv, with evident relief, "That's terrible!"

Rahv's response to the case of Ezra Pound was troubled and ambivalent. As between the poet incarcerated in Saint Elizabeth's Hospital and the Philistines of *The Saturday Review of Literature* who attacked the award of The Bollingen Prize to him for *The Pisan Cantos* in 1949 by the Poetry Fellows of The Library of Congress, he left no doubt that he was on the side of Pound. Yet he found his company embarrassing. In 1940 in "The Cult of Experience in American Writing," he had commented on Pound: "What is so exasperating about Pound's poetry . . . is its peculiar combination of a finished technique (his special share in the distribution of experience) with amateurish and irresponsible ideas." It is not simply that he disagrees with Pound's political conclusions but that he cannot take him seriously as a social and political thinker. Reviewing a book by John Harrison entitled: *The Reactionaries: Yeats, Lewis, Pound, Eliot and Lawrence: A Study of the Anti-Democratic Intelligentsia* in 1967, Rahv writes:

I am inclined to object to Mr. Harrison's rather gummy use of the label "fascist" in his indictment of all five writers under consideration, just as I object to Empson speaking, in his Introduction to the book, of "the political scandal of their weakness for Fascism." Not that I deny that for a time Pound and Lewis supported the fascist cause . . . In their social and polit-

*ical thinking all these writers were sheer amateurs . . . unable
to grasp that politics is a specific medium—of action in history and society . . . They were drawn ideologically to authoritarian positions but were not in any definite way committed
(not even Pound, who is by far the most vulnerable) to the
shifting demands and intolerable dogmas of any given political party. Not one of them was in any meaningful sense a
political man or even capable of consistent political thought.
Their social political unworldliness shows through all their
denunciations of liberal ideas . . . What they can be truly accused of is presumption in undertaking to speak pretentiously
about matters they knew little about . . .*

A passage such as this indicates that it was fortunate for
Rahv to have been spared becoming a cultural commissar
during his own Communist phase. Such a line of argument
might have made his loyalties suspect to his comrades.
As a matter of fact, Rahv had thought along these lines
even during his revolutionary period, and there is an article
of his dating from 1936 ("A Season in Heaven") urging
a more tolerant attitude toward T. S. Eliot's religious play
Murder in the Cathedral, which was at odds with the attitude
taken by his less independent political associates of the time.

Rahv's separation of literary technique from substance
in the case of Pound deserves to be noted. He clearly dis-
approves of the position of critics like Mark Schorer who
emphasize technique in the literary artifact almost to the
exclusion of all other qualities (Schorer speaks of "technique
as discovery"). Rahv writes: ". . . how are we going to reconcile Mr. Schorer's point of view with Proust's precept
that style is essentially a matter not of technique but of
vision? The implication of that precept is that the technique
of a true artist is dictated by an inner need and can be
imitated only superficially. Vision is inimitable." He finds
Schorer's view at odds, too, with that of another impressive
authority on the matter: "Let us recall T. S. Eliot's statement about Massinger—that he was a brilliant master of
technique without being in the proper sense an artist. This

can only mean that even though without technique we can do nothing in art, technique is not nearly enough."

Rahv also regards the substance of art as something that is independent of his personal attitude toward it. Thus he cannot subscribe to F. R. Leavis' strictures upon Eliot's supposedly unhealthy attitude toward sexual subjects in his work: "For my part," writes Rahv, "I cannot see why an attitude of sexual disgust is not as valid a theme for poetic expression as an attitude of affirmation, of health and sanity. The value of literary art cannot be judged by the bias of its ideology or world-view, but rather by its rendering of felt experience, the intensity of its existential commitment, above all the incontrovertible force of its concrete enactment." Yet it is interesting that when the situation is reversed—when, for example, instead of embodying a negative attitude toward sex, the art-work becomes the vehicle of what Joyce playfully describes as a "kinetic" approach and Rahv labels pure pornography, he aligns himself with what he describes as the moralistic bias of Leavis: "[Leavis] may be too moralistic and exclusive in his approach, but the currently modish idea that morality has nothing to do with literature is a sheer perversion, an accommodation to the indulgence of degeneracy that marks the arts in our age—an indulgence that on no account will deny artistic status even to obvious pornography." He has many reservations about the criticism of Leavis, yet there are qualities of Leavis which resemble his own: "What I chiefly like about Leavis' work are its Johnsonian qualities: the robustness, the firmness, the downrightness. He is not one to beat around the bush, to play the diplomat, to cultivate ambiguity, or to shun controversy."

It is important to remember that Rahv refused to exaggerate the function of the critic or to detach it from its ancillary role with respect to literature, which was perfectly capable of existing and going on without it. He was willing to grant, however, that a Matthew Arnold at the present time might be useful in restoring adequate literary standards.

(In Rahv's essay, "Criticism and the Imagination of Alternatives," the critic who, to his mind, turns out to be most relevant to our needs is—Matthew Arnold!) Critics forgetful of their subordinate role, to his mind tend egotistically to inflate the importance of their discipline and thus to pervert it. He gives two examples: "John Middleton Murry contends that criticism performs the same function as literature itself, that of providing the critic with a means of expression; and Rémy de Gourmont speaks of criticism as a subjective literary form, a perpetual confession on the critic's part. 'The critic may think,' he writes, 'that he is judging the work of other people, but it is himself that he is revealing and exposing to the public.' Needless to say, this is a notion I do not subscribe to. In my understanding of criticism, it is a medium first and foremost of the critic's response to literature and only indirectly, by refraction as it were, of his response to life."

Unlike some other critics, Rahv is never patronizing in his tone toward those he takes to be masters of the art of literature. He is there not to teach lessons to them but to learn from them. If he occasionally makes use of Freudian insights, it is not with any reductive intention, and he does not leave us with the feeling that he thinks he has cleared up all of the mysteries that surround art. His lack of critical arrogance and his humility toward literature itself reward him with sensitive insights, as in the following passage from his introduction to Kafka's stories, in which he begins by making a contrast between Joyce and Kafka:

. . . the difficulty of understanding [Kafka] is on a different plane from that encountered in reading a novelist like Joyce . . . Whereas the obscurities of the latter are inherent in the elaborate stylization of his material and in his complex structural designs, in Kafka's case it is the meaning alone that baffles us. Both in language and construction he is elementary compared to Joyce, yet many readers have been mystified by his fictions. But the mystification is gradually

*cleared up once we learn to listen attentively to his tone and
become accustomed to the complete freedom with which he
suspends certain conventions of storytelling when it suits his
symbolic purpose. Thus when we read in the first sentence
of "The Metamorphosis" that the clerk Gregor Samsa awoke
one morning to find himself changed into a gigantic insect,
it is a mistake to think that by means of this bold stroke
Kafka intends to call into question the laws of nature. What
he calls into question, rather, is the convention that the laws
of nature are at all times to be observed in fiction; and having suspended that convention in the very first paragraph
of the story, from that point on he develops it in a logical
and realistic manner. The clerk's metamorphosis is a multiple
symbol of his alienation from the human state, of his
"awakening" to the full horror of his dull, spiritless existence, and of the desperate self-disgust of his unconscious
fantasy-life, in which the wish to displace the father and
take over his authority in the family is annulled by the guilt-
need to suffer a revolting punishment for his presumption.*

Those who are disposed to stress Rahv's "narrowness"
may cite the very small number of contemporary American
writers whom he chose to encourage. In the end he seemed
to think that of the generation born in the time of the
First World War two novelists were best assured of survival:
Saul Bellow and Bernard Malamud. The fact that Bellow and
Malamud as well as Rahv himself were Jewish and that both
were initially published in *Partisan Review* did not escape
notice. Rahv himself complained of the widespread tendency
(on the part of Jewish apologists as well as their critics)
to yoke disparate writers together on the basis of what he
regarded as superficial characteristics or resemblances while
ignoring some of the deeper qualities that separated them
from one another. Writers for Rahv are above all unique
individuals; their visions (despite historical contexts) are in
the end personal and inimitable, though the power with
which these visions are expressed may (as in the case of

Kafka notably) inspire innumerable and for the most part vain attempts at imitation. If there were affinities between writers, they were likely to be produced by similarities of temperament and aesthetic attitudes rather than by racial, national, or social origins. Turgenev and James were drawn to each other, for example, by the same qualities that bound them both to Flaubert. On the subject of classification of American writers on the basis of both their origin and their principal subject matter (a critical attempt was made to establish the validity of such rubrics as ethnicity, for example, by drawing an analogy between them and long-recognized categories like "regionalism" in American literature), Rahv made certain pertinent observations in an introduction to a Malamud reader in 1967:

Generally speaking, he has been assimilated all too readily to the crowd of American-Jewish writers who have lately made their way into print. The homogenization resulting from speaking of them as if they comprised some kind of literary faction or school is bad critical practice in that it is based on simplistic assumptions concerning the literary process as a whole as well as the nature of American Jewry which, all appearances to the contrary, is very far from constituting a unitary group in its cultural manifestations. In point of fact, the American-Jewish writers do not in the least make up a literary faction or school. And in the case of Malamud, the ignorant and even malicious idea that such a school exists has served as a way of confusing him with other authors with whom (excepting his Jewish ancestry) he has virtually nothing in common . . . The truth is that many writers are Jewish in descent without being in any appreciable way "Jewish" in feeling and sensibility; and I am noting this not in criticism of anyone in particular but simply by way of stating an obvious fact usually overlooked both by those who "celebrate" the arrival of American Jews on the literary scene and by those who deplore it. It is one thing to speak factually of a writer's Jewish extractions

*and it is something else again to speak of his "Jewishness,"
which is a very elusive quality and rather difficult to
define . . .*

Having said this, Rahv proceeds to write a model analysis
and differentiation of various types usually accommodated
under the broad umbrella of "American-Jewish writers" and
to define Malamud's particular position with regard to it:

*What is mostly to be observed among these (American-
Jewish) writers is ambivalence about Jewishness rather than
pride or even simple acceptance . . . [They] either back away
from their Jewishness or adopt an attitude toward it which
is empty of cultural value; it is only in their bent for comic
turns that they call to mind some vestigial qualities of their
ethnic background . . . Malamud differs from such literary
types in that he fills his "Jewishness" with a positive content. I mean that "Jewishness" as he understands and above
all feels it, is one of the principal sources of value in his work
as it affects both his conception of experience in general
and his conception of imaginative writing in particular. One
can see this in the very few instances when his characters
touch on literature in their extremely articulate but "broken" speech . . .*

Rahv writes with high appreciation of the achievement of
Malamud, yet his critical sense is constantly alert to the
faults he finds in him. This is especially true in the case of
the novel *The Fixer* which, of the four novels that Malamud
had written at the time of Rahv's essay, "has proven to be
the most popular. But despite its impressive sales figures, it
seems to me to be the weakest of his longer narratives; and
its success can be traced to fortuitous circumstances."
When the public is led to read a writer by those it accepts
as intellectual guides, the results are often regrettable in
that the inferior works of the writer which sometimes follow in the wake of his masterly ones serve only to dis-
tract attention from their betters and reap the rewards

which rightfully belong to them. Rahv's conclusion is that:

> . . . *as a whole Malamud succeeds far more frequently in his short stories than in his novels; and of all his stories, surely the most masterful is "The Magic Barrel," perhaps the best story produced by an American writer in recent decades. It belongs among those rare works in which meaning and composition are one and the same. Who can ever forget the matchmaker Salzman, "a commercial Cupid," smelling "frankly of fish which he loved to eat," who looked as if he were about to expire but who managed, by a trick of the facial muscles, "to display a broad smile"? The last sentences of this tale are like a painting by Chagall come to life . . . The rabbinical student who, as he confesses, had come to God not because he loved Him but precisely because he did not, attempts to find in the girl from whose picture "he had received, somehow, an impression of evil" the redemption his ambiguous nature demands . . . It seems to me that "The Magic Barrel," a story rooted in a pathology that dares to seek its cure in a thrust toward life, sums up many of the remarkable gifts of insight and expressive power that Malamud brings to contemporary literature.*

In discussing Saul Bellow, the matter of his Jewishness is of less concern to Rahv, perhaps because it is less central and more peripheral to Bellow himself. Rahv discusses the novel *Herzog* in 1964 with little attention to the Jewishness of the protagonist, though it is more important in relation to some of the other characters—Gersbach, for example, whom Rahv describes as "a purveyor of the latest cultural goodies, like Buber's 'I and Thou' relationship, the more portentous varieties of existentialism, and Yiddishisms of phrase and stance." There is another allusion to a possible Jewish component of the book in Rahv's discussion of Bellow's style. In the first paragraph, he had called Bellow "the finest stylist at present writing fiction in America." In the last paragraph, he returns to this theme and says, "Bellow's style in this narrative, as in most of his fiction,

provides a very meaningful pleasure in its masterful combination of the demotic and literary languages. At once
astringent and poetic, it neither muffles nor distends his
themes. Among the elements back of it is, no doubt, a
deep sense of humor derived from his Jewish background
and thoroughly assimilated to his sensibility. This style is
sensibility in action."

But if Bellow's ethnic background enters in some measure
into his style, it still remains for Rahv a very subordinate
consideration, because he regards Bellow's intelligence as
his most important quality, and intelligence is something
objective and without discernible connection to either race
or nationality. Saul Bellow to Rahv was "the most intelligent
novelist of his generation" and "the most consistently
interesting." Bellow is important for Rahv because he represents a new departure in American literature, in which,
with few exceptions, "experience" has been more important
than an intelligent analysis and assimilation of the meaning
that may be derived from it. "It is important," writes Rahv,
"to stress this element of intellectual mastery in Bellow,
for in the milieu of our creative writers intellect has by
no means played a conspicuous part. Hence the immaturity
of even the best, like Hemingway for instance, and the
aborted careers of not a few other gifted writers, aborted
among other things by the repetition compulsion that results
not so much from neurotic disturbance, though that may be
present too, as from thematic poverty and narrowness of
the mental horizon. To be sure, intellect is not art; in some
ways it might even be said to be corrosive in its effect on
artistic production. But without intellect it becomes impossible for the artist, the verbal artist particularly, to transform
into consciousness what is offered by experience and the
manifold and at times infinitely varied and subtle emotions
it gives rise to . . ."

In retrospect it appears to me that Rahv, in his immediate
response to *Herzog*, may have overestimated its literary
quality somewhat when he wrote: "For some time now the

critical consensus has been, expressed not so much formally in writing as in the talk of literary circles, that *Seize the Day*, published some nine years ago, was [Bellow's] best single performance. However, I think *Herzog* is superior to it, even if not so tightly organized and in fact a bit loose on the structural side. For one thing, it is a much longer and fuller narrative than *Seize the Day*, which is hardly more than a novella . . ." Rahv was inclined to rate the importance of the novel as a literary form about as highly as critics once did the epic, and he was loath to think that a smaller and less ambitious effort might in the end be more successful and aesthetically satisfying. Yet, as we have seen, he had recognized, in the case of Malamud, that his most durable artistic artifact might be a short story. The arguments against *Seize the Day* which Rahv marshals in the passage to which I have alluded are less persuasive now than when they were originally made.

There is something in this case which Rahv could hardly have been aware of in 1964 or indeed by the time of his death in the early 1970's: the epistolary invention by Bellow in *Herzog* (highly praised by Rahv) heralded an increasingly direct dialogue between the novelist and the public which would proceed through *Mr. Sammler's Planet* and *Humboldt's Gift* to his dispensing with fiction altogether in the reportage of *To Jerusalem and Back*.

Later on, Rahv might have seen *Herzog* in a rather different light from that in which he was able to perceive it in 1964. Despite this, it seems clear that he should still have welcomed the award of The Nobel Prize to Bellow in 1976 and that he could hardly have felt that it contributed to a lowering of literary standards as the previous one to Steinbeck had done. If anything about the award would have shocked him, it might have been the Swedish Academy's special notice of the novel *Henderson, the Rain King*, which Rahv had not regarded seriously enough to mention in praising *Herzog*, as one of the principal works which entitled Bellow to the great prize.

What Rahv sought for consistently was disinterested judgment that rose above the flux of ephemeral fashion and personal bias of all kinds. To say of Rahv, as Kazin does, that he was primarily "a pamphleteer, a polemicist" or that "for Rahv, a piece of writing was not real unless it appeared in the immediate social setting of a magazine and evoked an immediate social response in conversation, rebuttal, polemic" seems to me to misconceive his aims completely. It is clear from the nature of his tastes and judgments that they were the results of an enormous amount of private reflection and that it was the long preparatory period which preceded his public pronouncements that lent them their particular weight. He was certainly, in my experience of him, a sociable man and enjoyed the quick give-and-take of personal interchanges and conversation, but this was only a superficial aspect compared with something much deeper. Back of the talk and all the clever improvisations there was a great deal of lonely thinking. I did not have the impression, knowing him in his later years, that he was primarily a social rather than a private man.

His intellectual ideal was detachment and objectivity. The classic to him was the standard art aimed at, or, to use Arnold's term, the touchstone. He was concerned with the qualities that constituted the classic, and he did not lightly bestow the honorific term upon many works. This concern with the classic was somewhat unusual in his intellectual circle, and it was what brought him quite close in sympathy to both Arnold and Eliot (and perhaps even, if he had not been so alien to his conservative politics, Irving Babbitt). One of the striking passages in Rahv's criticism occurs in his introduction to an essay in 1938 which was inspired by the infamous "Moscow Trials"; in it, he makes a memorable suggestion concerning the true meaning of a classic. The essay is called "Dostoievski and Politics: Notes on *The Possessed*":

The tendency of every age is to bury as many classics as it revives. If unable to discover our own urgent meaning in a creation of the past, we hope to find ample redress in its competitive neighbors. A masterpiece cannot be produced once and for all; it must be constantly reproduced. Its first author is a man. Its later ones—time, social time, history . . . To be means to recur. In the struggle for survival among works of art, those prove themselves the fittest that recur most often. In order to impress itself on our imagination, a work of art must be capable of bending its wondrous, its immortal head to the yoke of the mortal and finite—that is the contemporary, which is never more than an emphasis, a one-sided projection of the real. The past retains its vitality insofar as it impersonates the present, either in its aversions or ideals; in the same way a classic work renews itself by impersonating a modern one.

The thought about time in its creative and recreative role recalls to my mind a passage in Proust which might have inspired it: "The world was not created once and for all but is created anew every time an original pair of eyes looks at it."

The true test of a critic, according to Proust, is not what he has to say about old works (except perhaps in those rare instances in which he has been instrumental in rediscovering their worth and relevance to a generation that has forgotten them) but what he has to say about his contemporaries. Judged by this criterion Rahv should fare well. His judgments, both positive and negative, have been increasingly sustained in a respectable number of the cases in which he chose to express himself. He was not the facile kind of reviewer who discovers masterpieces with every leading article he is commissioned to write. He did not have a ready stock of superlatives on hand. And even when a writer inspired him with enthusiasm, it was rarely without reservations. A good example is Solzhenitsyn, whom he recognized early as a successor of Tolstoi and Dostoievski but hardly a replacement for them or a real rival to them aesthetically. In his review of *One Day in the Life of Ivan Denisovitch*, he compared the protagonist Shukhov to

Platon Karataev, the idealized peasant in *War and Peace* who is the real carrier of the author's letter to the world. The comparison revealed "a significant difference between them. For Karataev, standing somewhat apart from the other characters in *War and Peace*, who are portrayed with surpassing realism, is in the main a mythic figure, an abstraction of Christian goodness, while Shukhov, in no way dependent on religious doctrine or precept, is invested with a goodness that is altogether credible, altogether imbedded in the actual." He also detected a resemblance between Solzhenitsyn's theme and the "theme that Dostoievski developed, though in a manner quite different, in his *House of the Dead*, another account of life in a Siberian prison, published almost exactly a hundred years ago." Despite these lofty comparisons, Rahv does not overestimate the new author's literary abilities: "As a novel it is not, in my view, the 'great work of art' that some people say it is; its scale is too small for that. But it is a very fine book in which not a false note is struck."

He rejected the Machiavellian interpretation placed upon the book by some readers who saw in it an instrument of one of the competing cliques in the Kremlin or even of the new dictator who had encouraged its publication, the so-called new Stalin who was busy demolishing the old one, Nikita Khruschev himself: "It is senseless to see its meaning serving the partisan interests of any faction . . . The integrity of this story is inviolable."

Rahv appears to have been optimistic in his interpretation of the publication of the book and the account of its popular reception in Russia as "some kind of breakthrough toward freedom in Soviet writing." But he added, in sentences that are significant and unexpected: "Thank God, the world is still unpredictable after all. No one, not even the most astute Kremlinologist among us, could possibly have foreseen that the party hierarchs would be prevailed upon to permit the publication of a work so devastating in its implications." Rahv's profound revolt against the stifling certainties of the closed Marxist system finds expression in this passage.

At such times he was inclined to be as antisystematic as Dostoievski's protagonist in *Notes from Underground*. The extreme individualist, like the extreme romantic, is one for whom the world is continually surprising, as it was for the philosopher Henri Bergson who described reality as "a perpetual gushing forth of novelties." I do not wonder that Rahv was so avid a reader of the newspapers that the closing down of *The New York Times* for some months by a printers' strike in the early 1960's seemed to daze and completely bewilder him as if it had made him feel helpless amid the welter of events in a world whose configurations succeeded each other as arbitrarily as those of a kaleidoscope.

What Rahv abhorred above everything else, in the period when I knew him, were *mechanical* reactions to reality, which was to him always fresh and surprising. He recognized immediately the devices by which the lazy-minded are able to avoid thinking about the finer nuances of unrepeatable situations. To be sure, the refusal to avail oneself ever of ready-made responses put quite a strain upon a person. One felt that to be sensitive and intelligent in his eyes, one would have to live according to the advice which Henry James gave to those who aspired to be real writers rather than mere journalists: "Try to be one of those upon whom nothing is lost!" The trouble is that in living up to such an ideal, one might be worthy of the description applied to James himself by T. S. Eliot, namely that "he had a mind so fine it could never be violated by an idea!" The word "idea" in this sentence (used in conjunction with the verb "violated," with its connotation of sexual force) must be understood to mean empty generalization, the equivalent of what may be described as a mechanical response. *Thinking* in the true sense begins only when one takes account of the unique individual characteristics and eccentricities to be found in every living situation.

It is Rahv's skepticism of all systems and mechanical responses to an ever new and changing world of reality that lies back of what he himself describes as his existentialist view of art, a view that is projected most successfully perhaps in one of his major essays, "Tolstoy: The Green Twig and the Black Trunk." Here is how he describes his general view of art: "Art and reason are not naturally congruous with one another, and many a work of the imagination has miscarried because of an excess of logic. 'There may be a system of logic; a system of being there can never be,' said Kierkegaard. And art is above all a recreation of individual being; the system-maker must perforce abstract from the real world while the artist, if he is true to his medium, recoils from the process of abstraction because it is precisely the irreducible quality of life, its multiple divulgements in all their uniqueness and singularity, which provoke his imagination."

This philosophic approach to the nature and problem of art in general leads directly to the concrete exemplification of its validity in the analysis of a particular aspect of one of Tolstoy's most celebrated works. The passage in which this occurs is important enough for an appreciation of the quality of Rahv's "practical" criticism to be quoted at length:

The Tolstoyan characters grasp their lives through their total personalities, not merely through their intellects. Their experience is full of moments of shock, of radical choice and decision, when they confront themselves in the terrible and inevitable aloneness of their being. To mention but one of innumerable instances of such spiritual confrontation, there is the moment in Anna Karenina *when Anna's husband begins to suspect her relation to Vronsky. That is the moment when the accepted and taken-for-granted falls to pieces, when the carefully built-up credibility of the world is torn apart by a revelation of its underlying irrationality. For according to Alexey Alexandrovitch's ideas one ought to have confidence in one's wife because jealousy was insulting to oneself as well as to her. He had never really asked himself why his wife deserved such confidence and why he believed that she would always love him. But now, though he still felt that jealousy was a bad and shameful state, "he also felt that he was standing face to face with some-*

*thing illogical and irrational, and did not know what was to
be done. Alexey Alexandrovitch was standing face to face
with life, the possibility of his wife's loving someone other
than himself, and this seemed to him very irrational and
incomprehensible because it was life itself. All his life Alexey
Alexandrovitch had lived and worked in official spheres,
having to do with the reflection of life. And every time he
stumbled against life itself he had shrunk away from it.
Now he experienced a feeling akin to that of a man who,
while calmly crossing a precipice by a bridge, should suddenly discover that the bridge is broken, and that there is a
chasm below. That chasm was life itself, the bridge that
artificial life in which Alexey Alexandrovitch had lived. For
the first time the question presented itself to him of the possibility of his wife's loving someone else, and he was horrified
at it." . . . It is exactly this "standing face to face with life,"
and the realization that there are things in it that are irreducible and incomprehensible, which drew Tolstoy toward the
theme of death . . .*

There can be little doubt that Rahv's views of literature
evolved over a considerable period of time. In 1939, years
after breaking with the Communists, he could still write in
an editorial in *Partisan Review*: "From [Chateaubriand's]
René to *The Waste Land*, what is modern literature if not
a vindictive, neurotic, and continually renewed dispute with
the modern world?" But twenty-seven years later, in 1966,
he would be sharply critical of Leslie Fiedler for asserting
(more shrilly, it is true) much the same thing: "Highbrow or
truly experimental art aims at *insult*; and the intent of its
typical language is therefore exclusion. It recruits neither de-
fenders of virtue nor opponents of sin; only shouts in the
face of the world the simple slogan, *épater les bourgeois*, or
'mock the middle classes,' which is to say, mock most, if
not quite all, its readers." Rahv comments caustically on
this statement of Fiedler's: "Now, it is patently impossible
to recognize such 'highbrow or truly experimental' writers
as, say, Proust, Gide, Sartre, Mann, Kafka, Joyce, Yeats,

Eliot and Stevens in this singular definition. Its emphasis is wholly on the writer's putative attitude toward his pro- spective readers rather than toward himself."

Yet Rahv's objection to Fiedler may have been not so much a matter of substantive disagreement as it was a pro- test against his stylistic sensationalism. From the beginning of his career to its end, Rahv would probably have agreed with the unidentified writer to whom he alludes in a memorable sentence: "A close observer of the creative pro- cess once finely remarked that the honor of a literature lies in its capacity to develop 'a great quarrel in the national consciousness.'" Rahv goes on to apply the moral of the quoted passage to the most celebrated examples of American fiction in our century: "The modern American novel is implicated in 'the great quarrel . . .' To my mind the prin- cipal theme of this novel from Dreiser and Anderson to Fitzgerald and Faulkner, has been the discrepancy between the high promise of the American dream and what history has made of it . . ." After quoting the eloquent conclud- ing passages of *The Great Gatsby*, he adds: "Art has al- ways fed on the contradiction between the reality of the world and the image of glory and orgastic happiness and harmony and goodness and fulfillment which the self cherishes as it aspires to live even while daily dying."

What Rahv seems to blame is hysteria in the response rather than legitimate dissatisfaction with the world as it is, a dissatisfaction he fully shared to the end of his life. He did not have the sort of temperament that permitted him to be happily "at ease in Zion." Confronting the reality about him, he saw only "people in the aging twentieth century, prostrate amid their material affluence and spiritual bank- ruptcy." His perception of the actual situation did not differ markedly from that of a man like Eliot, whom he found in general a sympathetic figure, though he was hardly prepared to follow him into any church as a way out of the impasse. "The true function of criticism," Rahv wrote in his last essay on Eliot, "is more frequently to resist the *Zeitgeist* rather than acquiesce in its now rampant aberrations."

(The formulation reminds one of that passage in Goethe's table-talk in which he cautions us to bring to bear against the aberrations of the present day "masses of universal history.") A fully balanced account of any literary phenomenon is difficult to achieve, and it is for such an achievement that Rahv chooses to praise Eliot in reviewing a volume of his prose after his death:

> *To my mind the most admirable piece of criticism in the book is the essay "From Poe to Valéry"—a marvel of precision and insight. Eliot begins by giving us his impression of Poe's status among English and American readers and critics, an impression accurate enough, and then proceeds to develop his own estimate of him. I take it to be the definitive estimate; I certainly find it far more convincing than either the wholly negative, virtually demolishing view that Yvor Winters adopted in* Maule's Curse, *or the somewhat implausibly positive opinion of Poe to which [Edmund] Wilson has committed himself.*

Rahv himself was always correcting some departure by other critics from precision of observation or from common sense. Such errors are often committed by those whom he suspects of being excessively literary in their preoccupations—that is to say, those for whom literature seems to be a free-floating balloon of fantasy without any ballast of reality to bring it down to earth on occasion. Of such a critic he can think of nothing more devastating to say than that "the actual is seldom real to him." A critic like Leavis, on the other hand, though suffering from some other defects in his eyes, is free from a misleading "purist aestheticism." He goes on to say, "I think F. R. Leavis was essentially right in remarking some years ago that 'one cannot be seriously interested in literature and remain purely literary in interests.'"

But the unavoidable fusion of "impurities" in the literary process must not permit us to regard real writers as mere mouthpieces or public-relations people for the causes they mean to propagate. "It is only in becoming a mouthpiece," says Rahv, "that the writer defeats himself." It goes without saying that writers worth reading do not suffer such self-defeat. A writer like Whitman boasted of the "contra-dictions" and "multitudes" with which he was informed, but this does not mean that writers who do not make a show of their contradictions do not contain them. One must be sure not to miss the writer's latent content or to think of him as more unified than he actually is.

The best examples of the contradictions between the latent and manifest content of literary works of art were for Rahv to be found in the Russian literature of the nine-teenth century, and these contradictions had a great deal to do with the fact that it was precisely this literature that managed to rise most successfully above its parochial and national limitations to interest the whole world in a way which only the great classics of the more or less remote past had done hitherto. It was the very intensity of the intel-lectual and emotional struggle waged by the greatest Russian writers of the past with their demonic experiences that enabled them finally to wrest a benediction that was intel-ligible to all of mankind. In one of Rahv's numerous defenses of the great "reactionary" Dostoievski, the "nay-sayer" to the Revolution, he tells us that

to recognize the achievement of the Russian novel of the nineteenth century is to recognize Dostoievski's supremacy as a modern writer. His one rival is Tolstoi. Only dogmatists of progress, who conceive of it as an even and harmonious development, can presume to commit Dostoievski to a museum of Romantic antiquities. It is true that he labored to give his genius a religious sanctification, that in his philos-ophical and political views he ran counter to progressive thought. But it must be kept in mind that in the sphere of imaginative creation progress does not simply consist of knowing what is true and what is false from the standpoint of scientific method. Dostoievski not only renovated the traditional properties of Romanticism, but also discovered

inversions and dissociations in human feeling and con-
sciousness which to this day literature has but imperfectly
assimilated.

Rahv deserves to be read and remembered for a number of
good reasons. The first is that his writing itself is very
good, not showy or effervescent but sincere in its enthusiasm
and with deep thought behind it. He has little else in common with the author of *Erewhon*, but Samuel Butler's
statement about literary style describes the practice of
Rahv well: "A man should be clear of his meaning before
he endeavors to give it any kind of utterance, and, having
made up his mind what to say, the less thought he takes how
to say it, more than briefly, pointedly, and plainly, the
better." The reason for Rahv's relatively limited literary
output could not be better expressed. He took up his pen
only when he had something urgent to say, and he then
said it in concentrated form. If some of his critical contemporaries had shown the same restraint and self-criticism,
the volume of their works might have been reduced and what
remained might stand up better beside his work now.

He also seemed to share (at least when I knew him)
Butler's antipathy to all zealotry (Butler's favorite maxim,
we are told, was *surtout point de zéle*). Because extremism
of any kind seemed so alien to him in the period in which
I knew him, it is not easy for me to imagine him in his
Communist phase. Since he soon divorced himself from it,
one may conclude that the original relationship was based
on mutual misunderstanding. That he shunned fanaticism
of any kind, while recognizing its temptation for the young,
is evident in the kind of praise which he chose to bestow
on Eliot after his death:

As he grew older Eliot was never fanatical about his literary
ideas and opinions, and he mixed grace with courage in
retracting quite a few of them, as on the subject of Milton,
for instance; nor did he ever lose sight of the literary subject
in expounding his religious convictions. The one interlude

of fanaticism in his career that I recall occurred in the early 1930's, and its upshot was After Strange Gods. *This book, harsh and even supercilious in tone, has not been reprinted for a long time, probably because its author regretted its publication in the first place. The fanaticism has been voiced mainly by his disciples, who did their master little good by converting his insights, perhaps inseparable from their specific contexts, into dogmas; and Eliot does in fact express (in his last published writings) his irritation at having his words, uttered decades ago, quoted as if he had written them yesterday . . .*

Yet a man of integrity must accept responsibility for his entire past, even that part of it which he may have subsequently rejected and feels self-conscious about. Rahv, in his own case, did not seek to avoid such responsibility. He had no objection to historians and anthologists disinterring items dating from his Communist past during his anti-Communist period, even when there was reason to suspect that this was not an altogether disinterested intellectual exercise but was designed to embarrass him politically. An instance that occurs to my mind is the reprinting of the essay by Rahv and William Phillips, "Recent Problems of Revolutionary Literature" (copyrighted by International Publishers in 1935). In this essay, the authors had loudly proclaimed that "the profile of the Bolshevik is emerging in America, heroic class battles are developing, new human types and relations are budding in and around the Communist Party . . . The assimilation of this new material requires direct participation instead of external observation; and the critic's task is to point out the dangers inherent in the *spectator's* attitude . . ." (The allusion in the italicized word may have been an ironic one to the title of a "reactionary" periodical of the time, to which Communist fellow-travelers like Theodore Dreiser were contributing articles embarrassing to their comrades.) There was nothing about the insight or the hectoring *Daily Worker* editorial tone of the article that the later Rahv could have taken any pride in.

The later Rahv is better represented by the 1939 *Partisan* editorial in which he rather plaintively observes that "all we have to go on now is individual integrity." This quality could have been singled out in so particular a way, it seems to me now, only by one who himself possessed it. Though he apparently regards it as a minimal recommendation for a serious writer, integrity in the degree to which it is revealed in his work as a whole is not a widespread literary characteristic, and in retrospect it certainly does not appear to be the least of the reasons for our continued interest in what he has to say. Adopting his own terminology for a moment, it may be said that the contradictions of his career were a reflection to some extent of the unhappy history of the United States in his time (and, more specifically, of the great economic depression beginning in 1929 in which he suffered certain traumatic reversals, like so many of his fellow-citizens), while its consistency was the laborious achievement of his own moral character. Integrity may be described as the ultimate saving grace of the individual. Rahv's is not a consistency that is mechanical or easy to grasp. It is not of the simple-minded kind that Emerson once described as foolish; least of all is it the product of a little mind. Or even, in the true sense of the word, of an especially "narrow" one. On the contrary, the consistency and integrity discovered in the writings of Rahv now seem merely the outward signs of the depth of thinking and feeling in the writer himself.

Chapter 8

Philip Rahv: The Last Years

Alan Lelchuk

Philip once told me of how, when he was eight or nine years old, Russian soldiers were bivouacked in his village, Kupin in the Ukraine. The soldier who stayed in Philip's house, a tall, blond, handsome Russian—Philip remembered these details a half century after the fact, with fondness—the young soldier gave the Jewish boy several books to read, among them Dostoievski and Tolstoi. Thus began Philip Rahv's literary education, and also his serious acquaintanceship with his own (written) Russian language, since in the Greenberg (real name) household the basic language was not Russian but Yiddish. In a word, Ivan Greenberg was an authentic *shtetl* boy. The points of irony here are many. One of them certainly stretches forward from the nine-year-old Jewish child to the man who became, several decades later, one of the great literary critics of the *English*-speaking world (a feat which may be more remarkable than that of the novelists who began with one language but made their reputations in another, like Conrad, Nabokov). But what I would rather emphasize here about the incident is what remained, to my mind, a fundamental aspect of Philip Rahv's life throughout: his deep-rooted sense of personal exile. Exile in the land of his birth and childhood because of the family *Jewishness*; exile in the land of his adulthood, America, because of his Russian and Jewish sides and his socialist beliefs; exile even in Palestine, his stopping-off spot early on, because of his literary ambitions. And even once in Oregon he felt strange, he told me, precisely because he was accepted casually, by the young woman who loved him and the employer he worked for (in radio advertising); the rich and painful paradox of the cripple missing his wound! Philip frequently bemoaned the fact that a literary person needed very special surroundings to feel at home. Was this a way of saying that no place was special enough for him to feel at home?

Certainly it was not the university, where he spent the last fifteen years or so of his life. An autodidact who never finished high school—let alone attended a university— he didn't put much store in academic degrees, or in their relation to talent or intelligence. Most universities, he felt, were just glorified high schools anyway. Nor was he at home with most of the students who were passing through, on their way back to that commercial and philistine society, America. Yet, to be sure, to those few students whom he believed to be literary, or who at least aspired in that direction, he could be open, accessible, and an extremely valuable teacher—a teacher in the old sense, as shrewdly interested in life as he was deeply learned about literature and culture. More like a personal tutor then than a mass education functionary, Philip was as willing and eager to talk about the dilemmas of a real romance as of the dilemmas of Anna Karenina, regardless of a student's age or sex. The main qualifications were active intelligence, eagerness to learn, a spark of life. Perhaps here, in pedagogy rather than in politics, Philip at last practiced and believed in authentic democracy. And though he was known to be a powerful and nonstop talker, he also had the capacity to listen. In the early going, anyway.

In some very complicated ways, I think it was this sense of exile that helped to establish our own friendship, which began when I first came to Brandeis in 1966 and carried through—through some choppy waters and serious wrecks— to the night before he died. At our first few meetings he found out pertinent details about my own biography— mainly my own dead father's Russian upbringing and communist dreams as an immigrant here, and my youthful hostil-

ity to him partly because of that embarrassing politics, a
subject which fascinated Philip, who urged me to write
about it in fiction. Anyway, after uncovering these details,
he decided, early on, that in some ways we were destined
to be close. Or more precisely, that I was fitted emotionally and biographically to serve as a kind of adopted
son to him, in place of the son he never had. I don't mean
to make myself the subject here, but rather to use myself
and the relationship as a way of trying to understand
Philip's affective life, that aspect of his personality from
which he frequently sought exile, almost in a conscious
way. A childless man all his life, he seemed better constructed for the role of spiritual father than real one.
(Like how many others who, unfortunately, have to serve
the other role?) Uprooted from his own family, and staying
that way with a too-determined pride—for example, most
people never dreamed that Philip's brother lived down the
turnpike, in Providence—he nevertheless seemed to me to
be filled with strong family yearnings, though they were
constantly being defeated by ideological priorities. A family man without a family of his own, just the feelings, fur-
tive, flickering; a painful incongruity.

In any case I found myself going to dinner regularly at
his home in Boston, a lovely Back Bay brownstone where
he and his wife, Theo, treated me with great openness and
immediate warmth. There, over excellent meals, we discussed literature, leftist politics, childhoods, cooking, students, writing, women, *Partisan Review*, and his hopes for
a new magazine. And of course his enemies, an important
and growing subject. (These included the "huckster" Mailer
for dominating the New York literary scene by means of
his tough guy personality and grabbag of subliterary tricks;
the new academicians, who were squeezing the life out of
literature with their endless varieties of fashionable criticisms, derived from the French, a group that he found
much more repugnant than the old New Critics, whom he
disputed but respected—a list of opponents that increased
with his own frustrations, unfortunately, so that personal

enmity became more and more confused with intellectual difference.) Also, he was most curious about the younger generation, especially as the New Left was developing, though like most of the older generation of leftists, he never quite understood that it was more a politics of sensibility than a system of strategies and ideological positions. Yet he asked about that sensibility with sincere interest—which rock stars were the best, whether marijuana (or other drugs) increased or decreased your sexual potency, what really went on in the new liberated dormitories. And when he was given a new stereo set one Christmas, by his affectionate step-daughter Theo, whom he was very fond of, he immediately bought records of the Beatles and Dylan, to hear and judge for himself. But if Dylan's "A Hard Rain's A-Gonna Fall" brought tears to his eyes, with its vision (to Philip) of nuclear catastrophe, he was at the same time appalled when such rock groups became the subject of study in the pages of *Partisan Review*. What some saw as an exciting mixing of categories—pop lyrics and music analyzed with a literary seriousness—Philip saw as a confusion of realms, a deliberate and dangerous confusion.

For all his interest in theory, however, Rahv surprised me with his material and epicurean sides. Or at least nudged my innocence about the Rules for Socialists. For example, Philip might be talking to you about the crucial failures of American cold-war policy, but he would interrupt suddenly to check out the pork chops Hungarian and their special sauce. A man who could hardly boil an egg at age forty-five, he had been astonished by a dinner cooked by Nicholas Nabokov one evening, and decided then to learn the craft. In a few years the devout Trotskyite had become a very competent Claiborne, sticking with French recipes for food, Russian formulas for revolution. His determined and disciplined way of learning to cook was no different from the way he learned most things, languages, literature, philosophy—on his own, without teachers or classes, just himself and books. In dress, too, his feeling for the material worth of reality flashed, with his snappy ties, pastel-colored shirts, spiffy sports jackets. These interests, developed only in his maturity, demonstrated not only Philip's practical side but also his growing ease as an accepted socialist in a hopelessly capitalist society. Knowing how to eat and dress well seemed also to serve the literary man in the sense of advancing his knowledge of manners; a man who didn't *know* society, Philip always said, couldn't really know or judge the full range of literature. So what would have seemed frivolous distractions for the younger radical now were permitted their uses in the adult's education. Besides, wasn't there a renowned gentleman of revolution who, whether he was exhorting the bohemians, shopkeepers, or intellectuals, in Switzerland or Russia, always dressed impeccably? Putting forth the most radical ideas while appearing in the most bourgeois costume? Lenin, not Trotsky, was the useful model here.

Rahv had the air of a tasteful diplomat or fashionable cosmopolitan, rather than of an English professor. His style was not tweeds, vests, and pipes, but dangling cigarettes and fine suits; only a long pencil protruding awkwardly from a shirt or jacket pocket betrayed the smooth appearance. Even in his fifties his face retained a certain boyish handsomeness, especially when he smiled, lighting up his swarthy complexion. The frame was heavyset, not fat; and a bad fall at Brandeis, which caused him to use a cane for years, added to his authority. Images of the man: A Russian bear with a shrewd practical eye. A dark eminence with an earthy sense of humor. A lady's man, more at home with Ladies than with women.

Philip in those first years was instructive and affectionate, and it was only later that my own—and his—ambivalence emerged. (Inevitable ambivalence, I should say, not merely because of a charged father-son relationship, but also because was there anyone who provoked ambivalence as a response more than Philip?) But again, early on, he offered me a full course in leftist politics and literary judgment, and, equally valuable, encouraged and criticized my own writing. Later on, he told me what he liked and disliked in *American Mischief*, making several valuable suggestions for the manuscript. A Trotskyist-Leninist in his politics, Rahv was a democrat in literature, a fierce and tested democrat as a result of the Stalinist-Proletarian wars of the Thirties. To my mind, were it not for his particular moment in history, his strong egalitarian feelings might have found a different political vehicle than Bolshevism to express them. It was to his credit, however, that you could always debate his views with him, once he saw that you were serious, not frivolous, in your views—"serious" meaning that the politics came from conviction, not idle or academic considerations. And if he took time to shift his ground, he could eventually do it. Few people recognized that in his last few years he did shift ground importantly, coming around to believe, in his most poised moments, that the true tragic politics of the century existed because of the disparity between egalitarian impulse and necessary political deed, and while he never gave up on the *idea* of political revolution, he did grow skeptical of the old way of doing it. For him this was an important concession. Although it should be said that even earlier, in the hothouse atmosphere of the sixties, while intellectually decrying the tactics of the young militants, he neverthe-less had sided with them emotionally and had criticized severely older leftists who stood on the sidelines and berated the young. (See his debate with Irving Howe in the *New York Review of Books.*) Clearly his generation, with its wars and wounds, influenced his personality more than he admitted, or in retrospect perhaps, would want to admit. In general, however, Rahv was a bigger and more flexible, and infinitely more humorous, man than his political philos-ophy at times suggested.

In any case, Philip, who could be as tough as he was warm, cruel as kindly, went through some major upheavals in his last years. He became a different Philip Rahv from the one I had known and experienced. It is very difficult to give full justice to his life here, in so skimpy a space; it deserves a longer telling. But at the heart of it was pain and turbulence, much pain and bewilderment even—a new emotion for him, I think—starting with a catastrophic fire that left him bereft of Boston home, manuscripts, and annotated library, and his wife. It is impossible to measure here the full effects of this accident upon his personality and outlook, and perhaps even—even crucially—his work. To my knowledge it was the first major blow struck upon his life; the sudden interruption of routine, for a man of routine like Rahv, probably staggered him as much as the human tragedy. Certain feelings Philip made sure to keep private and guarded, from himself especially, and while I witnessed up close the immediate devastation wrought in the months afterward, the deeper wounds lay there, buried, probably unlooked at. Had he believed in the power of psychiatrists, it would have been an excellent time to seek one out; but psychoanalysis, as practiced in America, had long ago been written off as a luxury for the bourgeois. (No reflection upon Freud, this judgment; Rahv had great respect for Freud, and wrote a first-rate and too-little-known essay on Freud and Literature.) Philip's pride, a strong force in his writing, frequently was a barrier in his life. Anyway, during those months, I was involved with a Philip Rahv unknown to the public or to most of his friends, a man vulnerable, near-helpless, and childlike in dependence. One didn't imagine him this way. The heavyweight terror had suffered a technical knockout and was still reeling and struggling to recover in a Boston hotel room.

Starting *Modern Occasions* a year or two later brightened his mood considerably, since if there was one place he felt at home, it was on and with the printed page, with words and ideas, writing and editing, making his presence and opinion felt in the culture. Like most writers, his real identity was dramatized there, in his literary judgment and outstanding prose. The two years that we worked together on the magazine, 1970–72, were another sort of education for me, at once exciting, disconcerting, and inimitable. It was not a democratic magazine in any sense of the word, and it prospered and suffered because of that, I imagine. For me it was a great pleasure to see Rahv returning to his beloved combat, writing his brilliantly packed essays in polemics, against this false political trend or that turn to the right in a supposedly liberal journal. It was good to see him put on his gloves again; he was a terrific counterpuncher against sham, stupidity, injustice, and other onslaughts by middlebrows and massbrows parading as standard-bearers of the culture. To shift metaphors, running a magazine for him was like running a war, in which this critic (Erlich) was used in the battle against Structuralism, say, that philosopher (Elevitch) in the fight against the new hip psychiatry; the General also had it in his power, I learned to my dismay, to accept stories or pieces which he didn't really like but which were useful in terms of the names involved, or else, simply personal dispensations. No matter how much I and the other young lieutenant fought against such decisions, we were overruled; the General knew best. Eventually that sort of old Army dictatorship disturbed me sharply and, worse, hurt the magazine.

But mainly it was uplifting to observe the respect and rewards that the name Rahv brought in from the intellectual and creative world. Pieces began to arrive from poets, novelists, critics, essayists, more for the honor of publishing with Rahv than for the little money and little actual exposure one could earn from a piece. In terms of audience, of course, Philip never believed in size, but rather in influence; it was not *how many* you were reaching, but *who.* Yet, when the audience reached almost four thousand subscribers by the end of the second year, Philip was heartened; after all, he said, it had taken *Partisan Review* some two decades plus to reach, at its apex, ten thousand. And just as *PR* had been a home for the best in literary and cultural thought in the thirties and forties, so *Modern Occasions* began to draw in quality again. Just as the young Rahv had elicited contributions from the likes of Orwell, Wilson, Eliot, Stevens, Trotsky, Trilling, Arendt, Auerbach, McDonald, Howe, Ellison, Silone, Styron, F. W. Dupee, so in the space of two years with the new magazine there appeared Sartre, Chomsky, Dickey, Lowell, Roth, Bellow, Brustein, Kramer, Aiken, J. V. Cunningham, Hardwick, McCarthy, and the usual selective assortment of newer writers and critics. Of course there was a fine irony present in the older days, when Rahv the refugee and exile was making a home for the most gifted men and women of his time. Now, however, the special feel of sanctuary was gone; to use a phrase of his, "the intellectuals were in," meaning they could get published anywhere and were in demand, great demand. A situation that frustrated Philip, rather than elating him, despite his success in getting writers to write for him; his old pride had been precisely in making that home, for political enemies (like Eliot) as well as friends, all those with serious talent. (He loved to narrate his many coups in judgment, as when he received in the mail one morning from Saul Bellow his *Seize the Day*, with a note explaining how the *New Yorker* had just rejected it. Or how Eliot had surprised his agent by asking him to publish sections of "Four Quartets" in *PR*. Or the discovery by accident, when Philip was out to improve his self-taught German and ran across a volume of criticism in a Fourth Avenue second-hand stall by someone named Auerbach; it was *PR* that published the first translation of *Mimesis*.) If the feeling of sanctuary was missing, so too was something else, a clear and direct Enemy. For while a great thrust of the old *PR* was its anti-Stalinist polemics in literature and politics, the thrust now for Philip was much more ambiguous, since the New Leftists held no purge trials, and looked to Port Huron and Berkeley not Moscow for ideas; and since, concerning literature, they really were not interested. Again, agreeing with their basic impulses, he disagreed strongly with their methods of activism—not the activism itself, it should be said—and found himself caught in between. Articles and editorials appeared which gave off contradictory signals about where *MO* stood, politically and culturally. Such uncertainty was anything but Philip's style; and instead of making a serious stand behind that ambivalence, as an earned, deserving attitude, Philip retreated from it, in confusion, flailing out against more easy targets.

Also, significantly, much of the new literature was being produced by a generation far removed from Philip's, and its aims and methods were also far removed from his sensibility. The new emphasis on the subjective mode and the increased openness concerning the sensual life, for example, were strange, if not outright alien, developments. Even in his own writing. Though he had often wished in the later years to write a memoir of his life, he acknowledged that it would be very difficult for him to do. His own inimitable prose style, surely one of the most sophisticated styles of any twentieth-century critic, was founded squarely on the objective mode, in which the personality of the writer was effaced completely in the service of content. A far cry from the contemporary way, to be sure. Which is to say, in summary, *Modern Occasions* still was a place for *quality* in the midst of the modish, the slick, the flashy, the schlock, but it lacked the right age, the right circumstances, the right sensibility, perhaps even the right Philip Rahv to make itself the cultural force that *PR* had once been. After the first year Philip himself began to sense this inadequacy, I believe, decrying the times with a surplus of virulence. He who couldn't change began to blame the times for changing.

But though remote from contemporary culture, Rahv, to my mind, continued to have a serious influence. He existed as a grey eminence of literature, in the wings rather than on the stage proper. His positions had been staked out earlier, and his performances were there for all to see. Against his standards of excellence, especially those regarding the classics of nineteenth- and twentieth-century Russian and American literature, the best of the newer critics had to measure themselves, whether they named him or not. One remarkable feature of Rahv's essays was his method of designing, as well as defining, the underlying scaffolding for his edifice of taste, while dealing with a specific writer. An essay on Tolstoi, for example, would include within it a substantive discussion of realism, differentiating its varieties in Tolstoi, Dostoievski, Chekhov; or in talking about Dreiser there would be a survey of naturalism, starting with the Continental version in Zola and leading to the alteration in the American vision. Thus a specific essay contained within it much broader statements and definitions (something like

E. M. Forster writing on Sinclair Lewis and the virtues and limitations of "photographic realism"). A modest-sized essay packed enough intellectual weight to provide a full-scale education in the subject. Rahv's economy of intelligence here—combining as it did breadth of knowledge with depth of insight and the virtues of the literary historian enhanced by those of the analytical critic—is most impressive; it places him, I believe, among the finest critics in twentieth-century literary criticism.

His death, along with the deaths of Wilson and Auden (and, probably, of Trilling), brings to an end an era of culture, in fact, and marks the end of a breed of critic in the Anglo-American world. In the seventies there would be no more clear authority of taste, normal accepted literary standards, in the world of literary criticism. The full chorus of voices from the gallery, about what and who were good, would now not only be heard, but would *count*. Whether this sort of democratization has led to a state of cultural incoherence and chaos, as I think, or else to a more healthy give and take of views seems to me to be one of the dominant literary questions of our time, yet to be answered. But what remains undebatable, I sense, is that the quality of criticism as practiced by Rahv and Wilson and Auden is no longer being practiced and may never again be practiced. Other aims, other arts, other temperaments, other circumstances dominate now and seem to ensure that the making of a literary critic of the likes of these is highly improbable in the future. It may very well be that it was not merely some literary critics who died, but an essential component of what we call literary culture. What the effect of this absence will be upon the creative sides of literature remains to be seen.

Rahv lost his one last home, too: *Modern Occasions* finally went under for lack of sufficient funds, and Philip found it difficult to concentrate on his own writing. For a man who lived so much within the medium of the written word, whose strongest and best impulses often found their place in his written work, not being able to write with the old rhythm was tantamount to dying. Certainly it was an enormous shock to his system. Whether this stoppage was a cause or an effect of the breakdown in his new marriage is hard to tell; but certainly the two circuits of breakdown crossed and touched each other, with untold damage. He had married a woman unlike any he had ever known, not an upper-class lady with credentials and money, but the pretty daughter of a West Virginia farmer, a once-married academic with a 14-year-old son. Hence when trouble began between them and she reacted with an anger much stronger than his previous wives, Philip was unprepared, furious, helpless. Used to analyzing and judging domestic difficulty in novels with sympathy, subtlety, and the controls of distance, Rahv found himself torn apart by the real-life dilemma thrust upon him. Reality was getting harder and more real, it seemed, from fire to writing disability to separation-traumas to increasing illness. No longer boxer, no longer general, no longer editor or writer, he was having a hard time just being a reasonable man.

More and more at the end, his inner chaos—its frustrations and pains leading to an unabated cynicism in all human dealings—separated him from the pleasure and consolation of friends. For sure his friendships and sense of friendship in the last few years were badly deformed, deranged. There was hardly an intimate friend in the end, among the well-known poets and writers, ex-wives and ex-prodigal sons, ambitious acquaintances and kindly colleagues, for whom he didn't feel and express a cutting ambivalence, at best. Warm in their presence, he was cruel behind their backs. But this weak streak should be understood, I think, within the context of his approaching end, and his sharp consciousness of it—perhaps willingness for it. Not writing, festering in his idleness, bruised by the bitter divorce battle, he lost much of his generosity, patience, humor, and overall balance. Friendship was a major casualty. Thus the ironic paradox of a man who needed such friendships more than ever, suddenly losing the mental framework to sustain them seriously. More and more people came around, including old

acquaintances, friends, wives, students; but they were there
mainly to fill up his time and dejected solitude, not his heart.
Or his mind. Those had closed.

Pitiable and painful were the moments in the last months
when he would talk about the turmoil of his life interrupting
his concentration. The fire burning him up would emerge
plainly, powerfully. He wanted death, and resented it; and
resented wanting it; resented others for not wanting it, not
having it. Besides resentment, there was helplessness; lum-
bering about his kidney-shaped living room like a bear shot
by a hunter, dazed by what had hit him, badly wounded,
wondering when the end would be. At times in the past we
had discussed the possibility of his using a tape recorder for
his work, but it was like suggesting to him that he take up
the bicycle, or motorcycle. Machines of any sort, especially
for writing, were not for him. He needed, he said, the security of his wooden shelf, built by carpenters on the walls of
all his studies, and on which he wrote, standing up, in long-
hand, with a pencil, with a Quotations and Ideas notebook
at his side, thoughts and phrases that he had culled from
his classics, for pre-writing stimulation. No typewriter, no
tape recorder, just the yellow pencil and lined sheets of
paper and the shelf. A Galapagos creature in this age of
electric typewriters and electronic devices. At the very end,
in the last week of his life, a close mutual friend and myself
did persuade him to talk to us along with the recorder, to
begin serious work again. Plans were made for his Dostoievs-
ski book to be completed, at long last; and also we would get
going on a long-promised project, that personal memoir of
literary life during the thirties and forties. This excited him.
The stories that he knew about famous literary figures, like
several he told us, would cause a scandal, he felt. He laughed
about them—and threatened. He loved to tease himself and
others with the thought that one day he would overcome
his timidity, personal and ideological, and become the
naughty raconteur. Indeed Rahv would have made a fine Duc
de Saint-Simon of the Literary Court, given his eye for
detail, his ear for rumor, his nose for aroma. More impor-

tantly, the thought that the actual writing ordeal was going to be *bypassed* by means of talk with friends (and tapes) cheered him immensely. It was a good last week and last night for Philip, a badly fatigued man riddled with domestic trouble, physical illness, and torturous self-doubt.

What was especially pleasant about the last few meetings between us was a return of intimacy, whereby talk of all sorts flowed freely again. He never lost his large curiosity about people, or his exact memory for details, especially the scandalous and humorous ones. There was always that interesting dysjunction about Rahv, the kind of awe about the man inspired by his writing, alongside the earthy informality he encouraged in person. A fierce polemicist and powerful authority in print, he was, like many powerful men of the mind, invariably lonely for human company, and therefore could be most approachable and down-to-earth as a man. If you were intelligent, he wanted to talk with you; if you were imaginative, he wanted to hear your stories; if you were pretty or charming, he wanted to have you around visible; if you were ordinary, he could be courteous; if you were pretentious, he was merciless. The prospect of the two new projects suddenly ahead of him revived the more wholesome aspects of his personality, and it was gratifying to see his dark face lighten, his grey eyes come alive from within their deep hiding places. When he smiled mischievously at his naughty stories that last night, like a boy telling tales out of class, I thought of how it was not only an aspect of his humor but also an outlet for his feelings. To my mind there was much more raw feeling and emotion in Philip than he liked to admit even to himself; and if that suppression in the social-political self was one of the costs of his largeness as a critic, so be it. To me that strong feeling was always embedded there, down deep; it was a crucial source of his high taste and outstanding discrimination as a literary critic; it was that which allowed some to become his close friends so quickly, and to retain feeling for him, despite the political self and many of its deeds. For while there was the tyrannical and dogmatic man, there was also that man of feeling and great talent, and the mischievous boy. I was grateful at the end for the return of the more personal note, for both our sakes.

In his will he bequeathed a good part of his estate to Israel. This surprised many friends and family and shocked old political and literary associates. It seemed most improbable to think of Rahv as a Zionist, given his apparently total commitment to Trotsky-Lenin Bolshevism; yet there was no doubt in my mind in the eight years or so I knew him that he was a Zionist. Even back in 1966 when I first met him, he never once allowed his Internationalist beliefs to violate his sense of historical justice about the state of Israel, or his socialist theories to distort the socialist and humanitarian realities of life in Israel. Furthermore, there were his strong feelings about Jewishness and the Jewish people and the land they had transformed by hard labor; at least twice as a young man, once for a considerable period, Philip had lived in Palestine, seriously contemplating settling there. What decided him against *aliyah* was not political reasoning but his large ambitions in literature; Palestine and Hebrew were too small a stage to act on, he felt, for a serious reputation to be made in the field of literary criticism. Hence, America. But meanwhile he had learned more than a little Hebrew, had helped to place his mother in a retirement home there, and had followed the country's progress closely. His ardor for the Israeli Cause increased, rather than diminished, as time wore on. His attitude toward the '67 victory was one of exultation for example, and he cheered at the television newsreels like a young fan cheering on a favorite team's touchdown. (He was always a greater fan of wars than sports, armies than teams; military history and strategy was a serious pastime. This was the main reason why he enjoyed Solzhenitzin's *1914*, for example). He only wondered when the rise of antisemitism would begin seriously in this country. And in the last year or two he said again and again that if he were starting over, it would be in Israel, not here. America had become too corrupt culturally and politically, while most of the socialist countries, especially Russia and China, had betrayed the high ideals of *the* (Russian) Revolution. In Israel, he felt, one could still see many socialist principles in operation—in the kibbutzim and moshavs, in State ownerships of the land and the natural resources, etc.—without the sacrifice of life, limb, and liberty. For a man who had shunned determinedly most American Jews—the nonintellectual, the Hadassah or shtetl type— Philip took a great pride in the new Jew being created in Israel: strong, self-sufficient, unabashedly Jewish, even heroic. In exile from himself and from his Jewishness, he possibly viewed that Israeli as unspoken alter-ego or condition of selfhood which he himself had missed out on but now, his Diaspora existence exhausted, he could aspire toward, aloud—even more, perhaps long for. Indeed, at the end it was only Jewishness and Israel that filled him with anything approaching tender emotions—in this case, longing and lament. His emotions at the end, shaky and volatile as they were, nevertheless suggest strongly that beneath the confirmed atheist and determined rationalist there lay a soul in longing for a final authority of peace and justice, and that that authority, whether a God or not, could only be Jewish. Interesting perhaps that at the end, in his personal affairs of state, in money—which he prized dearly—the emotion that showed through was tribal emotion.

Notes on Contributors

ROBERT ALTER, Professor of Comparative Literature at the University of California, Berkeley, is the author of *Rogue's Progress: Studies in the Picaresque Novel*; *After the Tradition; Partial Magic: The Novel as a Self-Conscious Genre*; and other works. He is a contributing editor to *Commentary*.

ROBERT BRUSTEIN is Dean of the School of Drama and Artistic Director of the Repertory Theatre at Yale, In 1980 he will assume the directorship of the Loeb Drama Center in Cambridge and will join the Harvard faculty. Among his books are *The Third Theatre*; *Revolution as Theatre: Notes on the New Radical Style*; and *The Culture Watch: Essays on Theatre and Society*.

NOAM CHOMSKY is Institute Professor in Linguistics and Philosophy at the Massachusetts Institute of Technology. Among his recent books are *Human Rights and American Foreign Policy*; *Essays on Form and Interpretation*; and *Reflections on Language*.

ARTHUR EDELSTEIN has served on the literature faculties at Hunter College, Brandeis University, and The College of William and Mary. His essays have appeared in *The Southern Review, Modern Occasions, Commentary*, and other periodicals.

MILTON HINDUS, Professor of English at Brandeis University, is the author of *Charles Reznikoff: A Critical Essay*; *A Reader's Guide to Marcel Proust*; *F. Scott Fitzgerald: An Introduction and Interpretation*; and other works. He is editor of the American literature section of the *Encyclopedia Judaica*.

ALAN LELCHUK, Writer in Residence at Brandeis University, is the author of three novels: *American Mischief*; *Miriam at Thirty Four*; and *Shrinking*. He was Associate Editor of Philip Rahv's periodical *Modern Occasions*.

HOWARD NEMEROV holds the Mallinckrodt Distinguished University Professorship of English at Washington University. Among his most recent books are *Figures of Thought*; *Reflections on Poetry and Poetics*; and *Stories, Fables and Other Diversions*. His *Collected Poems* were published in 1978 and won a Pulitzer Prize and a National Book Award.

RICHARD POIRIER, Professor of English at Rutgers University, New Brunswick, was an editor of *Partisan Review* from 1963 to 1972. Among his books are *Robert Frost: The Work of Knowing*; *The Performing Self*; and *A World Elsewhere*.

STEPHEN WHITFIELD, Assistant Professor of American Studies at Brandeis University, is the author of *Scott Nearing: Apostle of American Radicalism*. His essays have appeared in *Virginia Quarterly Review, South Atlantic Quarterly, Yale Review*, and other periodicals.

Library of Congress Cataloging in Publication Data
Main entry under title:

Images and ideas in American culture.

    CONTENTS: Edelstein, A. Introduction.–The literature and language of politics: Chomsky, N. Foreign policy and intelligentsia. Whifield, S. J. Totalitarianism in eclipse.–The politics of literature and language: Alter, R. Mimesis and the motive for fiction. [etc.]
    1. United States–Civilization–1945-   –Addresses, essays, lectures. 2. Criticism–United States–Addresses, essays, lectures. 3. Rahv, Philip, 1908-1973–Addresses, essays, lectures. I. Edelstein, Arthur. II. Rahv, Philip, 1908-1973.
E169.12.137   810'.9   78–63584
ISBN 0-87451-164-X